D1606119

THE SUPERSTOCK INVESTOR

THE SUPERSTOCK INVESTOR

Profiting from Wall Street's Best Undervalued Companies

Charles M. LaLoggia
Cherrie A. Mahon

McGraw-Hill

New York   Chicago   San Francisco
Lisbon   London   Madrid   Mexico City
Milan   New Delhi   San Juan   Seoul
Singapore   Sydney   Toronto

Library of Congress Cataloging-in-Publication Data

LaLoggia, Charles M.
  The superstock investor : profiting from Wall Street's best undervalued companies /
by Charles M. LaLoggia and Cherrie A. Mahon.
      p.   cm.
  ISBN 0-07-136083-2
    1. Stocks—United States. 2. Investments—United States.
  3. Corporations—United States.   I. Mahon, Cherrie A. II. Title.

  HG4910.L35 2000
  332.63'22—dc21   00-060922

McGraw-Hill
A Division of The McGraw·Hill Companies

1   2   3   4   5   6   7   8   9   0   AGM/AGM   0   9   8   7   6   5   4   3   2   1

ISBN 0-07-136083-2

This book was typeset in Palatino by Hendrickson Creative Communications.

Printed and bound by Quebecor World/Martinsburg.

This publication is designed to provide accurate and authoritative information in regard to the
subject matter covered. It is sold with the understanding that neither the author nor the publisher is engaged in rendering legal, accounting, futures/securities trading, or other professional
service. If legal advice or other expert assistance is required, the services of a competent professional person should be sought.

—From a Declaration of Principles jointly adopted by a Committee of
the American Bar Association and a Committee of Publishers

C O N T E N T S

Chapter Eight

If Everybody Knows Everything, Then Nobody Knows Anything   65

ACKNOWLEDGMENTS

I would like to thank the person who inspired this book and without whom it would not have been written: my friend, my business partner, and Director of Research, Cherrie Mahon. This book was actually born when I met Cherrie in 1998. She was a stockbroker at the time and was endlessly inquisitive about my newsletter, research techniques, and rather unusual approach to stock selection in comparison to what she was learning at the major "mainstream" brokerage firm that employed her. She seemed to recognize that my way of thinking was different from anything she had been exposed to, and her constant search for answers forced me, for the first time, to think about and explain, in detail, the thought processes that went into the recommendations in the newsletter. In a way, Cherrie's interrogating and seemingly endless curiosity forced me to turn an approach that had been based mostly on instinct and experience into an understandable and, I hope, instructive set of principles and guidelines that can be used by any investor willing to take the time and effort to learn how to use them.

Obviously, I have done a lot of writing over the years, but writing a book is different. If it were not for Cherrie, this book would not have been born—and if it were not for Cherrie, I probably never would have had the determination to complete it. Her support throughout this process was invaluable.

Charles M. LaLoggia

Introduction

If you'd been born in a cave and had lived there your entire life, with no knowledge of radio or television signals, you would probably be skeptical if someone were to tell you the air waves were filled with conversation, political commentary, advice for the lovelorn, hot stock tips, music, and even pictures. Of course, without a radio or television you would not be aware of the existence of such signals. The signals would be all around you, but you'd be oblivious to them without the means to pick them up.

Similarly, if you are accustomed to a certain way of reading the financial news, you can pick up "signals" that a certain stock that seemingly has nothing much going for it will soon rise dramatically in price. Why? Because something is about to happen which will literally *force* the stock market to recognize that stock's true value. I call such stocks "superstocks," because they can leap above any kind of market in a single bound.

I began publishing my stock market newsletter as *The CML Investment Letter*—currently named *Superstock Investor*—in December 1974. Along the way I developed a reputation for being able to spot neglected companies that were about to become stock market stars—not because they suddenly became supergrowth companies or had developed a ground-breaking new technology, but because something was about to happen that would send that stock price to a much higher level that better reflected that company's value as a business. Usually, that "something"—an outside event, or what I call a "catalyst"—had the effect of pushing the stock price higher in one sudden jump rather than gradually over time. Seemingly, that

1

outside event came out of the blue. But in reality that event was the logical conclusion to a series of events that began with a single clue, or Telltale Sign, that strongly suggested what the ultimate outcome would be.

This book shows you the clues, or Telltale Signs, that can point you toward stocks like these. I know these Telltale Signs exist because I have been using them for 25 years to pick countless takeover targets. My success in recognizing these signs is a matter of public record, as you will see. During one particularly productive 55-month period through September 2000, a total of 48 of my recommended stocks received takeover bids (see Table I–1).

I want to make one thing perfectly clear at the outset, though: What you will learn in this book is not a "get rich quick" method of investing. There are no sure things in the stock market except this: *There are no sure things!* I have seen countless systems and approaches to stock selection and market timing come and go. Many work for a while—sometimes for quite a while—and then fall into disfavor and disrepute because they simply stop working. Nobody knows why. Some resurface years later and begin working again, "discovered" by a new generation of investors.

But that is not what this book is all about. This approach is not a "system"—rather, you will learn a new way of thinking and a new way of observing the day-to-day financial news that passes your way. This new way of thinking is not meant to supplant any other approach to investing you may already be using—*it is meant to supplement it.* It can become a way to add to the mix of your investment portfolio by uncovering interesting and usually off-the-beaten-path stock ideas that can not only be profitable, but also rewarding on a purely intellectual basis. In addition, you will find that the stocks you uncover by using this method will usually march to their own drummer and will not be as affected as most stocks by the short-term emotional winds that buffet the stock market.

In effect, this approach will provide you with a sort of "offline" portfolio of stocks that travels along its own path, with each stock in the portfolio responding to events that are, for the most part, divorced from the events affecting the rest of the stock market.

Almost all of the 48 stocks that received takeover bids during that 55-month period ending in September 2000 were on my newsletter's recommended list because, based on the approach described

T a b l e I–1

Charles M. LaLoggia's 48 Takeover Bids in 55 Months

	Months Held	Percent Gain (or Loss)	Percent Annualized Gain (or Loss)
Sep '00 Advest	1	+19	+230
Sep '00 AXA Financial	12	+70	+70
Sep '00 Donaldson, Lufkin	8	+85	+127
Aug '00 PaineWebber	21	+119	+88
Dec '99 Pittway	3	+41	+164
Dec '99 Dexter Corp	5	+36	+86.4
Nov '99 E'Town Corp	11	+38	+41.4
Oct. '99 SJW Corp	10	+100	+120
Sep '99 Nichols Research	19	+10	+6.3
Aug '99 United Water Resources	9	+77	+102.6
Aug '99 Copley Pharmaceuticals	11	+23	+25.1
July '99 Red Roof Inns	9	+30	+40
June '99 Aquarion	7	+50	+85.7
June '99 Sugen Inc	42	+169	+48.2
Mar '99 Frontier Corp	28	+156	+54
Jan '99 Alarmguard	21	+21	+12
Dec '98 Brylane	2	+52	+312
Nov '98 Genovese Drug Stores	27	+219	+97.3
Nov '98 Pool Energy Services	56	+53	+11.3
Aug '98 Clearview Cinemas	6	+75	+150
Aug '98 American Stores	2	+25	+150
Jul '98 Life Technologies	2	+20	+120
Jul '98 Grand Casinos	7	+46	+78.8
May '98 Union Texas Petroleum	8	+21	+31.5
May '98 Giant Food	28	+36	+15.4
Feb '98 Harvey's Casino	1	+32	+384
Feb '98 Arbor Drugs	17	+163	+115
Dec '97 Showboat	25	+16	+7.7
Nov '97 Holmes Protection	10	+43	+51.6
Nov '97 Renal Treatment	28	+261	+111.8
Sep '97 Rexel Corp	23	+110	+57.4
Sep '97 Rohr	27	+124	+55.1
Sep '97 Riviera Holdings	1	+0	+0
Sep '97 WHG Resorts	5	+100	+240
Aug '97 Protection One	7	+105	+180

Continued

T a b l e I–1

Charles M. LaLoggia's 48 Takeover Bids in 55 Months
(continued)

	Months Held	Percent Gain (or Loss)	Percent Annualized Gain (or Loss)
Jul '97 Rotech Medical	36	+143	+47.6
May '97 Logicon	40	+292	+87.6
May '97 Smith Food & Drug	7	+50	+85.7
May '97 Vivra	36	+119	+39.6
Feb '97 UNC Inc	6	+100	+200
Dec '96 ADT Corp	9	+50	+66.6
Dec '96 Roosevelt Financial	12	+22	+22
Oct '96 Ornda Healthcare	4	+16	+48
July '96 Fay's Drugs	7	+87	+149.1
July '96 Bally Corp	2	+20	+120
Jun '96 Community Health	11	+40	+43.6
Apr '96 Hemlo Gold	12	+29	+29
Feb '96 Loral Corp	10	+15	+18

in this book, I considered them takeover candidates. No "magic" insights will be revealed here; instead, this book will describe what I have observed to be true over 25 years—that a certain event or development tends to lead to another, which ultimately results in the birth of a "superstock." Think of this book, and the approach it describes, as a road map. The map will point out guideposts and landmarks that can lead you toward a takeover target that suddenly jumps in price because an event has occurred and the stock market has no choice but to value it at—or very near—its intrinsic value as a business.

In the same way professional poker players can see certain behavioral patterns and use them to their advantage, you will learn to spot certain Telltale Signs that may seem meaningless or unimportant to most investors but will be highly significant and meaningful to you. These signs will point you in the direction of potential superstocks.

Let me repeat that the approach to investing you are about to learn is not a system. The key to this approach is *interpreting the news.*

This type of interpretation involves experience and a determination to delve into areas that most investors have neither the time nor inclination to examine. To be honest, it isn't easy to implement.

Over the past 25 years, I have explained my approach to countless thousands of subscribers, as well as journalists and the viewers and listeners of many television and radio programs. The approach to interpreting the news has never stopped working, for two reasons. First, it is far too complex and involves far too much judgment, experience, and willpower for most investors. Second, it involves human nature—it describes what companies and their management and major shareholders tend to do during the years, months, or weeks prior to an event that forces the stock price higher. In other words, it describes the sort of rational decision-making and human behavior patterns that tend to emerge when someone—either inside or outside the company—believes a stock is severely undervalued and intends to do something about it. And that type of behavior is not likely to change, no matter how many people learn to recognize it.

To that extent, the telltale signs discussed in this book will always be valid. And to the extent that using these techniques involves not only experience but also the inner confidence to believe what you are seeing—and sticking to your convictions even when there is little or no support from Wall Street—well, I just can't imagine this approach becoming so popular that it simply stops working.

A question often asked about investment books is: Does the system—in this case, the interpretive approach—always work?

The answer here is a resounding no! There is no sure-fire key to stock market riches. There have been plenty of times when the "Telltale" Signs you'll read about here seemed to point directly to a future superstock, only to turn out in the end to be unprofitable.

Does that bother you?

It shouldn't, because reality should never bother you on any level—it should only serve as a means for better understanding the way the world really works. Every mistake along the way—every road you take or stock you buy that does not work out as hoped—should be considered a learning experience that will make the next experience more likely to succeed.

I can only say that if you follow the clues described here, you'll end up with more winners than losers.

Now, I will describe some really interesting things I have learned over the years. It's an approach to investing that has served me well, and if you learn to use it, it will do the same for you.

THE BULLS, THE BEARS, AND THE HORSES

The recent trend toward microanalyzing the stock market on a minute-by-minute basis has less to do with investing than it does with providing a "fix" for stock market addicts. In his classic book *The Money Game*, author George Goodman, writing under the name "Adam Smith," says that most people are not in the stock market to make money; they are in it for the excitement. And if you were to catch a stockbroker in a moment of candor, you would probably discover that many have reached the same conclusion. A large part of the stock market's explosive popularity in recent years is that the advent of financial television and the Internet has turned investing into a form of entertainment that provides a welcome diversion from the predictability of day-to-day life.

I completely understand this, of course, having spent 25 years of my life transfixed by the stock market. Watching the minute-by-minute analysis on financial television and having a real-time quote system on your desk is part of the appeal of the whole business. Nothing wrong with that, although this book is a way of pointing out that there is another way to approach the business of picking stocks, one that allows you the opportunity to get up from in front of your television set to get a glass of water and maybe even do a little gardening.

There are many people who will tell you that the stock market is actually just like horse racing, and if you stop to think about it, they may have a good point. As every horse bettor knows, there is nothing quite like the adrenaline rush one gets when your bet is down, the bell rings, the starting gate opens, and the track announcer says, "They're off!"

This, of course, is precisely the feeling a day trader gets at nine-thirty each morning when he or she is tuned in to CNBC. The only difference is that the chairman of Time Warner is not standing at the starting gate ringing the bell.

It is probably no accident that as the stock market has become increasingly popular and accessible to the masses over the past 15 years, the horse-racing industry has gone into a steady decline.

Financial magazines are multiplying like rabbits while the *Daily Racing Form* has been sold and resold several times as its circulation eroded year after year.

Let's face it: Wall Street is beating the horse-racing business at its own game. While a horse race can provide periodic bursts of entertainment and excitement, each race lasts only a minute or two and is followed by a period of boredom and slowly building anticipation until the next race begins. On Wall Street you get nonstop action for 6½ hours 5 days a week, and if you're a real glutton for punishment, you can buy a sophisticated quotation system that allows you to sit around all night watching after-hours trading, and the opening of the Asian markets and the start of European trading in the predawn hours.

Wall Street never stops. How can horse racing compete with this?

For one thing, they might try out the concept of horse brokers. In New York State there are Off Track Betting parlors scattered all over the place. What's the difference between this and brokerage firm branch offices? There are no horse brokers. The only thing these OTB parlors lack are salesmen with clients who can be badgered over the telephone to bet on the horses and generate some commission business.

And why stop there? To support the sales force—excuse me, the horse brokers—OTB could even hire analysts to write research reports. If you are a "value" investor who concentrates on fundamentals, your horse broker could send you a report on the pedigree and training performances of a good-looking prospect in the seventh race at Belmont Park. Or if you are a "momentum" player who concentrates on technical analysis with a preference for following the "smart money," you could get a frantic call from your horse broker doing his best James Cramer imitation moments before post time about some mysterious movement in the odds that could indicate somebody knows something.

"Who cares why the odds are going down?" he would scream into the telephone. "This is a momentum horse! Get your money down now, before it's too late!"

The similarities are endless. Was the jockey holding his horse the last time out so the trainer can turn him loose today and cash a big bet at large odds? Has that corporation been overstating its earnings to keep the stock price up so insiders can bail out at high prices? You want to take a shot at big money? Forget options—play the daily double—here are our top picks, for speculators, of course. What's that? You're wondering what to do with your pension funds? Why, that calls for a more conservative approach—how about allocating 5 percent of your account on the favorite, to show?

One reason the stock market fascinates so many of us is that there are so many ways to approach it. This frantic moment-to-moment approach, in which the market is treated as though it were a racetrack or a casino, is certainly a valid way.

This book is about a different way.

PART ONE

The Making of a Superstock Investor

CHAPTER ONE

A Defining Moment

LALOGGIA'S DICTIONARY

Su-per-stock (soo-per-stok): A stock that has the potential to rise significantly in price regardless of what the general stock market is doing. This significant rise in price is due to a specific potential event, or "catalyst," usually a takeover bid, which, if it occurred, would force the price higher.

Since most stock market investors are obsessed with growth, perfectly good companies with consistent profits—many of which are cash rich with little or no debt—are passed over, shunned by the majority of investors seeking growth and earnings momentum.

Yet, a great deal of value can often be found in such stocks. The problem is, these neglected and undervalued stocks can remain undervalued for a long period of time, creating "dead" money, while other stocks provide solid gains.

These *superstocks* generally sell far below their actual value *as a business*, but nobody cares because the company's earnings may be erratic or even trending lower and the company's growth potential may be unexciting.

A number of events, or "catalysts," can force a stock trading at undervalued levels to move instantly closer to its true value as a business. The most efficient catalyst is a takeover bid, where a company or individual—and sometimes even the management of the company—

offers to pay a premium over the prevailing price to buy all outstanding shares. Other catalysts include a massive partial stock buyback at a premium. In this scenario, the company offers to acquire a large percentage of the outstanding stock at above-market prices. A third catalyst is a large onetime cash or stock dividend, where a company distributes accumulated cash or shares in a wholly owned subsidiary to its shareholders. A fourth type of catalyst occurs in a spinoff, where a company tries to establish the inherent value of a subsidiary by selling a small piece to the public in an initial public offering, thereby calling attention to the value of its remaining ownership.

These potential catalysts, as well as others, can suddenly turn a previously boring, uninteresting company into a superstock—a stock that rises dramatically in price, usually over a one- to two-day period, regardless of what the overall stock market is doing.

A LIGHTBULB GOES ON

The early 1970s were a difficult time for the U.S. economy and also for the stock market. A sharp rise in inflation in 1972–73 resulted in sharply higher interest rates, which in turn plunged the economy into a severe recession. The Dow Jones Industrial Average plummeted from the 1000 level to its ultimate low near 570.

In the midst of this economic and financial downturn, many companies saw their earnings evaporate and turn into huge losses. Companies cut or reduced dividends on their common and preferred stocks.

By April 1975, as inflation began to ebb and interest rates began to go down, I noticed an interesting phenomenon. Some of the companies that had plunged into the red and had been forced to eliminate dividends were moving toward profitability again.

I also noticed that some of the preferred stocks that had stopped paying dividends were "cumulative," which meant that all unpaid dividends would accumulate and have to be paid in full before any dividends could be paid on the common stock.

One such company was LTV Corporation, which had suspended the dividend on its $5 Cumulative Preferred stock back to 1970. By April 1975, $22.50 of dividends "in arrears" had accumulated. LTV's earnings were turning sharply positive by 1975, and its shareholders, who noted the improvement, had begun to push for dividends on the common stock.

LTV issued a statement that it would soon "consider" its dividend policy at a special meeting of the Board of Directors. But the only way LTV could pay a dividend on its common stock would be to first pay all of the cumulative preferred dividends in arrears. In other words, anyone who had bought the $5 Cumulative Preferred—then trading at about $57 a share—stood a reasonable chance of getting a lump-sum payment of $22.50 a share. Also, if the regular $5 preferred dividend were reinstated, the stock would probably move higher.

So, if a certain event took place—the payment of the $22.50 per share in back dividends—LTV Preferred stock would literally be *forced* higher, no matter what the general stock market did.

Using this reasoning, I recommended LTV $5 Cumulative Preferred. Not long afterward, LTV's Board of Directors announced it would pay the $22.50 in back dividends and reinstate the $5 annual preferred dividend. The price of LTV Preferred soared when this news was announced.

With this "taste" of what would become superstock investing, I looked for a company in a similar situation—and found it. Like LTV, Avco Corporation had a cumulative preferred stock (the $3.20 Cumulative Preferred) trading on the New York Stock Exchange. Like LTV, Avco had fallen on hard times and suspended dividend payments on the preferred, and they were accumulating "in arrears." And like LTV, Avco's earnings had taken a major turn for the better, and its common stockholders were pushing for dividends on the common shares, which could only be paid if the arrears were paid on the cumulative preferred stock.

I recommended Avco $3.20 Cumulative Preferred in August 1975 at 18½. After Avco paid all of the arrears on the preferred stock and reinstated the annual $3.20 dividend, the stock was selling at $47. This literally forced the stock market to revalue the preferred stock at a higher level since that $3.20 annual dividend would have created a yield of almost 18 percent, based on the original price of 18½—far too high a yield. To adjust for the fact that the dividend was once again being paid, the price of the preferred stock would have to rise. In other words, based on this anticipated development—the reinstated dividend—this stock *had* to go up.

Remember, though, higher earnings do not necessarily mean that a stock *has* to go up, even if those earnings beat analysts' expectations. A fat, new contract does not mean a stock has to respond to the news. What we should look for is a development that *makes it absolutely necessary for a stock to rise dramatically in price to reflect the new reality of the situation.*

THE LESSON LEARNED

Here's what can be learned from these two successful recommendations. Sometimes it is possible to anticipate a certain specific event which—if it were to take place—would literally force a stock price to move higher, *no matter what the overall stock market is doing at the time.* There are plenty of situations where a certain event could elevate a stock out of the usually unpredictable world of Wall Street and into another world.

It is these events that create the world of "superstocks."

CHAPTER TWO

A Superstock Is Born

On August 3, 1998, American Stores, a supermarket and drugstore company, jumped 5¾ points, or 25 percent. American Stores was the largest percentage gainer on the New York Stock Exchange that day, a day on which the Dow Jones Industrial Average dropped 96 points. The following day the Dow fell 299 points, and American Stores once again bucked the trend, rising another 1¾₆.

With that performance, American Stores joined the ranks of the superstocks—stocks that have the ability to rise quickly and substantially in price no matter what the general stock market is doing.

What propelled American Stores into the ranks of the superstocks? A takeover bid from Albertsons, a supermarket operator which, like many other supermarket companies, was seeking to expand by acquiring other companies. When Albertsons made its takeover bid for American Stores, it offered a big premium over American Stores' previous closing price. American Stores shares simply had to move sharply higher. It made absolutely no difference what the stock market did on that day. An outside "catalyst" was propelling the price change, and American Stores shareholders watched their stock soar in price as the general stock market collapsed over a 2-day period.

Takeover! There is no sweeter sound for an investor than to wake up to discover that a stock is the subject of a takeover bid at a huge premium over the previous day's closing price. It's not uncommon for takeover bids to drive a stock price higher by 25 percent, 50 percent, or even more in a single day—usually in a single trade, right at the opening bell, following the announcement that Company A is offering to buy Company B.

And while, to a casual observer, it may seem that these takeover bids that create instant profits usually come out of the blue, in fact many takeover bids do not occur as a random bolt, but as a final, predictable event that is the culmination of a series of other events. They are the logical conclusion to a series of interrelated developments that, when properly noticed and analyzed, can clearly point the way to many takover bids that seem totally unpredictable to outside observers who don't know what to look for.

And here's the best part: Because many takeover bids involve neglected, undervalued, and out-of-favor stocks, you will not necessarily be incurring an inordinate level of risk when you pepper your portfolio with these genuine takeover candidates. The only risk you'll be taking is opportunity risk—and even that usually turns out to be a temporary problem. A neglected takeover candidate that just sits there while the trendier momentum stocks hog the spotlight can be frustrating to own. But when your takeover candidate shoots up 25 to 50 percent in one day on news of a takeover bid, you will be paid back in spades for those periods of temporary underperformance.

And remember this: While undervalued takeover candidates that do not respond to the general market can be frustrating to own when the market is going up, they can be rewarding when they march to their own drummer while the rest of the stock market is marching off a cliff, as many investors learned in 2000.

In this book you will learn how to spot the Telltale Signs of a seemingly sleepy, out-of-favor stock with nothing much apparently going for it that could suddenly turn it into a superstock and chalk up huge gains as a result of a takeover bid. This is not a "get rich quick" system, backtested by computer, and guaranteed to make you rich.

This is a book for investors who recognize that successful investing requires research and clear, original thinking. It's for investors who understand that brains are often confused with bull markets, and that in a rising market *anyone* can look like a genius. Those with the experience or insight understand that the true test of investment acumen comes when the general stock market is going against you. Then, and only then, are the benefits of shrewd stock selection clearly apparent.

Every example of a takeover success story in this book was predicted, thoroughly analyzed, and fully documented in my investment newsletter, *Superstock Investor*. These are actual case studies that show how the clues observed along the way clearly pointed to the ultimate outcome—a profitable takeover bid.

American Stores, for example, had tipped its hand a few months prior to the takeover bid. We had already alerted subscribers to the ongoing takeover trends in both the supermarket and drugstore industries, and chalked up several winners that became takeover targets in those industries. As you will learn later, one of the strategies to identify a potential takeover target is to monitor stocks in takeover-lively industries that are acting suspiciously well relative to other stocks in the industry or relative to the stock market in general.

American Stores was added to my Master List of Recommended Stocks for that very reason. During a 4-day period in the spring of 1998, while the Dow Jones Industrial Average was plunging 500 points, American Stores was moving slowly and steadily higher, completely disregarding the spreading weakness in the overall stock market. That performance, combined with the established takeover trends in both the supermarket and drugstore industries—two businesses operated by American Stores—suggested that American Stores was acting like a potential superstock.

When American Stores received a takeover bid from Albertsons on August 3, investors enjoyed large profits while the broad stock market was declining sharply—precisely the result a superstock is supposed to deliver.

By the time you finish this book, you'll know how to identify such potential superstocks as they tip their hand. And by then you'll have a framework to help you get started.

CHAPTER THREE

Stock Selection

For most investors, the traditional method of stock selection goes something like this:

You're sitting in your office trying to figure out where to go to lunch and the phone rings. It's your broker.

"Hello, Mr. Spinelli?"

"Yes?"

"Tom Hayden, from Dewey, Pickum & Howe."

"Oh. Hi, Tom."

"Listen, Mr. Spinelli, our research department has come out with their stock pick of the week."

"I'm thrilled. What is it?"

"General Electric. We think it's a great company at these prices."

"You need a research department to tell me General Electric is a great company?"

"Well, no, the thing is, we think they're going to beat the street estimates by around a penny a share."

"General Electric has tripled over the past four years. It's doubled over the past year and a half. *Now* you tell me to buy General Electric?"

"Well, we—"

"What else do you like?"

"We like Dell Computer."

"Dell Computer?"

"Yes. Our research department thinks it's a—"

"I know, it's a great company. What else?"

"Uh . . . IBM?"

"Listen Tom, no offense, *but* I can hear about every one of these stocks a hundred times a day on CNBC. I can give you the entire list by heart. I already own six mutual funds and these stocks are in every one of them. Every one! Why don't you guys recommend a stock like WMS Industries? That's a great turnaround story that nobody's talking about. Plus, the Chairman of Viacom has been buying this stock on the open market and he owns 25 percent of the company. He obviously thinks it's undervalued. Maybe he'll make a takeover bid."

"WMS Industries?"

"Yeah."

"Uh . . . Let's see. Here it is. Well, they have no debt. And they have lots of cash."

"Exactly. It's a great situation."

"Well, no . . . You see, if they have no debt and they have lots of cash, we probably wouldn't recommend it."

"Why not?"

"Well, because they probably wouldn't need to do any investment banking business."

"Any what?"

"Investment banking business. See, if they wanted to do a stock or bond offering, we could be their investment banker and then we'd recommend the stock. That's how it works with smaller companies."

"It does?"

"Usually, yes."

By the end of this conversation, you have learned an invaluable lesson about Wall Street: Much of the time—perhaps most of the time—mainstream Wall Street research has less to do with picking stocks than it has to do with generating business. It is no accident that less than 1 percent of brokerage firm research reports are sell recommendations. Brokers do not want to offend potential investment banking clients. And it is also no accident that smaller companies with lots of cash and no debt are usually overlooked by the bigger research departments on Wall Street. This is because these poor outfits, flush with cash and owing nothing, face the dreaded double whammy: Not only are they too small for the big institutions that generate the big commissions to bother getting involved with, but they are also not even potential investment banking clients for the brokerage firm. So, given a limited universe of stocks to deal with and limited time, what kinds of stocks do you think the brokerage analysts are going to cover and recommend?

I once had a conversation with a gentleman who ran a fast-growing health care company whose earnings were growing at 40 percent a year. The company had more than enough cash, no debt whatsoever, and no intention of raising any money. Larger companies in his industry that were loaded with debt and doing secondary stock offerings were selling at 30 to 40 times earnings and were recommended by every major brokerage firm on Wall Street. This poor guy's stock was trading at 13 times earnings and going nowhere. I called him up to see if I was missing something, like perhaps there was a mass murderer on the Board of Directors.

"We can't get anybody to talk to us," the president moaned.

"Why not?" I asked.

"Because we don't want to do any banking business with the brokerage firms."

I asked him if he was joking.

"No," he said. "They all say the same thing. Do a little convertible bond. Do a little secondary offering. Acquire somebody, let us be the banker on the deal. Then we can follow the company."

That conversation was a real eye-opener. But, it is a familiar refrain because when I am looking for takeover candidates, the focus tends to be on companies with lots of cash and little or no debt. These companies tend to make more tempting takeover targets. And, the irony is that since these are precisely the sort of companies neglected by Wall Street research departments, these cash-rich, low-debt companies tend to lag behind the market due to a lack of analytical support. By lagging and trading far below the values accorded the average stock, these financially strong companies tend to trade at a huge discount below their true values as takeover targets.

What this means to you as an individual investor is that the Wall Street behemoths have left the playing field wide open for anyone who wants to be an independent thinker and look for individual stocks that are being left behind and are selling at great values. The obsession with large-cap stocks and servicing the big institutional clients has resulted in big research departments becoming little more than marketing arms of the sales force, something that has always been a fact of life on Wall Street but never to the extent that it is today.

Imagine some poor junior analyst trying to convince his or her boss to recommend WMS Industries.

"Mr. Gerard?"

"Yeah."

"I have this report I'd like you to look at."

"It's a buy recommendation, isn't it?"

"Yes."

"Because we don't want to offend anybody. That's bad business."

"Yes, I know."

Mr. Gerard looks at the report. "WMS Industries, huh? Market cap is only $500 million. That's pretty small for us. How much do they want to raise?"

"Excuse me?"

"How much money do they want to raise?"

"Uh . . . I don't think they want to raise any money."

"What do you mean they don't want to raise money? Look here, they have no debt. Don't they want to borrow some money? Sell some bonds?"

"Well, see, their cash flow is quite strong and they have a lot of cash, and . . . Sumner Redstone, Chairman of Viacom, has been buying stock on the open market, and—"

"Do they want to acquire somebody?"

"Not that I know of."

"Well, then, what are you bothering me for? Get out of my office! Come back when you can recommend something that will generate us some revenue."

Eventually the analysts learn how the game is played and their research tilts farther away from the smaller, financially strong companies. And as time goes on, all the analysts are looking over their shoulders as they play the same game, and the focus begins to narrow to a progressively smaller group of stocks, the same stocks you hear about day in and day out, *ad nauseam*, on CNBC, CNNfn, and every other financial program and publication. The buy recommendations proliferate, no matter how high the stocks go, because almost everybody says buy and nobody wants to offend a potential client. Earnings disappointments are overlooked: The silver lining is always found. Eventually, all this positive commentary and concentrated buying on a small group of large-cap stocks creates a situation where these stocks are so overvalued relative to their small-cap counter-parts that the pendulum must inevitably swing the other way.

Years ago Doug Flutie electrified the college football world when he threw a "Hail Mary" touchdown pass with no time left on the clock and Boston College scored an upset win over the mighty Miami Hurricanes. That play, which has been shown thousands of times, capped a stellar collegiate career for Flutie. But after he graduated, Flutie was able to secure only part-time employment in the National Football League and was eventually banished to the Canadian Football League, where he became not a superstock, but a superstar.

Flutie's shortcoming, as far as the NFL was concerned, was that he was too small. At 5 feet, 9 inches, Flutie simply could not see over the heads of onrushing linemen. So how could he find his receivers?

The logic seemed sound. If you're 5 feet, 9 inches, and six muscle-bound monsters standing 6 feet, 10 inches and weighing 300 pounds apiece are bearing down on you, it stands to reason that you might have difficulty spotting a wiry little guy 20 yards downfield. And so the NFL said, "Sorry, too short," and Flutie went on to lead several Canadian Football League teams to championships.

If you follow football at all, you probably know the rest of the story. Flutie returned to the NFL in 1998 as a backup quarterback with the Buffalo Bills, and when the starting quarterback went down with an injury, Flutie stepped in and almost took the Bills to the Super Bowl.

How did he do it, considering his diminutive stature relative to his opponents? The key is that Flutie did not try to match the onrushing linemen strength for strength or height for height. He refused to play their game. Instead, he used his agility to simply step aside, avoid the lumbering behemoths, and scramble around until he spotted the receivers and completed passes.

In his book *Supermoney*, author George Goodman, writing under the name "Adam Smith," used the analogy of the small but nimble quarterback to point out that individuals can compete with the giant institutional investors by "taking a quick look and stepping into the gaps between them." If you think of yourself as Doug Flutie, and you think of the index funds and other huge mutual funds and pension funds as lumbering, muscle-bound opponents, you will begin to see the tremendous advantage individual investors have today.

CHAPTER FOUR

Investing Paradigms: A New Way of Thinking about Stock Selection

A *paradigm* is a framework or model. As we learn and experience, we begin to establish various paradigms relating to all aspects of our lives. Eventually, we establish a framework with which we're comfortable. We begin to expect that certain ways of thinking or behaving will bring certain results, and we reach a certain comfort level between our actions and the reactions they will create. Sometimes the paradigms we establish serve us well for our entire lives. Other times, we become dissatisfied with the results our actions create and it becomes necessary to create a new paradigm.

When it comes to selecting individual stocks, 99.9 percent of investors and Wall Street analysts are operating using a dog-eared, shop-worn paradigm that is coming apart at the seams. They are all looking for the same thing: growth stocks with earnings momentum that will deliver strong earnings gains indefinitely into the future and enable these companies to justify their sky-high stock prices. There are two problems with this paradigm: First, it's been in existence for nearly 20 years and it's getting a bit creaky. In fact, it's probably on its last legs. The second problem with this paradigm is that it's not new; it's only a new version of other paradigms that have come and gone over the years. The late 1960s version, for example, was called the "One-Decision Stock Paradigm." In this version, certain stocks had earnings that would grow forever, which meant their stock prices would go up forever. That, in turn, meant that investors would never have to sell the stocks. Thus, only one decision was necessary—to buy them.

That paradigm eventually collapsed when it turned out that some perpetual growth industries (like bowling) reached their saturation points far sooner than analysts expected; other perpetual growth industries attracted competitors and price competition, thereby reducing profit margins (like calculators and CB radios); and economic recessions still surfaced from time to time, which had a tendency to affect all industries, turning growth stocks into normal, run-of-the-mill cyclical stocks.

This book offers a new paradigm—a new way of thinking about stock selection. Forget about earnings estimates and concentrate on asset values. Ignore the hot momentum stocks everybody is recommending and concentrate on industries and stocks that are out of favor. When you read *The Wall Street Journal*, ignore the market commentary and the earnings digest and instead look for items—especially small items—that involve industry consolidation, or takeovers. Listen carefully to CEO interviews on CNBC or CNNfn and pay particular attention to those who talk about "growth through acquisitions." Take note of every large merger announcement you see, and pay particular attention to the reasoning behind that merger. Get a list of the top 10 to 15 companies in that industry and zero in on those with little or no debt and high cash and/or working capital relative to their stock prices, on the theory that a merger trend in motion tends to stay in motion and that once a large merger has occurred in an industry, more will inevitably follow. Take note of every merger that falls apart, on the theory that the buying company will look around for another target. Also take note of situations where two companies are trying to acquire the same target, on the theory that only one of them can win the prize, and the company that loses out will eventually look around for another company to buy. Subscribe to the *Vickers Weekly Insider Report* and make a note of every outside company that is raising its stake in another company through open-market stock purchases. Take notice of every company that announces a stock buyback of 5 percent or more, and put a big red circle around those that operate in industries where a great deal of takeover activity has occurred. Make note of every company that enacts a "Shareholder Rights Plan" designed to make a takeover more difficult, based on the theory that the company wouldn't be bothering with such a plan unless it felt its stock was undervalued relative to its assets, and it was vulnerable to a takeover bid at an unrealistically low price. Make note of every company in a consolidating industry where 10 percent or more of the stock is held by a brokerage firm, a buyout firm, or an investment partnership that does not maintain long-term investments in the normal course of its business. The theory behind this is that a sophisticated stockholder will recognize the opportunity to maximize its investment and will act as a "catalyst" for a takeover bid. Take note of companies that are selling or spinning off noncore operations, especially when the parent company or the spinoff operates in an industry where takeovers are occurring, because corporate restructurings like this are often a prelude to a takeover bid.

Finally, subscribe to the Mansfield Chart Service or a similar service that presents charts organized by industry group. These enable you to see at a glance if a particular stock in an industry group is suspiciously outperforming its peers—often a sign that some sort of takeover development is brewing.

This way of thinking is new paradigm territory for 99.9 percent of investors and analysts. At first it may seem difficult and unusual, but if you have the courage to enter this new paradigm, you will find yourself in a fascinating new world where all sorts of new and exciting stock ideas will present themselves. You'll also find that this new paradigm is sparsely populated, which at first may be uncomfortable. But eventually, seeing things that others do not see will eventually turn out to be the source of great excitement and satisfaction. You will understand things that others do not understand. At times, you'll feel almost as if you can see the future, and you will marvel at the inability of others to do the same.

And if you think that's exaggeration, consider this real-life example of old paradigm thinking versus new paradigm thinking. In December 1998, I presented a front-page story in *Superstock Investor* entitled "Water Utility Industry Could Be on the Verge of a Takeover Wave." The article compared the water utility industry to the drugstore industry, which had undergone a rapid wave of takeovers over the previous 2 or 3 years. It noted that two major water utility mergers had recently taken place—the purchase of Consumers Water by Philadelphia Suburban, and the purchase of National Enterprises by American Water Works—and that a third smaller takeover of

Dominguez Water by California Water Service had just been announced.

In addition, I noted that I had seen interviews with water utility executives outlining clear and logical reasons for future takeovers in this industry. As a result, I presented a list of water utility takeover candidates, and I began to track this industry on a regular basis.

Later that month, on December 21, 1998, I appeared on CNBC and made the case for investing in water utility takeover candidates and specifically recommended two water utilities traded on the New York Stock Exchange, Aquarion (WTR) and California Water Services (CWT).

Just 6 months later, in June 1999, Aquarion received a takeover bid from Yorkshire Water PLC, a British water company, at a price of $37.05 per share, a 50 percent premium over my original recommended price for Aquarion. And remember, we are talking here about a water utility—a safe, stable stock with a dividend yield of nearly 5 percent. And yet, by focusing in on the developing takeover trend in the water utility industry, we were able to generate profits of 50 percent in 6 months!

On July 23, 1999, less than 2 months after the Aquarion takeover, CNBC presented an interview with J. James Barr, CEO of American Water Works, the largest publicly owned water utility. I was looking forward to this interview because I thought I might be able to glean additional reasoning and information regarding the takeover trend in the water utility industry. And if I were lucky, maybe I might get a hint of whether American Water Works was still looking to acquire companies, and if so, what region of the country they might be looking at. In other words, I was looking for clues that might lead me to a takeover target.

The interview began on a promising note. Mr. Barr stated that his goal was to continue to grow the business, and he said that one of the keys to continued growth would be an ongoing policy of acquiring other water utility systems. So far, so good.

Unfortunately, what followed was as classic an example of old paradigm thinking as you could possibly hope not to see. Here were the questions Barr was asked:

1. What are the possibilities of turning saltwater into drinking water?

2. What about turning glaciers into drinking water?
3. What about turning icebergs into drinking water?
4. How difficult will it be for you to raise rates?
5. Do you think there might come a time when government could confiscate your assets in the event of a water shortage?
6. What contingency plans have you developed in the event terrorists attack the nation's water supply?

Terrorists? Glaciers? Icebergs? These ridiculous questions are the type that make superstock investors all across America groan with disappointment. A superstock investor would have immediately focused on Mr. Barr's comment on growth through acquisitions and tried to pin him down with questions like these:

1. What kind of water utility companies are you looking to buy?
2. What region of the country are you looking at for new growth opportunities?
3. How big might a potential target be in terms of revenues?
4. What might the characteristics of a potential target be?

Anything at all to try to get a clue as to where American Water Works might strike next in terms of taking over a water utility. That's what investors would want to know. Those questions are designed to make you money in the stock market. But those questions were never asked. (At least we discovered that Mr. Barr isn't too worried about terrorists. That may be comforting to know, but it is not going to make you any money in the stock market.)

That, in a nutshell, is the difference between old paradigm and new paradigm thinking. If you're thinking in terms of takeover targets, you always look for clues and you are always on the lookout for an opening to receive new information and new insights. But if you're not used to thinking in these terms, you miss golden opportunities, such as those the CNBC interviewers missed, to bring new information to the surface.

The American Water Works interview was just one more example of how the vast majority of Wall Street analysts and commentators think in old paradigm terms. It illustrated why the new paradigm is so sparsely populated, and how information and evidence that is in plain view for everyone to see can be completely overlooked by the majority of investors and the people from whom they receive advice and information.

Just 10 months after this noninterview, American Water Works made a takeover bid for SJW Corp. SJW was on my recommended list as a takeover candidate. Suppose, for the sake of discussion, one of the CNBC interviewers had asked J. James Barr which region of the U.S. American Water Works might be looking at in terms of potential acquisitions. Suppose he had mentioned the western United States. This would have enabled superstock investors to zero in on the handful of publicly traded western water utilities as possible targets—SJW prominently among them. But the question was never asked.

And why wasn't the question asked? Well, certainly not because the CNBC interviewers are not good at what they do. It is extremely rare for any CEO to appear on CNBC and not be peppered with precisely the right questions. But in this particular interview CNBC missed the mark, and the reason is that they were talking to a CEO who operated in an obscure industry with a limited analytical following. Up until the takeover wave began to unfold, the water utility industry consisted of only a handful of public companies that generated very little news and even less excitement. For this reason, these stocks were completely off the Wall Street radar screen. In fact, even some of the handful of analysts who actually followed these stocks were behind the curve in picking up on the takeover potential in this group. So, it is perfectly understandable that this particular interview came off as though a group of people were struggling to make small talk at a boring cocktail party.

Making yourself aware of every industry—even an obscure industry like water utilities—that is beginning to consolidate through takeovers requires a new way of thinking about the financial news. The fact that you are reading this book indicates that you are likely to be receptive to this new way of thinking. In a few minutes I am going to take you inside the "superstock paradigm" and show you how to think and invest within that new framework.

But before you get to that paradigm you will have to traverse a Wall Street landscape that is full of potholes, dead ends, and hot air that can easily throw you off course. So let's take a brief look at some more of that landscape.

CHAPTER FIVE

The Twilight of Index Investing

A lemming is a member of the rodent family with a powerful herd instinct. They are noted for moving in packs, but then, many animals are pack animals, so this may not seem so unusual. Lemmings, however, take their herd instinct to a ridiculous extreme: They follow each other into the sea, often jumping off cliffs, which results in mass drownings. Although this sort of behavior may strike you as incredibly stupid, the same thing happens on Wall Street virtually every business day.

On Wall Street, the herd instinct is a powerful force indeed. Professional money managers, once they have been around for a while, discover there is great comfort in doing pretty much the same thing everybody else is doing. A certain style of investing, once it proves successful, tends to remain in style, year after year, until investors come to believe that this is the way things will be done forever and that no other style makes sense. Recently, the Wall Street lemmings have been running full speed toward the cliff of index investing, the fad of the moment that is sort of the bizarro world of superstock investing.

We all tend to base our view of the future on our most recent experience. This tendency to extrapolate trends of the recent past indefinitely into the future is perfectly natural—and on Wall Street it is extremely dangerous.

The history of the stock market is replete with examples of "can't miss" investing techniques that were successful for a while and then simply stopped working, victims of an overpopularity that eventually created the seeds of their own destruction.

In the 1960s, for example, small-cap stocks were all the rage. Well-known large caps were viewed as too boring, too predictable, and having limited growth prospects. Instead, investors wanted young companies with small revenue bases that might someday turn into larger companies that would bring huge stock price increases to their happy stockholders. The next Xerox. The next IBM. The next this, the next that. The next lemming.

As is always the case on Wall Street, brokerage firms and mutual fund companies were more than happy to create the products investors craved, and a slew of small-cap mutual funds were born, all of which were looking for the next IBM and all of which began chasing smaller-cap stocks. Eventually, the bargains disappeared, victims of too much money chasing the same stocks. How many IBMs could there have been, after all? The entire small stock sector crashed. The pendulum had swung too far toward small caps, and it was time to shift gears.

More recently, the focus has been on large-cap stocks—the same large caps everybody used to shun. If you've heard it once, you've heard it a thousand times: The best way for individual investors to make consistent profits in the stock market is to buy an "index" fund that tracks the performance of a broad-based stock market index like the Standard & Poor's 500 Index, which, in turn, represents a cross section of America's most solid, time-tested companies.

Don't try to pick individual stocks.

Don't try to outsmart the stock market.

Don't go too far off the beaten path trying to find overlooked values. All pertinent information is so readily available and so well analyzed by the Wall Street geniuses that it is already processed and "discounted" by the market. If you're an individual investor, don't even bother trying to find an edge. It can't be done.

Baloney.

Like lemmings, stock market commentators and mutual fund managers, and investors who listen to their advice, have run headlong toward the large-cap/indexing craze. It sounds so simple, who can resist it? This mantra has been repeated so often that you might think that the larger-cap stocks that dominate the major indices have outperformed their small-cap counterparts virtually 100 percent of the time since the stock market was created. One would think that earnings momentum has always been the stock market's holy grail and that value, asset-oriented stocks have always trailed the field.

And yet, those assumptions are not true. I'm not going to bore you with an historical examination of how the stock market favored different types of stocks at different times, except to say this: The infatuation with large-cap stocks has come and gone numerous times over the long history of Wall Street, and it will dissipate again, just as it has in the past. Trends ebb and flow, investment philosophies come and go, and every investment mania—that is, the recent obsession with indexing and large-cap stocks—contains the seeds of its own destruction.

Just a brief look at the past will prove the point. Figure 5–1, which tracks the relative performance of the S&P Low-Priced Stock Index to the S&P Big-Cap Index back to 1930, shows that smaller-cap stocks and larger-cap stocks have taken turns outperforming each other. A rising line means lower-priced stocks were leading the market; a falling line means the larger-cap stocks were leading the market. Good luck trying to glean anything from this chart, except for one thing: *things change.* For most of the 1960s small-cap stocks were outperforming large caps. In the early 1970s large-cap stocks were the star performers, but from 1976 through 1984, the small caps outperformed the large caps.The large caps took over from 1984 until 1991, then the small caps had a run from 1991 through 1995, and since then, the large caps have taken over once again.

What can we learn from this? For one thing: Anybody who tells you that the undisputed path to investment success is to index your investments to the S&P 500, which is dominated by large-cap stocks, has a limited sense of stock market history, has never seen this chart, or is a salesperson for an index fund. For another: No single investment style works best all of the time, and an intelligent lemming with a strong survival instinct had better learn that there comes a time when it's better to stop following the crowd.

Early in 1999 the "value gap" between large-cap and small-cap stocks was at the highest level in history. What this means is that price/earnings ratios accorded the large-cap stocks were at the *highest level ever relative to small-cap stocks.*

F i g u r e   5–1

Relative Leadership Index

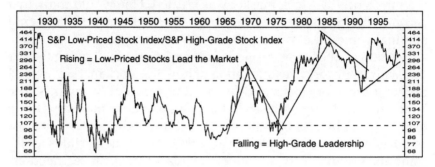

This fact, combined with the historical evidence shown in Figure 5–1, should at least raise the question: Are we fast approaching the twilight of large-cap and index investing? Is the pendulum about to swing the other way? And if it is, is superstock investing going to be the best way to beat the stock market over the next several years?

Experts: What Do They Know?

When you get to a fork in the road, take it.
Yogi Berra

By taking the fork in the road marked "superstock investing," you often will find that you have little, if any, analytical or "expert" support. This may produce an uncomfortable feeling at first.

This chapter is designed to get you over that feeling.

Once you begin to think in terms of the "new paradigm" of stock selection, you will have to get used to the idea, when you go off the beaten path, that you're not going to have a lot of company. In investment terms, the path in this book is definitely the road less traveled.

It's perfectly natural for any investor to feel more comfortable when buying a stock that is recommended by a large number of "expert" analysts. And yet, as you will see, the more analysts who are following a particular stock, the less likely it becomes that you can come up with any significant insight that hasn't already been factored into the stock price. Not only that, the more analysts who recommend any given stock, the greater the likelihood that all of the positive news and potential surrounding this particular company is already more than reflected in the stock price. This means that the slightest disappointment will result in an immediate and significant drop in the stock, which could wipe out months or years of profits in a single day.

In *Heaven Can Wait,* James Mason, an emissary from heaven, reveals a basic truth of life when he tells Warren Beatty that "the likelihood of a person being right increases in direct proportion to the number of people attempting to prove him wrong." This is another way of saying that if you are looking for truth, insight, or really great stock ideas, don't be afraid to go down that untrodden path—and don't waver simply because most people don't think the way you think or can't see what you see.

When you apply the principles described in this book to your stock selection process, you often will wind up with stocks that for one reason or another have been neglected or are out of favor. And yet, the Telltale Signs you'll learn to spot will strongly suggest that, beneath the surface of a sleepy, out-of-favor stock, a metamorphosis is starting to take place that has not yet become apparent to the mainstream Wall Street establishment, i.e., the "experts."

By the time you finish this book, you will recognize many of these Telltale Signs that metamorphosis is in the making, but that will be only half the battle. Even after you've spotted a potential winner, analyzed the situation correctly, and taken the plunge by buying the stock, you will probably have to suffer through a frustrating period during which whatever was blindingly obvious to you is completely overlooked by the experts who influence stock prices.

It can be pretty lonely and sometimes spooky when you're strolling down the untrodden superstock path.

To help you get through these inevitable periods of frustration when your confidence in your own judgment will be tested, and to help you remember that it is perfectly possible for you to be right while the "experts" are wrong, we'll show you some world-class examples of expert opinion that turned out to be completely off the mark.

WHAT IS AN "EXPERT," ANYWAY?

One wonderful definition is that an *expert* is "somebody from out of town," which is another way of saying that distance lends enchantment.

Another definition, and probably the best one for our purposes, would identify an "expert" as anybody who manages to get quoted in a newspaper or magazine or has a publicist with enough clout to wrangle an interview on television or radio. Considering the explosion of media outlets in recent years devoted to finance and investing, including the proliferation of financial Web sites, this definition of an "expert" would have to be considered fully diluted, if you get my drift.

"Experts" have always had a difficult time predicting the future, although this has never stopped any of them from making predictions. And it probably will not surprise you to learn that the U.S. government ranks right up there when it comes to the list of "experts" who have made pronouncements about the future that have turned out to be spectacularly wrong.

For example, every now and then over the past 30 years we have been subjected to an "energy scare" and we are told that energy supplies are running out. Every time these energy scares have surfaced, they turned out to be false alarms. But did you know that dire predictions of an imminent "energy doomsday scenario" have been going on for the last 115 years?

Take a look at the list of predictions about energy supplies from various U.S. government agencies given in Table 6–1, and remember it well the next time some bureaucrat or Wall Street analyst tells you that oil or gas supplies are running out.

But even a genuine, card-carrying expert with a track record of accomplishment and insight can be completely out of sync in any given situation and therefore way off the mark. Why? For one thing, even genuine experts are out there taking their best educated guess, just like the rest of us. And they can be influenced, like everybody else, by the subconscious idea that a trend in force for a long time will simply continue, indefinitely, into the future. And that means that most experts are not very good at identifying major turning points in the economy, the stock market, or the individual stock that has been in favor or out of favor for a long time.

One rule of thumb that has developed over the years is that whenever a certain trend in the economy or the stock market manages to make the cover of a general-interest magazine like *Time* or *Newsweek*, it's time to consider the possibility that this particular trend has pretty much run its course. A classic example of this phenomenon is the *Newsweek* cover, dated December 2, 1974, entitled, "How Bad a Slump?" When this issue of *Newsweek* hit the stands, the economy was in a severe recession, the stock market had been sliding for two years, inflation and oil prices had spiraled out of control, and interest

T a b l e   6—1

"Expert" Oil Supply Predictions from the U.S. Government

Year	Prediction
1885	Little or no chance for oil discovery in California (U.S. Geological Survey). Little or no chance for oil to be discovered in Kansas or Texas (U.S. Geological Survey).
1891	Little or no chance for oil to be discovered in Kansas or Texas (U.S. Geological Survey).
1908	Maximum future supply of oil to be discovered in the United States will be 22.5 billion barrels (U.S. Geological Survey). (*Note:* By 1949, 35 billion barrels had already been discovered, with another 27 billion barrels proven and available.)
1914	Total future U.S. production of oil will be a maximum of 5.7 billion barrels (U.S. Bureau of Mines). (*Note:* By 1976, another 34 billion barrels had been discovered, with no end in sight.)
1939	U.S. oil supplies will last only 13 more years (U.S. Department of the Interior).
1947	Sufficient oil for U.S. energy consumption can no longer be found in the United States (U.S. State Department).
1948	End of U.S. oil supply almost in sight (Secretary of the Interior).

Source: Herman Kahn, *The Next 200 Years* (William Morrow & Co., New York, 1976).

rates were in the stratosphere. So "How Bad a Slump?" seemed a perfectly legitimate question to ask. What nobody knew at the time was that the slump had already ended, the stock market had already hit bottom, and both inflation and interest rates had already peaked.

A more recent example of a magazine cover signaling the end of a financial trend was the December 27, 1999, issue of *Time* magazine in which Amazon.com founder Jeff Bezos was named *Time*'s "Person of the Year." That issue of *Time* coincided with the exact peak of Amazon.com's stock price, which proceeded to fall from $113 to as low as $19.38 over the following year. This does not imply that Jeff Bezos did not deserve the honor—only that *Time*'s cover story resulted in large part from a very newsworthy trend (the incredible stock market performance of the Internet stocks), which had been in force for a long time and which by that time had reached a ridiculous extreme. *Time*'s cover story signaled the end of the bull market not only for Amazon.com but for every other Internet stock, all of which plunged dramatically during 2000, and many of which actually went completely out of business.

This strategy of betting against magazine covers should not be confined to economic and investing issues, by the way. Here is another classic example of expert opinion that was off the mark. In the October 17, 1988, issue, *Sports Illustrated* ran a cover story on the invincible Oakland A's, who were about to face the Cincinnati Reds in the World Series.

"The 1988 A's," the story said, "are the best team the American League has sent to the World Series since Charlie Finley's teams of the early 1970s. These A's may be even better." Having thus been anointed one of the greatest baseball teams of all time, the A's went on to lose four straight World Series games to the Cincinnati Reds.

The "experts" aren't very good at predicting recessions either.

Economic recessions do not announce their arrival the way Jack Nicholson announced his arrival in *The Shining*—by breaking down a door with an axe and scaring Shelly Duval out of her wits as he announced: "Honey! I'm home!" Rather, recessions tend to arrive on muffled oars, quietly, arousing little or no suspicion until one day the Commerce Department announces that, "Guess what? We have been in a recession for the past 6 months. Have a nice day, and good luck paying off those loans that you took out to expand your business at precisely the wrong moment."

Yet another classic example of the "experts'" inability to predict recessions was evident in July 1989, when *Fortune* announced there would be "No recession this year or next." Of course, the recession of 1990 was already in the process of beginning, but none of the experts *Fortune* relied on saw it coming.

Just take a look at thr chronology of headlines in Table 6–2 to see how much help the "experts" will be in preparing you for the next recession.

T a b l e   6–2

Chronology of Headlines

Source	Headline
Fortune, July 17, 1989	"No Recession This Year or Next"
Newsweek, September 1989	"Is there Ever Going to Be Another Recession?"
New York Times, February 1990	"Economy's Slide May Have Ended, Greenspan Says"
Investor's Business Daily, January 1991	"It's Official: The U.S. Is in a Recession, But It Won't Last Long, Government Says."

You can also use the media to call turning points in both interest rates and oil prices. Here's a classic. On September 16, 1987, *The Wall Street Journal*'s front page lead story was headlined: "The Bond Bears: Debt Securities Prices May Slide for Years, Many Analysts Think."

The implication was that interest rates would be rising for years into the future. This front-page story, amazingly enough, coincided with the exact peak in long-term interest rates. When this story appeared, the 30-year Treasury bond was yielding around 10.25 percent (see the arrow on the chart in Figure 6–1).

Bond prices then embarked on a relentless 6-year rally, which carried the yield on the 30-year Treasury down below 6 percent by late 1993.

In another classic example, Associated Press managed to catch the exact bottom in crude oil when it ran a story on March 9, 1986, entitled: "No Bottom to Oil." Again, check the arrow on the chart in Figure 6–1. This story managed to appear at the precise bottom in the

F i g u r e   6–1

Examples of How the Media Can Call Turning Points

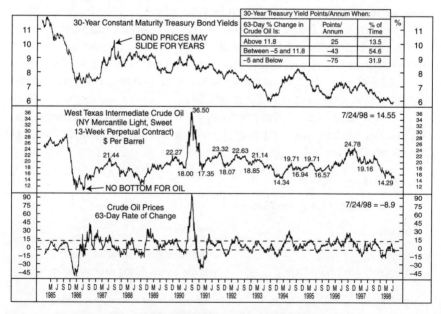

Source: Ned Davis Research, 2100 Riveredge Parkway, Suite 750, Atlanta, GA 30328.

price of oil, which rose from $12 to $36.50 a barrel within 4 years of the story's appearance.

How did *The Wall Street Journal* manage to run a lead story that was negative on bonds at precisely the peak in interest rates? How did the Associated Press proclaim that there was no bottom in sight for oil prices at the exact bottom for oil? They did what came naturally: They got used to a persistent trend and felt compelled to write about that trend for their readers. When *The Wall Street Journal* and Associated Press reporters went to their "expert" sources, these sources had also gotten used to a trend that had been in force, and simply extrapolated that trend into the future. It's always easier to explain what has been happening than to stick your neck out and suggest that something new is about to transpire, which is why you tend to see the media make a very big deal out of trends and people just as they are about to fizzle out.

Pack rat that I am, I have numerous examples of the media shining the spotlight on the wrong trend or the wrong person at precisely the wrong time. Here is one more example, a cover story dated October 26, 1987. This issue of *Fortune* hit the newsstands the very week of the 1987 stock market crash, and it said: "Why Greenspan Is Still Bullish." On October 19, 1987, the same week this issue appeared, the Dow Jones Industrial Average fell 508 points, a 1-day plunge of 18 percent.

Of course, following the monstrous stock market decline, the very same news magazines that had been touting prosperity and a forever-rising stock market shifted gears and began running cover stories about the coming recession and possible depression. The message of the stock market debacle, we were told, was that "hard times" were coming and that investors and businesspeople should batten down the hatches. Wrong again. The media went overboard on the meaning of the 1987 crash, just as it went overboard on the rally that preceded the debacle. The consensus of the media and its "experts" following the 1987 crash was that this could be just the beginning, a harbinger of severe economic problems for the world financial system. Even Robert Samuelson, *Newsweek*'s economic columnist and a man about as mainstream as you can get, ran a column after the crash entitled "The Specter of Depression," in which he asked the question: Did the market crash serve as a warning that an economic depression was imminent? His answer, delivered not entirely convincingly: "Probably not."

As it turned out, the 1987 stock market crash meant nothing at all. It was not an omen of anything, just a blip on the road to a continuing bull market and a U.S. economic advance that continued, with only brief interruptions, for more than a decade.

But you sure wouldn't have guessed that in October 1987 if you had listened to the "experts."

In the fall of 2000 the stock market was weakening as it became apparent that the economy was slowing down dramatically, and pundits were debating whether the slowdown would turn into a recession. On Friday, December 22, *The New York Daily News* ran a banner headline on page 5: "EXPERTS: NO RECESSION." I don't know about you, but I did not find this headline reassuring.

WHY EXPERTS CAN BE WRONG

So, what is it with these "experts" anyway? How can so many well-informed people be so wrong so often?

Part of the problem may be that the pool of "experts" is getting diluted.

A few years ago, before the proliferation of talk shows and the Internet, you had to be well versed in a particular subject before you were invited to appear on television or radio.

Not anymore. These days, talk shows have multiplied to such an extent that the supply of "experts" has increased to meet the demand. Of course, common sense will tell you there is a limited supply of experts on any particular subject, but this doesn't seem to matter very much because there is so much babble sprouting up in all forms of media that it's possible to say almost anything, no matter how outlandish or uninformed, and get away with it.

The proliferation of Internet financial sites has also created demand for more "experts." Every site needs columnists and "analysts" to expound on the daily developments on the financial scene. Most of them are excellent writers, and it sure *sounds* like they know what they're talking about. But who are they? What are their backgrounds? How much experience do they have? Have any of them ever even experienced a bear market or anything other than "momentum" and "index" investing?

It's tough to tell if you're reading truly informed analysis or just plain nonsense that has been created to provide content.

This nonsense cuts across ideological boundaries. No matter what your personal, political, or business agenda, it is possible to put your own "spin" on almost anything—even historical matters that are not really open to debate—and chances are you will not be challenged. And even if you are challenged, so what?

Rush Limbaugh, for example, has blamed the oil shortages and gasoline lines of the 1970s on Jimmy Carter, saying that "those gas lines were a direct result of foreign oil powers playing tough with us because they didn't fear Jimmy Carter." But the first—and worst—OPEC oil price hike took place between 1973 and 1974, during the administration of Richard Nixon. Not only that, but one reason for OPEC's initial oil price hike was the Nixon policy of wage and price controls, which caused OPEC to feel it was not receiving a fair price for its oil.

Everywhere you look, "experts" are spinning facts to promote an agenda. To this day, Democrats still try to deny that the economy performed well under Ronald Reagan.

Oliver North, who lied to Congress and was rewarded with the Republican nomination for senator from Virginia and then with a nationally syndicated talk show, refused to criticize Jerry Falwell for selling videotapes accusing President Clinton of murder, and responds to a question on *Larry King Live* by calling the tapes "alleged tapes," which apparently means that North could not even bring himself to acknowledge that such tapes even exist. If he *had* acknowledged their existence, after all, it would have reflected badly on Falwell, a philosophical and political ally.

Everybody, it seems, has an agenda. Cigarette company executives testify to Congress, under oath, that they do not believe nicotine is addictive. Even the sports world is not immune. In 1994 umpires confiscated the bat of Cleveland Indians slugger Albert Belle after the Chicago White Sox accused Belle of using a corked bat. American League officials X-rayed the bat, cut it in half, and then announced that the bat was illegally corked and suspended Belle for 10 days.

When the media confronted Belle's agent, the agent borrowed a page from the O.J. Simpson defense playbook and claimed the incident was "concocted by the Chicago White Sox."

So, given the surging supply of "experts" and the heightened probability that any given expert you may be listening to is promoting an agenda, don't be terribly concerned if you seem to have uncovered an exciting stock or two that is totally bereft of analytical "sponsorship."

Even Federal Reserve Chairman Alan Greenspan is a "spinner" with an agenda. In his book *The Agenda*—an appropriate title for this discussion—author Bob Woodward says that Greenspan managed to convince then–Treasury Secretary Lloyd Bentsen, early in President Clinton's first term, that the bond market would respond favorably if the Federal Reserve were to begin raising interest rates. Bentsen, impressed with Greenspan's reasoning, performed the spin on Clinton, who bought it hook, line, and sinker. Greenspan, Bentsen, and Clinton then performed their spin for the financial community, and everyone involved began to believe their own baloney to such an extent that they were all genuinely surprised when the bond market and the stock market headed lower following the Federal Reserve's interest rate hike.

So, one reason why an "expert" may be off the mark is that he or she is selling you a bill of goods, i.e., *promoting an agenda, rather than trying to get at the truth.*

Another reason experts don't always hit the mark is that they are not really *trying* to deliver the goods for a different reason, and that reason is that they're not always rewarded for telling the truth—especially when the truth is something their superiors do not want to hear. Sometimes they are even *punished* for telling the truth.

In his book *1929 Again*, author Terry R. Rudd points out that "one of the underlying problems making it virtually impossible for knowledgeable people to tell us the truth is that we can't accept it without reacting unfavorably."

"When the recipient doesn't receive news in a manner beneficial to the giver, " Rudd writes, "there is no incentive for the giver to do so."

It is a well-known fact among Wall Street professionals, for example, that there is little mileage in taking a negative attitude toward the stock market or the economy. Optimism sells, and if you want to do business, you are almost always better off taking the rosy view of just about everything on the investment scene.

Perhaps the classic example of this fundamental truth took place on September 5, 1929, just a few weeks before the Great Stock Market Crash. Economist Roger Babson, speaking at a major business conference, made the following statement: "Sooner or later a crash is coming, and it may be terrific. Factories will be shut down . . . men will be thrown out of work . . . the vicious cycle will be in full reversal and the recession will be a serious business depression."

Now that is about as accurate as you can get in terms of predicting the stock market and the economy. Babson's reward was that he was ridiculed and criticized as a fearmonger. Rudd says that one major brokerage firm actually took out an ad in *The Wall Street Journal* raking Babson over the coals and stating that "we will not be stampeded into selling stocks because of the gratuitous forecasts of a well-known statistician."

The stock market actually began declining on the very day Babson made his historical forecast, and that particular drop became known as the "Babson Break." By late October the crash that Babson had predicted was under way, culminating on "Black Tuesday," October 29, 1929, the worst day in stock market history.

And what was Babson's reward for being so accurate? Some people had the temerity to criticize Babson for being early in his bearish prediction, and others actually went so far as to blame the stock market crash and the ensuing depression on Babson's "fearmongering."

This is a lesson that has been learned and relearned in varying degrees over the years by anyone who has had the misfortune of turning prematurely bearish on the stock market or the economy or having the nerve to issue a "sell" signal on a big-name company with a popular stock and a penchant for doing investment banking business.

Therefore, you should not expect much help from the "experts" when it comes to predicting bear markets, recessions, earnings disappointments at large, well-known companies that do a lot of investment banking business on Wall Street, or in other areas where the forecast of bad news might be met with, shall we say, a bad attitude.

One of the all-time great examples of an "expert" receiving an icy attitude toward his honest point of view is the Russian economist Nikolai D. Kondratieff, who was exiled to a labor facility in Siberia and died there after he wrote a 1925 treatise in which he suggested that capitalism was a perfectly legitimate economic system that would always recover from depressions if left to its own devices. This point of view was not something the Communists particularly wanted to hear, since Moscow had taken the position that capitalism was a flawed system that contained the seeds of its own destruction.

And so, the father of the "Kondratieff Wave," which turned out to be one of the more enduring theories of economics, was handed a pickax, or whatever they gave you when they shipped you off to Siberia, and is most likely preserved in ice for future inhabitants to thaw and scratch their heads at.

Not all experts receive such harsh treatment for trying to report the truth as they perceive it. Some of them, like the brokerage firm analyst who issued a negative report on one of Donald Trump's companies several years ago, merely got fired.

Others meet with a more subtle form of resistance.

Case Study: Sunbeam Corp.

If you want to get a feel for how difficult it can be for mainstream Wall Street analysts to say "sell" when they know they will incur the wrath of the company in question, their clients, the brokers who work for their firms, and possibly even their employers, consider the brouhaha that greeted PaineWebber analyst Andrew Shore in 1997 when he merely downgraded his opinion on Sunbeam Corp. from buy to hold.

Sunbeam stock had taken off like a rocket, rising from $12 to over $50 following the arrival of a reputed corporate savior named Al Dunlap. Dunlap had a history of cutting costs and streamlining operations at poorly managed companies, and in fact had just engineered a turnaround at Scott Paper, which was then sold to Kimberly Clark and resulted in huge profits for Scott Paper shareholders.

Wall Street expected Dunlap to perform the same miracle at Sunbeam, an old-line appliance manufacturer whose stock was in the doldrums due to what Wall Street perceived to be poor management of a potentially powerful brand name. Al Dunlap arrived, full of bravado, and proceeded to lay off employees, close down plants, and issue optimistic projections for the future. Wall Street totally bought Dunlap's performance, and Sunbeam shares took off. Virtually every analyst who followed Sunbeam sang Dunlap's praises and expected a breathtaking turnaround, followed by an eventual takeover of Sunbeam—in other words, they expected an exact replay of the Scott Paper scenario.

Mr. Shore, however, had his doubts. He was somewhat skeptical of Al Dunlap from the start, wondering how layoffs and plant closings could possibly turn a low-margin business, faced with cutthroat competition, into a growth stock phenomenon—but he recommended the stock along with everyone else based on the premise that Dunlap's name and reputation alone would probably take the stock for quite a profitable ride. The trick, he thought, would be to get out in time.

Finally, in 1997, Andrew Shore began to notice warning signs deep within the Sunbeam financial statements filed with the SEC. As it turned out, these warning signs were harbingers of huge problems lurking beneath the shiny surface of Sunbeam which eventually pushed the company to the brink of bankruptcy. Shore decided he would pull his buy rating on Sunbeam; yet, even though he suspected a massive deterioration of Sunbeam's financial situation, he could only bring himself to change his rating from buy to "neutral." But even this move, which in retrospect proved to be a timid and incomplete decision, made him a virtual Nostradamus compared to his colleagues.

The first reaction to Mr. Shore's decision to pull his buy recommendation on Sunbeam came from his research associate, who told Shore that he risked a negative reaction not only from Al Dunlap and Sunbeam, but also from PaineWebber clients and brokers. "You realize what you're doing here, don't you?" he asked Shore.

"If we're wrong we're going to be fired," Shore replied, "but we have to do this." Shore even felt compelled to contact the legal compliance department at PaineWebber to explain his downgrade of Sunbeam before the downgrade was issued.

When you stop and think about the fear and soul-searching that preceded a mere downgrade from buy to neutral, you have to laugh out loud. Here was a well-known and established security analyst literally shaking in his boots because he was going to downgrade a popular stock to neutral. He was so fearful of being fired—fired!—if he were wrong that he felt compelled to explain his decision in advance to the PaineWebber compliance department, just in case the stock continued to go up and he had to explain himself later.

On April 3, 1997, Andrew Shore got on the PaineWebber "squawk box" and reported his downgrade to PaineWebber's 5000 stockbrokers. Within minutes Sunbeam stock dropped $4 a share. Shortly thereafter, when Andrew Shore checked his voice mail, he was stunned to hear a barrage of "caustic and bitter messages." "Most of the callers," author John A. Byrne says, "wanted Shore fired."

Shore, according to Byrne who documented these events in his book *Chainsaw*, was "horrified by the content" of the messages, which ranged from calling him "stupid and irresponsible" to even worse.

"It was a nightmare," said Shore's assistant, who bore the brunt of the flak from clients and brokers reacting to Shore's downgrade.

The story had a happy ending for Andrew Shore. Shortly after the downgrade, Sunbeam shocked Wall Street with the announcement that earnings would come in far below expectations. Those who had acted on Shore's advice saved a bundle—and of course, the congratulatory calls began to flow in.

Lessons Learned

What lessons can we learn from this episode?

First, keep in mind that Andrew Shore never told anyone to *sell* Sunbeam. He merely downgraded the stock to "neutral." Investors were forced to read between the lines of the recommendation, and those who did were spared the bulk of the Sunbeam carnage; the stock eventually fell to $0.25, down 99 percent from its Dunlap-mania high, as the news from Sunbeam got progressively worse.

But even that downgrade to neutral caused fear and soul-searching for Andrew Shore, which gives you an idea of why so few "sell" recommendations emanate from the mainstream Wall Street research departments. And the venomous reaction from PaineWebber clients and brokers to the Sunbeam downgrade should also go a long way toward explaining why the "messenger" is often so reluctant to deliver the bad news. When the reaction is criticism and anger, what is the incentive to tell the truth?

Experts Are Pressured to Conform to Prevailing Ideology

"A sell signal from an analyst is as common as a Barbra Streisand concert."
Arthur Levitt, Chairman of the Securities & Exchange Commission

It is not just the company, clients, and brokers who exert psychological pressure on analysts to maintain a positive attitude on the popular stocks they follow, although that would be more than enough. There is also pressure from other analysts to conform to the bullish point of view. If you are a mainstream Wall Street analyst and you have decided to turn bearish on a stock or an industry that is being recommended by virtually all of your analytical colleagues, you had better have your facts straight and be prepared for some criticism, veiled and otherwise. Curiously, the inverse is not true: It is perfectly acceptable for an analyst to turn bullish on an industry when everyone else is bearish; trying to be the first to catch the bottom, apparently, is within the rules of the analytical game.

But if an analyst tries to catch the top by turning negative on an industry or an individual stock everyone else loves, watch out!

On November 22, 1999, *The Wall Street Journal* ran a story entitled "Bearish Call on Banks Lands Analyst in Doghouse." The story described the travails of Michael Mayo of Credit Suisse First Boston, and the doghouse to which Mr. Mayo was exiled was owned and operated by other Wall Street banking analysts who saw only blue skies ahead for the bank stocks. When Mr. Mayo peered into the distance and announced that he saw some storm clouds brewing for the banking industry he was treated like the Wall Street equivalent of a stinky wet dog trying to shake itself dry.

The head trader at Sun Trust Funds, said *The Wall Street Journal*, "angrily grabbed a picture of Mr. Mayo, blew up the photo on the copier, scribbled 'Wanted' over his face, and pinned it to her bulletin board." When questioned about this response by *The Wall Street Journal*, the trader replied that "my impression [of Mr. Mayo] as a human being is that he's somewhat self-promotional," as though this were a rare trait among analysts on Wall Street.

Another bank analyst, angered by the sell signal, referred to Mayo derisively as "Mayo-naise" in a conference call with clients, according to *The Wall Street Journal*. Other analysts also questioned Mayo's motives, both publicly and in private. Some of them whispered that Mayo was in cahoots with short sellers who were in a position to profit if bank stocks declined in price. Others said that he was gunning for publicity in an attempt to earn a high ranking in an upcoming analyst survey by *Institutional Investor Magazine*.

Even after Michael Mayo's negative call on bank stocks turned out to be accurate, the critics refused to let up on him. A few months after his cautionary report on the group, Bank One, a Wall Street darling, collapsed in price following the surprising news that problems at its credit card unit, First USA, would lead to lower than expected earnings. Mayo had put a "sell" on Bank One (ONE) at $59.81 a share; the stock ultimately fell as low as $23.19 following the disappointing earnings, a 61 percent decline.

But even that did not keep the critics quiet. Instead of giving Mayo his due for his gutsy and accurate call, the bank bulls decided that nitpicking was now called for.

Mayo's general negative attitude toward the bank stocks stemmed from his belief that the earnings growth being reported by many banks was of "low quality"; in other words, the accountants were becoming increasingly creative in their ongoing effort to give Wall Street the earnings momentum it craved and expected. Anyone who understands financial accounting knows there are about 50 different and perfectly acceptable ways to look at almost everything and that your earnings may be up 5 percent, up 10 percent, or even down 10 percent, depending on which way the accountants decide they are going to paint the picture this particular quarter.

Eventually, though, the accountants' bag of tricks gets depleted, and if a company is not growing all that rapidly—or worse, if creative accounting has directed analytical attention away from a festering problem—the piper must be paid.

This is not an uncommon occurrence with popular stocks that are under tremendous pressure to meet Wall Street expectations, and the general observation that a particular company or an industry, in general, has begun to resort to accounting gimmicks to meet Wall Street expectations—i.e., that reported earnings are of "low quality," as Mayo stated—is a valid and sufficient reason to turn negative. If you smell something rotten, you don't have to rummage through the garbage to figure out what it is—you can just walk away from it.

When Bank One revealed that problems had been brewing in its credit card operations and that its earnings would be way below expectations, that should have been enough to shut Mayo's critics up.

But it wasn't.

"Critics say," *The Wall Street Journal* reported with a straight face, "that Mr. Mayo had not pinpointed the credit card problem."

When another bank stock cited by Mayo as having "poor earnings quality"—National City Corp.—warned that earnings would be lower than expected, that stock took a nosedive as well. But, *The Wall Street Journal* pointed out, "Mr. Mayo didn't specifically have a 'sell' recommendation on that stock."

The overall tone of *The Wall Street Journal* story on Michael Mayo was that he was sort of a self-promotional kind of guy who sort of lucked out by issuing a generally negative call on the bank stocks and turned out to be right for the wrong reasons, and that he was not all that popular among colleagues and clients.

You can see that the bar is raised considerably higher when you are bearish than when you are a conforming bull. *The Wall Street Journal* could have run a story about the 99 percent of analysts who were incorrectly bullish on Bank One, for example, and interviewed *their* clients, to see how they enjoyed riding that stock down by 61 percent. But it didn't. Instead, *The Wall Street Journal* dissected Mayo's bearish (and correct) call with a fine-tooth comb, and created the impression that while he turned out to be right, he wasn't really all *that* right and that he was a publicity hound to boot.

Michael Mayo's reward for being bearish on the regional banks was to be fired. On September 29, 2000, he announced that Credit Suisse First Boston had terminated his employment. "It's hard to do investment banking for a client with an analyst who is negative on that client," a source told Reuters.

It doesn't work the other way around, by the way. If you're a cheerleader for a stock and it goes up, nobody complains that it didn't go up for the reasons you said it would. You're just a brilliant analyst who made the right call. But if you're a bear on the bank stocks because you think that earnings quality is deteriorating and that some banks have been stretching to make their earnings forecasts and that this cannot go on indefinitely—if you say all that and you turn out to be right—that is still not enough. You have to pinpoint *exactly* what the problem was or your correctly bearish call can be dissected, analyzed, and ultimately criticized anyway.

The whole thing would be funny if it were not so important to you, as an investor, and these cautionary tales involving Mr. Mayo and Sunbeam analyst Andrew Shore are meant to illustrate a truth: If you really want original, independent research and you think you are going to get it from Wall Street, you may be in for a big disappointment.

Back in the 1980s a group of penny stock brokers had just completed a public offering for a company that was trying to develop a cure for cancer derived from shark fluids. I ran into the brokers at a restaurant one evening and they were so enthusiastic about this company's prospects they could barely contain themselves. The stock had run up from $0.10 a share to $1.30, and there were plans for a secondary offering to finance further research into new drugs once the company had proven it could use shark fluids to cure cancer.

Everything was going swimmingly until the scientist who ran the company called the president of the brokerage firm with the bad news that the process doesn't work.

"What are you talking about?" the brokerage firm president said.

"We cannot cure cancer with shark fluids," the scientist said.

"Yes, you can," said the brokerage firm president.

"No, we can't," said the scientist. "The process doesn't work."

"Yes, it does," said the brokerage firm president.

The scientist was taken aback at this response. "I wish it *did* work," he said again. "But it doesn't."

"Hold on," said the brokerage firm president.

When the brokerage firm president returned to the line, the scientist found himself in the midst of a conference call with every broker in the office. For the next half hour the brokers browbeat the scientist into submission, trying to convince him that he could, indeed, cure cancer through the use of shark fluids.

The scientist tried his best to hold his ground. "It doesn't work!" he said pleadingly.

"It has to work!" screamed one broker. "Your stock is at $1.30, all of my clients own it, and we're almost ready to do your secondary offering!"

And so, at the urging of his "constituency," the scientist agreed to go back to the drawing board to try to find a cure for cancer using shark fluids, trying to fulfill the fervent hope of a group of penny stock brokers that such a cure could be found so that these brokers could do a secondary stock offering. Yet, the scientist knew full well, as he continued his research, that the process didn't work.

The scientist admitted, long after the fact, that listening to those guys nearly convinced him that he had missed something.

I was reminded of this story on December 1, 2000, when *The New York Times* reported that certain analysts were "skeptical" of computer maker Gateway's shocking announcement that it was lowering its revenues and earnings forecasts for the quarter because its sales had unexpectedly plunged 30 percent over the weekend following Thanksgiving. Like the shark fluid brokers, these analysts just could not accept the bad news that Gateway delivered. Instead of accepting the news and revising their forecasts, some analysts tried to convince themselves (and Gateway) that the sales slump didn't mean what Gateway said it meant, which was that business was turning rotten. Loaded with Gateway shares in client accounts and stuck like SuperGlue to their overly bullish forecasts, these analysts accused Gateway management of "overreacting," which only goes to show you that whether we're talking about shark fluids and penny stock brokers or computers and big-time Wall Street analysts, there are few things so constant as human nature. As songwriter Paul Simon reminded us in *The Boxer*, "a man sees what he wants to see and disregards the rest." That is a fundamental truth of Wall Street that every investor should keep firmly in mind.

So, one thing to keep in mind when you're listening to the opinion of an expert: Who is the expert's constituency? Or, to put it more bluntly, who pays the expert's salary? If it isn't you—and it usually will not be you—consider the possible agenda of the expert and/or constituency and view the expert's point of view in that light.

Even experts who are honestly taking their best shot and are not influenced at all by an agenda or a constituency can get things all wrong, as Figure 6–2 shows.

IT ALSO REALLY HELPS IF YOU CAN MAINTAIN SOME PERSPECTIVE

"To understand what the outside of an aquarium looks like, it is better not to be a fish."
André Malraux

Back in 1974, when I was working as a junior analyst on Wall Street, I used to circulate a weekly tongue-in-cheek stock market report among my fellow employees. The newsletter was mostly satire, poking fun at some of the idiosyncrasies and absurdities of Wall Street.

In the fall of 1974 the Dow Jones Industrial Average was trading below 600, trading volume was running at around 6 million shares, and on most days you could have organized a good racketball tournament on the floor of the New York Stock Exchange and not annoyed anybody because nothing much was going on down there anyway. Things were so slow that a major investment magazine ran a cover story entitled: "This Is Not Just a Bear Market. This Is the Way Things Are Going to Be from Now On." (The experts were wrong, of course.)

During lunch, we would sit around and lazily watch the ticker tape move across the top of our quote machines, that is, when it moved at all. In those days, the tape moved in fits and starts; a couple of trades would show up, then the tape would just sit there, and not move for 10 or 20 seconds, and then another solitary trade would be reported. Sometimes the tape would stop for such a prolonged period of time that we would tap the side of the computer screen, as if we were tapping the side of a pinball or videogame, trying to get the tape moving again.

F i g u r e   6–2

"Experts" and Their Statements

- It was "expert" Jimmy the Greek who declared "Impossible!" when someone asked him whether Cassius Clay (aka, Muhammad Ali) could last even six rounds with heavyweight champion Sonny Liston, just a few days before Clay won the title.

- It was "expert" Thomas Edison who said in 1922 that "the radio craze will die out in time."

- It was "expert" Harry Warner, President of Warner Bros., who in 1927, laughed at the idea of using sound in motion pictures, saying, "Who the hell wants to hear actors talk?"

- It was "expert" Emmeline Snively, Director of the Blue Book Modeling Agency, who told Marilyn Monroe in 1944: "You'd better learn secretarial work, or else get married."

- It was an "expert" (a United Artists executive) who turned down actor Ronald Reagan for the starring role as the President in *The Best Man* by saying: "Ronald Reagan doesn't have that presidential look."

- It was "expert" Jim Denny, manager of the Grand Ole Opry, who told Elvis Presley on September 25, 1954: "You ain't goin' nowhere son. You ought to go back to driving a truck."

- It was "expert" Ken Olson, President of the Digital Equipment Company, who said in 1977: "There is no reason for any individual to have a computer in their home."

- It was "expert" Charles H. Duell, Commissioner of the U.S. Office of Patents, who urged President William McKinley to abolish the Patent Office in 1899, based on the incredible logic that "Everything that can be invented has been invented."

- It was "expert" Professor of Economics Irving Fisher of Yale University who declared, on October 17, 1929: "Stocks have reached what looks like a permanently high plateau."

- It was "expert" Thomas J. Watson, Chairman of IBM, who declared, in 1943, "I think there is a world market for about five computers."

- It was "expert" Eric Easton, manager of the Rolling Stones, who said of Mick Jagger in 1963: "The singer will have to go."

Source: Christopher Cerf and Victor Navasky, *The Experts Speak* (Pantheon Books, New York, 1984).

On some days the trades were so few and far between we were able to sit around and comment at length on each trade that appeared on the tape before the next one appeared. This got me to thinking about the potential for a television program in which a group of analysts just sat around and commented on the New York Stock Exchange ticker tape all day long.

My friends got a big laugh out of that one.

A few days later I published my weekly stock market "report" in which I imagined what it would be like if Howard Cosell, Frank Gifford, and "Dandy" Don Meredith, the hosts of ABC-TV's *Monday Night Football*, were to host a live daily television program direct from the New York Stock Exchange.

As I envisioned it, Howard Cosell and Frank Gifford would be sitting in a booth high above the New York Stock Exchange trading floor, much as political commentators sit above the floor of a political convention, watching a huge ticker tape and providing a trade-by-trade commentary on the day's stock market action.

Meanwhile, Don Meredith, a former Dallas Cowboys' quarterback, would serve as the sideline commentator, roaming the floor of the NYSE, elbowing his way through the mass of traders and looking for expert analysis and inside scoops.

What a laugh, right? Little did I know.

There's nothing wrong with minute-by-minute analysis of the financial markets and the fact that so much market analysis and commentary is so short-term-oriented. There are many ways to skin the proverbial stock market cat, and many approaches to the market that can yield profitable results.

And, there is no use complaining about it. In the age of the Internet and instant information, when complete access to the floor of the New York Stock Exchange is available, you cannot expect that all of this will not be put to use. You can question whether it really matters what the stock market does on any given day, or during any given hour, and you can wonder if much of the short-term commentary you hear day in and day out is of much real value. (You can wonder, for example, how it is possible for a guest to sit there, on live television, and respond to question after question from viewers calling on the telephone, asking about a series of random stocks. How can this "expert" possibly provide a thoughtful, informed response on every single question?)

You can wonder about all of this, but you can't fight it, and besides, there is a market for this type of information. Plenty of investors apparently find it useful or there would not be such a wide audience for CNBC and stock message boards. Short-term trading, based on instant analysis, is a perfectly acceptable way to approach the stock market. Just ask any trader.

But it is not the only way. And the problem is since so much of the mainstream media has become fixated on this ultra-short-term approach to investing, there is a tendency to forget that there are other approaches that do not make you feel guilty if you leave your quote machine or turn off the financial television station for 10 minutes.

You can, if you wish, be made aware of every uptick and downtick of the market, all day, every day. You can know about every analyst upgrade and downgrade and why any stock is moving on any given day. You can know all of the important earnings estimates, down to the last penny; you will also know the "whisper number"; you will know if the company that has just reported earnings managed to beat the official estimate, the "whisper number", or both; and you can even hang around after the close to see if the lemmings are frantically buying or selling in after-hours trading, based on the burning issue of the moment, which in all probability will be replaced the next day by another, completely unrelated burning issue of the moment.

You can put yourself through this madness, if you like. But there is another way to deal with the stock market. You can decide to take a step back from the precipice of urgent microanalysis and deal with the stock market only from a vantage point that provides some perspective.

This vantage point involves looking for stocks that are showing signs that something significant is changing—for the better—on a long-term basis. You can look at neglected stocks that have fallen so far out of favor that you have to begin to remind yourself that this is a business, not just a piece of paper for Wall Street to play games with, and that if certain Telltale Signs are popping up, there is a good possibility that somebody will step in and force the stock market to value this neglected stock *at its proper value as a business*.

In this book, you will learn how to spot some of the Telltale Signs that will enable you to buy these out-of-favor stocks with confidence. We will show you how to determine when a formerly sleepy, seemingly uninteresting stock may be about to emerge as a huge winner.

In short, we have arrived at a fork in the stock market road—this book will take you on a trip down the road less traveled.

And once you've been down this road, you will never look at the frantic three-ring circus of urgent day-to-day stock market commentary and "expert" analysis in quite the same way.

CHAPTER SEVEN

What Is Value?

You've heard a lot about "value investing" recently, but what exactly does that term mean? Generally, value investing involves buying stocks that are out of favor and therefore undervalued relative to other stocks. That sounds like a sensible way to invest until you ask two key questions:

1. What is "value?"
2. Why can't a stock that is undervalued remain undervalued, theoretically, indefinitely?

It's all well and good to say that in the long run the stock market will adjust undervalued stocks to a more reasonable value, but as John Maynard Keynes pointedly reminded us, "In the long run we are all dead."

What we need is an investing approach that not only focuses on "value" but also provides for some sort of catalyst—some outside event—that will literally force the stock market to take an undervalued stock and reprice it at a higher, more appropriate value.

Let's start with this premise: A stock is worth what the stock market says it is worth on any given day—no more, no less. You can argue that a stock is overvalued or undervalued, but if you want to buy it or sell it, there is only one value that really matters: the price the stock market is placing on that stock right now.

Where does that price come from?

It comes from two places: *(1) earnings expectations and (2) the present value the market is willing to place on those earnings expectations.*

Think of a stock as representing a small piece of ownership in an estimated future stream of earnings. Those earnings are unknown, and investors rely on the best guesses of Wall Street analysts to determine what they'll be. When you buy a share of stock today, you're buying a stake in that future earnings stream.

Of course, analyst estimates of that future earnings stream may be wildly off the mark, which adds another major variable to the question of determining value. But let's assume, charitably, that the analysts are going to get it right and you know precisely what a company will earn over the next 10 years.

Even so, you would have only half the equation because the next question would be: What is that future earnings stream worth today? What the market is willing to pay for a given level of earnings is the *price/earnings ratio*. And if you think predicting earnings is difficult, you haven't seen anything yet.

Take a look at Figure 7–1, which shows the price/earnings ratio of the Standard & Poor's 500 Index going back to 1925. As you can see, the stock market at various points along the way has decided that stocks were worth anywhere from six times earnings (in 1949) to as much as 28 times earnings in 1998. And that ratio has gyrated wildly along the way, rising and falling sharply, so that a stock earning $2 per share could be worth $40 one year and only $20 the following year. Same company, same earnings—but a wildly different concept of value.

F i g u r e   7–1

S&P Price/Earnings Ratio

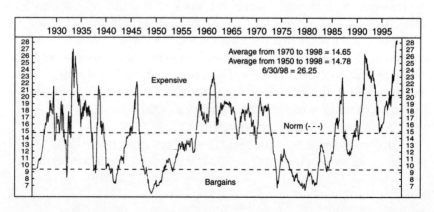

What causes price/earnings ratios to shift so dramatically?

The major determining factor is interest rates. When interest rates rise, price/earnings ratios tend to fall. When interest rates decline, price/earnings ratios tend to rise.

There are two reasons for the profound effect of interest rates on price/earnings ratios. The first has to do with how money managers behave. The stock market is one place where a money manager can invest funds, but there are other alternatives, and the relative attractiveness of those alternatives can affect the amount of money that goes into or out of stocks.

For some investors the stock market competes for funds with the bond market. Stocks carry risk, but long-term bonds carry less risk. A 20- or 30-year bond can have some awfully wild swings before the payoff (maturity) date, but some money managers look at long-term bonds as an alternative to stocks because at least they know these bonds will have a certain maturity value at a certain fixed point in time, at which time their original investment will be intact. Stocks, obviously, carry no such guarantee.

When other money managers are deciding whether to commit more or less capital to the stock market, what they're really looking at as an alternative is the "no-risk" alternative—cash.

By "cash" we mean money market funds or short-term treasury securities, where a dollar invested today will be worth a dollar tomorrow, unequivocally and with no other potential outcome. This is the riskless alternative to the stock market, and the interest rate a money manager can earn on this riskless alternative is perhaps the major variable that determines the price/earnings multiple placed on a given level of earnings.

Suppose, for example, you are managing a pension fund for a large company. Your job is to make sure that when employees retire they will receive their pension benefits. Your company has set aside a certain amount of money for this purpose and instructed you to invest it in such a way that when the benefits have to be paid, at some point in the future, there is enough money to pay them. A team of actuarial accountants has prepared a very nice booklet, complete with actuarial tables, that sits on your desk. And what this booklet tells you, basically, is that if you can earn 8 percent per year on the money that's been left for you to manage, there will be enough money to pay the retirees and everyone will be happy.

As you sit there and survey the investment scene, you see that long-term U.S. government bonds are yielding 6 percent. That will do you no good because you need to earn 8 percent or the retirees will be calling you up for loans so they can maintain their standard of living 20 years from now. The yield on money market funds, at 4.75 percent, is even less.

To earn the required 8 percent, therefore, you will have to take some risk—and that means you'll have to invest in the stock market. Although stocks do not come with guaranteed returns, they do offer upside growth potential. And since there's no other way to get the 8 percent you need, you take the plunge into the market.

Across the street there is another money manager in charge of another company pension fund. His job is just like yours, except his company has a lousy union and the pension benefits for its retirees are going to be a lot less than yours. According to the actuarial tables, the money manager across the street needs to earn only 6.5 percent on his investments to fund the retirement plan.

So, you're both in the same boat—at least for now. You need to earn 8 percent and the money manager across the street needs to earn 6.5 percent, but neither one of you can get what you want in bonds or money market funds, so you're both buying stocks.

Now, let's suppose interest rates start to rise. The yield on the 30-year government bonds jumps to 7 percent. This is still not good enough for you because you need 8 percent to fund the pension plan. But the money manager across the street now faces an interesting situation. He needs 6.5 percent to fund his plan; he can get 7 percent in U.S. government bonds. In order to do his job, all he has to do is buy bonds and go shoot a round of golf. He will also have a lot less stress. And he must now ask the question: If I can get the 7 percent I need in government bonds, why should I be taking risks in stocks? That is a very good question, and the answer will likely be that this money manager will begin moving at least a portion of the funds he has invested out of stocks and into bonds. And if the interest on "cash" investments, like money funds and short-term treasury bills, also reaches 7 percent, he will likely move a lot more money out of stocks.

In other words, as interest rates on less risky investments rise, a certain amount of money will leave the stock market to lock in that return. At 7 percent, a certain number of investors will determine that they do not need to take the risk the stock market entails. At 8 percent, a new round of money managers will make the same decision. Each uptick in interest rates will suck money out of the market because the lesser-risk return meets some investor's goal, which is one reason why rising interest rates almost always put downward pressure on the stock market.

The profound effect of interest rate movements on stock prices is the major reason Wall Street is so obsessed with Alan Greenspan and the Federal Reserve, even to the point where CNBC analyzes the size of Greenspan's briefcase as a potential clue as to whether the Federal Reserve is about to shift its interest rate policy.

There is another reason why rising interest rates usually mean lower stock prices. It's a bit more complicated but its worth knowing, and it explains a big part of the mystery of the wildly gyrating price/earnings ratios touched on earlier.

This concept is called "discounted present value," and what it boils down to is this: If you know what a company will earn over the next 10 years, what is that future earnings stream worth today? Again, what the market is willing to pay today for those future earnings is the price/earnings ratio.

Let's use this example:

Suppose Totter's Rollerblades Inc. (TRI) is estimated to earn a grand total of $50 per share over the next 10 years. This means if you buy one share of TRI today, you are buying a piece of that future earnings stream. What is that future earnings stream worth right now? Put another way, what amount would you have to invest today to have $50 ten years from now?

Answer: It depends on the level of interest rates. The higher the level of interest rates, the less you must invest today to get that $50 ten years from now. In other words, when interest rates are high, the *present value* of that $50 will be less than it would be when interest rates are lower. High interest rates will result in the present value of that $50 ten years from now being lower, while low interest rates will result in present value being higher.

For example, if you want to have $50 ten years from now and interest rates are 10 percent, you only have to invest around $19 today. But if interest rates are at 5 percent, you will have to invest $31 today to get that $50 ten years from now.

Think about that for a moment. Ten percent interest rates make the present value of $50 ten years from now worth $19. Five percent rates make the present value $31. In other words, given the earnings projections for Totter's Rollerblades Inc., the present value of those earnings can be worth anywhere from $19 to $31, depending on the level of interest rates. And if you think of a stock price in terms of present value, you can see how interest rates can have a profound effect on what Wall street will be willing to pay today for a projected future earnings stream. Same company, same earnings projections—the only difference is what those earnings are worth right now in any given interest rate environment.

That, in simplified terms, is how most stocks trade. For the most part they're at the mercy of earnings forecasts that are constantly changing and may or may not be on the mark, and they're at the mercy of interest rate movements that cause professional money managers to move into and out of stocks in general and that will alter the value of your investments as rates fluctuate, even if earnings estimates are accurate.

Given all of this, how can anyone define "value"?

Let me tell you one way.

When thinking of value, think of this: What would a company be worth to another company *as a business*? Every company has a certain value, which can be fairly well-defined, when viewed in this light. But this is a far different concept of value than the one under which Wall Street operates.

The actual value of a stock—*as a business*—is only fleetingly related, if it is related at all, to the gyrations of the stock market. Again, depending on shifting earnings forecasts or interest rate fluctuations, stocks can move all over the place, like a ship passing another ship on a foggy night, without even knowing it's there.

The only time this concept of value matters is when someone is willing to step up to the plate to pay that value. In other words, when a takeover bid takes place.

My concept of a "value" situation, therefore, is: *stocks that are selling at clearance-sale prices, significantly below their value as a business, where there is a reasonable possibility that someone will step up and offer to pay that value, thereby forcing the stock market to reflect that value in the stock price.*

When this happens, a normal, run-of-the-mill stock that is at the mercy of all of the variables discussed here becomes a superstock. It immediately rises to its true value level—*as a business*— and it is no longer subject to the whims of the stock market and all of the unpredictable variables that determine where most stocks trade.

You may think that choosing stocks that are likely to become takeover targets is an impossible task. The reason why you may think this way is that you've probably heard this refrain over and over again from Wall Street commentators who are obsessed with earnings forecasts and stock market projections and who have no experience when it comes to selecting logical takeover candidates.

But picking takeover targets is *not* an impossible task.

As an individual investor, you can uncover neglected and undervalued stocks that are not only selling at a discount to their value as a business, but that also have a reasonable possibility of being forced higher by a takeover bid.

By the time you finish this book, you will look at the stock market and at stock selection in an entirely different way. You will become aware of news items and the availability of certain types of information that most investors are completely unaware of.

You will be on the lookout for superstocks.

CHAPTER EIGHT

If Everybody Knows Everything, Then Nobody Knows Anything

By now you might be thinking: This is a book about the stock market, yet the stock market itself will not be a factor in any of the superstock takeover situations we discussed. Every one of these superstocks generated a profit for reasons totally unrelated to the trend of the general stock market.

Which is precisely the point. When you're dealing with superstocks, pegging your stock selections to specific events or "catalysts" related to a particular company that are likely to force the stock price higher, for the most part you're removing the behavior of the general stock market from the equation.

When you begin to think in terms of the new paradigm, you'll find yourself zeroing in on news items that relate to the stocks you're holding or to other stocks that could become potential superstocks. You'll find yourself paying attention to "micro" news items rather than "macro" news items. You'll become less interested in grandiose generalizations concerning the big picture and more interested in specific news items that will impact individual stocks you're following.

For example, you'll find yourself paying more attention to CEO interviews ("We believe the consolidation in our industry will continue and we intend to be one of the major players by making additional acquisitions"), merger announcements ("We will continue to look for opportunities to grow our defense electronics segment"), or "shareholder rights plans" ("Although we know of no specific plans to acquire our company, this shareholder rights plan will ensure that our shareholders will receive fair value in the event of a bid").

You will find yourself taking note of stock buybacks ("We believe our stock is undervalued") in consolidating industries. You will be paying close attention to 13-D filings that indicate an outside beneficial owner has increased his or her stake in a company. And your ears will perk up when you hear that a company plans to spin off one of its subsidiaries to "enhance shareholder value," *especially if the parent company or the subsidiary operates in an industry where takeovers are proliferating.*

You will even notice when an outside beneficial owner receives a hostile takeover bid, because one way the beneficial owner can ensure protection from such a bid would be to turn around and make an acquisition itself—and therefore, what company would be a more logical takeover candidate than a company that is already partially owned by the outside beneficial owner?

On the other hand, you'll pay less attention to durable goods orders, the consumer price index, the trade deficit, and whether Alan Greenspan might have gotten up on the wrong side of the bed this morning before he presided over the Federal Reserve's Open Market Committee meeting. You would be more interested in the fact that WMS Industries has announced that it will spin off its three Puerto Rico hotel/casinos as a separately trading company because you will have noted a takeover wave in the hotel/casino industry (see Chapter 13). Therefore, while the TV talking heads are wringing their hands over what Greenspan may or may not do, you'll be more interested in the possibility that the WMS spinoff might become a takeover target once the hotel/casinos are trading separately as a "pure play." (It did.)

You will also begin to realize that if Rexel S.A. plans to make a takeover bid for Rexel Inc. (see Chapter 9), it will make the bid whether or not housing starts were up last month, and it won't matter to Rexel S.A. if Apple Computer missed its earnings estimates by a penny. And you will know that Rexel S.A. is not going to scratch its takeover plans because some market strategist who has been bullish before now believes we may be headed for a 10 percent correction.

The superstocks you'll be tracking will be marching to their own drummers, and you'll pay less attention to what "the market" is doing and more attention to the stream of information and scattered clues and evidence that directly impact the themes, trends, and specific superstocks you're tracking.

If you're like me, you won't miss the market "analysis" at all. In fact, you may find it's a relief to get it out of your hair because so much of it is meaningless anyway.

The sheer quantity of financial commentary being offered today on television, radio, the print media, and the Internet requires constant explanation and interpretation of every stock market gyration, no matter how unexplainable it may be. As a result, financial commentators, stockbrokers, and analysts are expected to have an answer for everything.

Most investors understand that much of what passes as market analysis is nothing more than gibberish, but they tolerate it because even stock market gibberish tends to be a lot more interesting than most other topics of conversation.

For some of you this may be difficult to accept, especially if you are an avid follower of television financial reporting or if you have one of those stockbrokers who seems to have an answer for everything.

"How's the market?" you ask.

"Down 80 points," he says.

"Eighty points? Why is it down 80 points?"

"Profit-taking."

Now, you may not be the smartest investor who ever lived, but you're smart enough to know that since the market has declined in 17 of the past 20 sessions, it is definitely not profit-taking that's pushing the market lower today. Your broker knows that, too, but has to tell you something because he or she is supposed to know what's going on. Consequently, the broker will have an answer for any question you can possibly come up with.

How does the broker do this?

On any given day there are probably 5 or 10 potentially bullish news items and 5 or 10 potentially bearish news items on the Dow Jones news wire. Depending on which way the market has gone that day, one or more of these innocent items will be plucked from the tape, like some Miss America from the crowd in Atlantic City, and this news item will be used to explain what the market did that day.

Let us say that, at ten-twenty in the morning, the Dow Jones Industrial Average is down 200 points. There are four major items of interest on the news wire: (1) the President has announced that he will seek a tax cut, (2) Iraq and Iran are at it again, and an Iraqi fighter plane has been shot down, (3) the bond market is higher, and (4) durable goods orders jumped 5.2 percent last month. Item 2 is meaningless but could be trotted out to explain a falling market, if necessary. Item 3 is bullish. And items 1 and 4 can be either bullish or bearish, depending on how you want to look at it.

Your broker can use any one of these news items to put a "spin" on why the Dow Jones is down 200 points.

Your stockbroker is sitting at his desk.

The phone rings. It's you.

"How's the market?" you ask.

"It's down 200 points," your broker says.

"Two hundred points? How come?"

"Well, the market has been depressed by a couple of news items this morning. First, the President says he wants a tax cut, and that's bearish because the Fed may decide to raise interest rates to counteract the potential inflationary effect of a tax cut. Also, Iran and Iraq are fighting, and an Iraqi plane was shot down. And durable goods orders were up more than expected, which could be inflationary also."

"Oh."

On the other hand, the market might be up 200 points. With the very same items on the tape, the conversation would then go something like this:

"How's the market?"

"Up 200 points."

"Up 200 points? How come?"

"Well, the President says he wants a tax cut, and that's bullish for the economy and for corporate earnings. Also, durable goods orders were up 5.2 percent, another sign of economic strength. Also, the bond market is higher this morning."

"Oh."

Since that sort of instant analysis is only a game to pass the time, the tough questions rarely, if ever, get asked, such as: If the market is down 200 points because the Fed might raise interest rates in light of the President's tax cut proposal, how come the bond market is up? Or, what do Iran and Iraq have to do with the stock market?

Nevertheless, this ritual is repeated over and over again until the stock market closes. If the market turns around and manages to erase its 200-point loss and close higher, the "bearish" items will miraculously be interpreted as bullish, as in "Wall Street had second thoughts about President Clinton's tax cut proposal . . ." and so on.

Believe me, once you get used to thinking in terms of superstock analysis, you will begin to see these stock market commentaries in an entirely different light—that is, if you bother to see them at all.

Can you really invest in stocks while you completely ignore the stock market in general? Can you really ignore the stock market prognosticators and other talking heads who can always be counted on to have an explanation of what the stock market did on any given day, even if in truth there is no explanation?

Yes. Because when it comes to the trend of the general market, it's doubtful that any one person can have much more insight than anyone else. All you really need to know is this: When interest rates are rising sharply and the no-risk rate of return begins to exceed the inflation rate by more than 3 or 4 percentage points, it's time to think about reducing your market exposure.

Other than that, nobody knows anything.

Which brings me to William Goldman.

William Goldman is not a stock market analyst. He is the screenwriter of *Butch Cassidy and the Sundance Kid*, *Marathon Man*, and numerous other well-known motion pictures. William Goldman is also the author of a brilliant and entertaining book, *Adventures in the Screen Trade*, in which he coined a memorable phrase that summed up everything he'd ever learned about the movie business.

Here it is: "Nobody knows anything."

What Goldman was saying was that you could take all of the sophisticated market research, all of the experience of studio heads and producers, all of the box office grosses of predecessor films, and all of the marketing savvy of the best distribution people, and throw it all out the window. If all of the widely available information known to everyone in the movie business meant anything, everyone would be making nothing but successful movies—and that sure isn't happening.

Says Goldman:

- If anybody knew anything, B.J. Thomas's advisers would not have been so upset after the first sneak preview of *Butch Cassidy and the Sundance Kid*. After hearing Thomas's new song, "Raindrops Keep Falling on My Head," in the context of *Butch Cassidy*, they were convinced that Thomas had made a potentially fatal career move.

- If anybody knew anything, *Raiders of the Lost Ark* would not have been turned down by every studio in town before Paramount decided to make the film.

- If anybody knew anything, Columbia Pictures would not have told Steven Spielberg that it decided not to make *E.T.*, even after the studio spent a million dollars developing the film. (*E.T.* wound up at Universal.)

- If anybody knew anything, Paramount Pictures would not have offered *The Godfather* to 12 directors (all of whom turned it down) before they got around to offering it to Francis Ford Coppola, and they would not have offered the role of Michael Corleone to Robert Redford, Warren Beatty, Ryan O'Neal, Dustin Hoffman, and Martin Sheen before they got around to offering it to Al Pacino.

Now, if you think about it, you can apply William Goldman's premise to the stock market, but with a slight variation.

In the stock market, when everybody knows everything, nobody knows anything. Overall, the evidence seems to indicate that the stock market, as a whole, is a pretty good "discounting" mechanism that takes into account everything that is knowable at any given time. The more analytical attention that is focused on the market or on a sector of the market or on any given stock, the more "efficient" the market becomes at determining a fair value.

This being the case, I would argue that the only way for an individual investor to get an "edge" on Wall Street is to go off the beaten path and to focus on areas of the market where analytical attention is slim or nonexistent. It also follows that there's no "edge" to be had in terms of trying to outguess the general market, since virtually every analyst and investor is looking at the same information, which will therefore be pretty well discounted, just as William Goldman's movie studio executives are all poring over the same current and historical data regarding box office grosses. If all of this "macro" publicly available information meant anything, everyone would be making the right move all of the time—and they're not. This strongly suggests that the way to hit a home run is to take a left turn when the lemmings are turning right—to take the road less traveled, as it were.

The same holds true for large-cap stocks. A 1999 study by Peter Schliemann, a money manager formerly with David L. Babson & Co., revealed that stocks with a market capitalization of more than $4 billion had an average of 17 analysts following the company, while stocks with a market cap of less than $100 million had an average of less than one analyst following the company. *This means that some of these companies with a market cap under $100 million had no analytical coverage at all.* (I don't know for sure, but I'd be willing to bet that more than a few of the small companies with no analytical coverage had lots of cash, no debt, and no need for investment banking services from Wall Street. See Chapter 3.)

In terms of large-cap stocks, you can see how efficient the market is and how difficult it is for any investor to get an edge on the competition by the way these stocks react to surprisingly good or bad information. When a widely followed stock trading at $66 misses its earnings estimate, there is no chance for anyone to sell at anywhere near $66. Every analyst in town lowers his or her earnings estimate and downgrades the stock, and your $66 large-cap stock simply opens at $50. That is how the efficient market works with widely followed stocks: Everybody immediately takes the new reality into account and the market adjusts its perception of value instantaneously.

Since everybody expected earnings of, say, $0.60 for the quarter, everybody knew everything—therefore, they knew nothing. Now that everybody knows earnings came in at, say, $0.50, everybody knows everything once again—but they still know nothing since there is no way to take advantage of that information to avoid the stock price decline.

So, when it comes to analyzing the general market or the widely followed big-cap stocks, nobody on Wall Street really knows anything at all— or maybe we should say that nobody really knows anything more than anybody else—or anything really worth knowing.

When you're looking for an edge in an area of the stock market where everyone else is looking, you'll find that new business becomes old business pretty darn quickly—usually too quickly to be of any use to an individual investor. By the time you hear any new significant information about the market in general or big-cap stocks, it's a good bet that it will be old business already, no matter how new it seems to you.

Now, compare this instantaneous reaction to new business in the large-cap stocks to the way the market reacted to Laidlaw's announcement that it would sell 12 percent of ADT Ltd. to Western Resources (see Chapter 9) for $14 a share. Did ADT immediately jump to $20 or $25 a share based on the likelihood that this move would ultimately lead to a takeover bid? No, it did not. The stock moved up gradually, over time, providing numerous excellent entry points for tuned-in investors.

But if, say, IBM were to reveal that it had been buying shares of Dell Computer in the open market and that it had accumulated a 12 percent stake without talking it over with Dell's management, what do you think would happen to Dell's stock price? Most likely, the Wall Street analytical community would immediately take its best guess as to Dell's potential takeover value and the stock would rise toward that level almost immediately.

This did not happen, as we will learn, with ADT. Nor did it happen with Rexel, Inc., even though the parent company, Rexel S.A., methodically bought shares in the open market, giving off a blatant clue that a takeover bid was on the way. With both of these stocks, investors had plenty of time to accumulate shares prior to the eventual takeover *because the stock market was inefficient in pricing their stocks in light of this information.*

That is the difference between how the market processes information involving widely followed large-cap stocks and less well-followed small-cap stocks. In fact, you can safely say that the market's efficiency in processing significant information is directly related to the audience for that information—i.e., whether institutional investors and the analysts who are fighting for their commission business are paying attention will determine how accurately the market reflects new information.

You will find, over time, it is important to spend more time researching individual stocks that are off the beaten path and less time thinking about the overall stock market and the popular stocks of the moment.

Two very important points can be made now: First, if you really want to have an edge in the stock market, you can only gain that edge in terms of individual stocks, where it is sometimes possible to notice information and interpret that information in a way that can give you some unique insight into a particular situation.

In other words, where individual stocks are concerned, the prize goes to those investors who go the extra mile, who do their homework better than everybody else. Sometimes this involves digging deeper for information about the company itself. Other times it involves thinking in terms of cause and effect, where a seemingly unrelated news item in the maze of information released on a daily basis has a connection to a stock you are following. For example, when Brylane's outside shareholder, Pinault Printemps, began raising its stake in Brylane, I saw a connection to the Rexel takeover bid because Rexel S.A., which bought Rexel, was a subsidiary of Pinault Printemps (see Chapter 9). But how many investors—or professional analysts—would have known that if they had not lived through the Rexel takeover drama?

So, lesson number one is: Research individual stocks—and smaller stocks, at that—and don't try to predict the market or compete with every analyst on Wall Street tracking the large-cap stocks.

The second lesson is that a lot of valuable public information is available out there that is *not* reflected in stock prices, especially when you're dealing with stocks that are not widely followed by the mainstream Wall Street analysts.

So, lesson number two: If you *really* want to get an edge on Wall Street, you should focus your attention on smaller-cap stocks that are not widely followed by analysts and their institutional clients. That is where you are most likely to turn up information and see a connection somewhere that is completely public but that has not been properly reflected in the stock price.

This principle explains why stocks like Rexel, ADT, Brylane, and others could easily have been purchased for months on end at bargain prices even though it was becoming increasingly likely to anyone paying attention that a takeover bid was on the way.

When you start to focus more of your attention on individual stocks and less attention on the general market, you'll be better able to train yourself to think in new paradigm terms. You will notice a subtle change in the way you perceive the news. You'll think in terms of cause and effect, and see connections between seemingly unrelated companies and events that others do not notice.

The more you think this way, the more likely you will be able to identify potential "superstocks"—and the less interested you'll become in the daily blather that passes for stock market analysis.

PART TWO

Identifying Takeover Targets

CHAPTER NINE

Creeping Takeovers

Let's begin this chapter with an actual example of a company that received a takeover bid that was completely predictable to those who were tuned in to the superstock method of analysis. One of the best ways to spot a future takeover target is to focus on companies that are already partially owned by another company that is consistently adding to its stake by purchasing additional shares in the open market. Many times these continual open-market purchases are a prelude to eventual takeover bids at much higher prices.

To understand why this is so, put yourself in the position of the outside owner. Suppose you own 45 percent of a company whose stock is trading at $10. Suppose this company operates a business that is complementary to yours and has excellent growth prospects. And let's suppose further that your management team has decided it would be a good idea to acquire this company within the next 2 years.

If the eventual plan is to buy the 55 percent of this company you do not already own through a takeover bid or tender offer, you know two things. First, you will have to offer a premium over the stock's current trading price. And you also know that even though you already own 45 percent of this company, your offer will be subject to what is called a "fairness opinion." This means that even though you are, by far, the largest shareholder of the target company, the Board of Directors of the target company will have to seek outside advice as to whether your takeover bid represents a fair price for the shareholders. The Board of Directors will probably enlist the services of a brokerage firm that will dispatch a team of analysts to study the target company, the industry in which it operates, the valuations of its competitors, and the future growth prospects of the company you want to buy. All of this means that you'll probably have to pay a hefty premium over the stock's current $10 trading price—especially if the growth prospects you envision are apparent to the target company's management and to the financial advisers the target company retains.

Given all of this, what would you do?

What many outside owners do is embark on what is called a "creeping takeover." In a creeping takeover, the outside owner starts adding to his or her stake in the potential target company by purchasing shares on the open market. Week after week, month after month, the outside owner accumulates additional shares at prevailing market prices, gradually increasing the stake. If these purchases are made in a cautious and patient manner, they may not push the stock price up very much. In fact, the stock price may not go up at all since there is always stock available for sale in the normal course of trading. Simply bidding for stock and putting out the word to market makers that a bid is available should a block of stock come up for sale may be all it takes to accumulate an additional, sizable stake in the target company.

This approach makes all the sense in the world because if your ultimate goal is to acquire the entire company, and if you know you will have to pay a sizable premium once the formal bid is made, the more stock you can accumulate at low prices, the less the eventual takeover will ultimately cost you.

CASE STUDY: HOW REXEL S.A. ACQUIRED REXEL INC.

If you think like a potential acquirer and you keep an eye on outside owners who are accumulating additional shares of a company on the open market, you can act right along with them by purchasing shares in the potential target company. How can you do this? Any holder of 5 percent or more of a public company is deemed a "beneficial owner" and must report all additional purchases and sales of stock. Once a "beneficial owner" crosses that 5 percent threshold, each additional purchase of stock becomes a matter of public record. Later, you will learn where to find this information so you can buy right along with these outside beneficial owners. But first, let's look at Rexel Inc. and the "creeping takeover" engineered by its largest shareholder, Rexel S.A. of France.

We recommended Rexel Inc. in October 1995 at $10¼ for three reasons: Rexel S.A. had recently raised its stake in Rexel from 43.5 to 45 percent through additional open-market stock purchases, Rexel had turned itself into a *pure play* electrical supply distributor by selling off noncore operations, and Rexel had announced that it would buy back 10 percent of its own stock. As you will soon see, these are all "Telltale Signs" of a potential takeover target.

As you will see throughout this book, we will spend some time presenting original recommendations and ongoing analysis of these takeover targets, for one important reason: We're not discussing "theoretical examples" or how you "might have done this" or "might have done that." *We're concerned with actual recommendations and the actual takeovers that followed, and you need to see that the original reasoning that went into these recommendations was directly related to the ultimate outcome.* The purpose of this book is to train you to think like a takeover detective, to spot the telltale clues that often precede a profitable takeover bid. The precise reasoning that went into each recommendation is significant because it describes the thought process you should use to ferret out takeover candidates that will later emerge as superstocks.

Rexel was what could be called "sneaky strong," moving up gradually, meeting good buying support on pullbacks, and generally embarking on a gentle uptrend, month after month, no matter what the general stock market was doing.

In other words, Rexel was beginning to act like a superstock—marching to its own drummer, oblivious to the manic/depressive gyrations of the overall stock market. *A "creeping takeover" drama was unfolding: Such situations, for all their potential, tend to be a lot less risky than the average stock.* This, as you would guess, goes against everything you've ever learned about risk and reward, which is that if you want a big reward, you have to take a bigger than usual risk.

But when it comes to a "creeping takeover," this is simply not the case. The reason is that if the outside beneficial owner continues to purchase large blocks of stock on the open market, it's a strong indication that there is *good value* at those price levels. If the price declines, the outside beneficial owner tends to go into the open market to purchase more shares, thereby supporting the price. Every time an open-market purchase is made by the outside beneficial owner—and especially if these purchases take place at successively higher price levels—it becomes logical that when the price dips too far below that level, it is viewed as a bargain, not only by the outside beneficial owner but also by the handful of stock market partici- pants who focus on situations like this. The result is often strong support on pullbacks, no matter what the stock market is doing. So, even if there is no takeover—and sometimes, even if the overall stock market is exceedingly weak—situations like this tend to hold up very well, thereby creating less risk.

Tell *that* to the next know-it-all stock market pundit who tells you that investing in takeover candidates is "too risky for the aver- age investor."

Following a *Business Week* story on Rexel, the price bumped to $14; however, Rexel drifted back to where it had started, meeting support in the $12 area. Rexel met strong support at that price. And then the "creeping takeover" really got under way.

In the stock market, you can tell where the value is by who is doing the buying. That notion is seen clearly in the fact that a Rexel vice president had gone into the open market to purchase 4000 shares of Rexel at a price of $11⅜. This created what I call a "triple play" situ- ation, usually the most powerful of all signs that a stock is going high- er. *A triple play occurs when an outside beneficial owner, the company itself, and also its corporate officials (insiders) are all buying stock on the open mar- ket. This is just about as good as it gets in terms of identifying a severely undervalued stock that is going to go significantly higher.* While 4000 shares is not exactly a monstrous transaction, it was just one more clue that Rexel was heading a lot higher.

In February 1996 there was another major purchase of Rexel shares—Rexel S.A. bought another 150,000 Rexel shares at prices between $12 and $12½.

It was clear by March 1996 that Rexel S.A. had begun to "creep." The French company had once again gone into the open market to buy 59,100 additional Rexel shares, at a price of $12¾. The continu- ing purchases of Rexel S.A. suggested that Rexel could become a takeover target at any time.

So Much for the "Efficient Market" Theory

At this point the Rexel story becomes a bit more interesting for a dif- ferent reason. The information age has arrived in full force, and it's safe to say that there's virtually no piece of information on any public company that is not readily available to anyone who is interested in looking for it.

The problem is, fewer and fewer analysts are looking for the most significant information—but that leaves the playing field wide open for the rest of us.

Previously, you learned that Wall Street research is increasingly geared toward servicing those who generate the largest commissions— mutual funds, pension funds, hedge funds, and other large-scale investors who require big-cap stocks with lots of liquidity. Smaller-cap stocks and micro-cap stocks—and also stocks in out-of-favor industries that are too boring to interest the momentum players—are simply not followed as closely as their better known counterparts.

The theory of the "efficient stock market" is that all pertinent information is so widely available that anything you and I know has already been discounted. But the reality is this: When lesser known stocks become increasingly neglected by the Wall Street analytical community, it becomes increasingly common to see information that 10 years ago would have moved a stock sharply higher have literally no effect at all. The fact that Rexel S.A., for example, had upped its open-market purchase price for Rexel from the $9 area to the $12 to $12¾ area should have sent a strong signal that Rexel was a great value at a $12 to $12¾ price. If Rexel S.A., which one must assume had a pretty good handle on the value of Rexel, was buying stock at progressively higher levels, then it would seem logical that investors should follow Rexel S.A.'s lead. And certainly if Rexel shares traded below the $12¾ area that Rexel S.A. had been willing to pay, that would make Rexel a very good value. Right?

Not necessarily. Again, remember that we're dealing here with a neglected stock that was virtually not followed at all by mainstream Wall Street research. What seems a logical way of looking at this situation—namely, that Rexel would have been a logical buy anywhere below $12¾—simply did not register with the vast majority of Wall Street analysts and the investors who received their advice from them.

Which leads to an important point: You would be amazed at how much time you have to accumulate genuine takeover candidates that are undergoing a "creeping takeover" before Wall Street catches on to what's happening. And you would also be amazed at how often you can buy these "creeping takeover" candidates at a significantly lower price than the outside beneficial owner has been paying!

In the case of Rexel, Wall Street greeted Rexel S.A.'s continuing purchases up to the $12¾ area with a collective yawn, and Rexel shares drifted back below $12 again.

By midyear Rexel S.A. had made two additional purchases of Rexel Inc stock: 21,000 shares and 275,600 shares, both at $11½ to $11¾. To many investors, takeover bids may seem unpredictable and to come "out of the blue." But in other instances takeover bids are the culmination of a series of events that can point you in the right direction if you watch the evidence accumulate and you exercise patience. Such buys by Rexel S.A., while not proof that a takeover was imminent, provide a case study in how a parent company methodically raises its stake in another company before finally making a bid.

By the end of the summer in 1996, Rexel S.A. had made two additional purchases of Rexel Inc. stock: 46,000 shares at $13¼ and 175,700 shares at a price as high as $14¼. And there was continued scattered buying of stock by Rexel Inc.'s officers and directors.

In September 1996, Rexel S.A. purchased another 162,000 shares of Rexel Inc., at prices between $13¾ and $13⅞, an indication that Rexel S.A. was accomplishing a takeover by attrition through its continuing open-market purchases.

On November 7, 1996, I reported to my subscribers that Rexel S.A. had purchased another 79,000 shares of Rexel Inc. at $13¾. And yet, amazingly, despite the sizable open-market purchases by Rexel S.A. that I had been documenting, month after month, Rexel Inc. shares were trading in November 1996 right at $14, no higher than they had been trading at the start of 1996.

This proved two things: First, no one on Wall Street was paying the slightest attention to the Rexel situation. And, second, as I've said before and I'll say again, if you're going to invest in off-the-beaten-path stocks with genuine takeover potential, you're going to need patience and the courage of your convictions. It can be a maddening experience to have so much accumulated evidence of a probable takeover bid staring you right in the face only to see a stock move sideways or even lower due to Wall Street's disinterest.

And yet, the flip side of that coin is: The more evidence that accumulates and the longer the stock takes to react, the more time you have to accumulate shares with even greater confidence—which means the ultimate payoff, when it comes, will be even sweeter!

By the end of 1996, Rexel was still trading near $14 a share, right where it began the year, despite the fact that Rexel S.A. had spent most of the year adding significantly to its Rexel stake . . . *and despite the fact that Rexel S.A. had just paid as high as $14⅞ for an additional 167,000 shares.*

In the first week of January 1997, Rexel Inc. finally broke out to a new high. (See Figure 9–1.)

Then, in February 1997, I reported to my subscribers that Rexel S.A. purchased another 43,500 shares of Rexel Inc., paying as much as $15⅟₁₆, a new high for Rexel S.A.'s open-market purchases.

In March 1997, Rexel Inc. stock suddenly pierced the $20 level on very large volume. Prior to that, Rexel S.A. had purchased another small block of 8000 shares, paying a new high of $16¾.

One Last Chance

At this point you're probably thinking: How could Wall Street have missed this obvious takeover candidate for so long? Why did it take over a year for Rexel Inc. to really respond to the growing takeover potential? And why would Wall Street provide an opportunity for investors to buy Rexel shares at prices significantly below what Rexel S.A. paid for the stock at so many different points and for such

F i g u r e   9–1

Rexel Inc. (RXL), 1995–1997

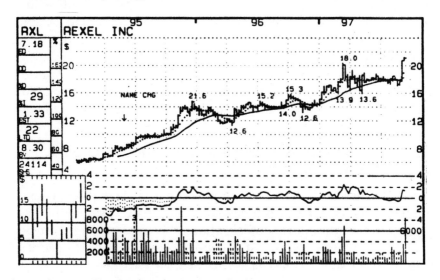

Source: Courtesy of Mansfield Chart Service, Jersey City, NJ.

extended periods of time along the way? There is an old saying that there are no free lunches on Wall Street, but in this case Wall Street provided a 12-course meal.

And then Wall Street provided dessert!

Shortly after it was announced that Rexel S.A. had just purchased another 184,000 shares of Rexel, paying as high as $20\frac{1}{16}$, Rexel shares dipped down to the $16 to $17 area and stayed there for several months. In other words, the perfectly efficient stock market, which sees all, knows all, and discounts everything, provided one last extended opportunity for investors to buy Rexel shares for significantly less than Rexel S.A. had just paid.

In April 1997, Rexel S.A. went into the open market and bought a small block of 10,000 Rexel shares at $16\frac{7}{8}$. The purchase made perfect sense; Rexel had just paid as high as $20\frac{1}{16}$ for 184,000 shares, so why not buy more at lower prices? By June 1997, Rexel stock had spent nearly four months trading listlessly between $16 and $18, despite the fact that Rexel S.A. had paid over $20 for the stock just months earlier. All told, Rexel S.A. had purchased a grand total of 1,734,900 shares of Rexel over the past two years.

Takeover Time!

Finally, in September 1997, Rexel S.A. announced a takeover bid for Rexel. The offer was initially at $19.50 per share, then ultimately raised to $22.50 per share. That takeover price represented a premium of 119 percent over our original recommended price of $10\frac{1}{4}$ in just two years.

The moral of the story is that even when you clearly spot the Telltale Signs that an event is about to occur that will drive up the price of an undervalued stock, you also may have to be very patient.

THE OTHER SIDE OF TAKEOVERS: SELLING BY A BENEFICIAL OWNER

This next case study illustrates another method of spotting takeover targets, which is the mirror image of the approach used with Rexel. In addition to monitoring stocks that are being bought by outside beneficial owners, *you should also take a close look at stocks where an outside beneficial owner has indicated a desire to sell.*

The reason for this is that, more often than not, the outside beneficial owner owns so much stock that an open-market sale is not only impractical but also makes no business sense. Since the objective of the beneficial owner should be to maximize the value of the investment, the proper way to get out of a large position in one company is to either sell the stake to another company that may want to buy the target company or perhaps urge the target company to put itself up for sale as a way of maximizing value for all stockholders.

In the vast majority of cases where a block of stock owned by an outside beneficial owner is sold to a third party, the third party will be thinking in terms of an eventual takeover.

Therefore, what seems to be a negative to "old paradigm" thinkers—that a large outside beneficial owner shareholder wants to sell its stake—is usually a sign that the target company is about to enter the ranks of the superstocks.

CASE STUDY: THE TAKEOVER OF ADT

An example of this approach is ADT Ltd., a security alarm monitoring company.

In February 1996 a small news item appeared about ADT Ltd., which at the time was the largest home security alarm company in the United States. The news item did not seem to raise any alarm bells on Wall Street. It seemed that Laidlaw Inc., a Canadian company that owned approximately 24 percent of ADT, had agreed to sell half of its ADT stake to a Kansas-based utility company, Western Resources, for $14 per share, roughly the price at which ADT shares were trading on the New York Stock Exchange. As part of the deal, Laidlaw had also granted Western Resources an option to buy the other 12 percent of ADT owned by Laidlaw by May 15, 1997.

One additional interesting part of the new item: ADT was actively attempting to sell its automobile auction business, which accounted for about 27 percent of its revenues. As you learned earlier, companies that sell or spin off "noncore" operations are often preparing to sell themselves as a pure play to a larger company. So the fact that a block of ADT shares had been sold to a third party, combined with the fact that ADT was setting itself up as a pure play, added up to this conclusion: ADT was about to be "in play" as a genuine takeover candidate.

My first response to this news item was to do a little research on Western Resources. Why would a midwestern utility want to buy a 24 percent interest in a security alarm company?

The answer was intriguing. Wester Resources, formerly Kansas Power & Light, was seeking to diversify into the nonutility business. In fact, recent press releases from Western Resources indicated that the company *had publicly stated it was thinking of expanding into the home security alarm business through acquisitions.*

Western Resources had already told Wall Street that it was seeking to buy security alarm companies. Following this public statement, Western purchased a 12 percent interest in ADT from Laidlaw at $14 and held an option to buy another 12 percent. And yet, ADT shares were sitting right there, in the $14 to $15 range, as though nothing fundamental had changed as a result of these two separate, but related news items.

ADT became part of the master list of recommended stocks in our *Superstock Investor* newsletter.

At the time, some utilities, including telephone companies, viewed home security companies as a cost-efficient "add-on" service. Due to these supposed economies of scale in a utility acquisition of a home security company, it seemed logical for Western Resources to eventually exercise its option to buy Laidlaw's remaining 12 percent of ADT and then to make a bid for the rest of the company.

The same reasoning suggested that two smaller companies, Protection One (ALRM), then trading near $11, and Holmes Protection (HLMS), then trading below the $8 area, were also potential takeover targets.

This analysis of the security alarm industry provided a detailed road map for investors for an upcoming takeover wave in the security alarm industry.

By mid-March Western Resources had exercised its option to purchase the additional 12 percent of ADT owned by Laidlaw at $14.80 per share. It was not expected that Western Resources would buy the additional 12 percent of ADT so soon, but since the option exercise price related to ADT's market price, Western Resources may have acted as quickly as it did because they thought ADT shares would move higher.

In May 1996 a rather curious development took place: ADT's management team had exchanged their low-priced ADT stock options (with an exercise price of $9 per share) for a larger number of higher-priced options (exercisable at $15 per share).

In effect, ADT management exchanged a guaranteed profit for a chance to make more money, but only if ADT rose significantly above $15.

Why did they do it? To me, there was only one possible conclusion: ADT management expected the company to be acquired at a price much higher than $15. And yet despite this growing evidence that ADT was about to be acquired at a price much higher than $15, you would have had no problem buying ADT shares in the $16 to $17 range.

Following my ADT update, subscribers were once again reminded that Protection One (then trading at $7¾) could also get caught up in a takeover wave involving security alarm companies.

On March 16, 1996, CNBC's Dan Dorfman reported on the recommendation of ADT as a takeover candidate. At the time, ADT shares had drifted back toward the $16 area again, demonstrating once again that *it is surprising how many chances you will receive to buy underfollowed stocks at bargain prices even when takeover storm clouds are obviously gathering overhead.*

In a May 3 report an item was included about a hostile takeover bid that Western Resources had just made for Kansas City Power & Light. It was reported that Western's bid for Kansas City Power & Light was unsolicitated and that it disrupted a friendly merger agreement that had already been negotiated between KCP&L and another company.

Western Resources had entered into an aggressive acquisition mode. One of the tricks to picking genuine takeover candidates is to look for companies that are already partly owned by other companies and have demonstrated they are in an acquisition mode. Western Resources' unsolicited bid for Kansas City Power & Light was a clear signal that Western was looking to grow through takeovers.

This observation demonstrates another strategy of picking takeover targets: *It pays to know the track record of the outside beneficial owners.* Just as our experience with Rexel S.A. and Rexel Inc. led us to the takeover of Brylane (see Chapter 10), this hostile bid by Western Resources for Kansas City Power & Light was a strong clue that Western Resources was in high-gear acquisition mode, and that should it want to buy ADT, would not easily take no for an answer.

Next, ADT announced a 5 million share buyback, another Telltale Sign that ADT was seriously worried about a takeover bid at an unreasonably low price. Remember the Telltale Sign: When a company whose stock is being bought by a third-party "beneficial owner" announces a stock buyback, it is usually a strong signal that (1) the company is worried about a takeover, and (2) the company believes its stock is severely undervalued and the potential acquirer will attempt a "low-ball" bid that might be above the current market price but still below the true value of the company as a business.

Both Western Resources and Kansas City Power & Light ran amazingly hostile advertisements about one another in *The Wall Street Journal*, again indicating Western Resources was in an aggressive acquisition mode. This type of aggressive action made an eventual bid for ADT all the more likely.

By this time ADT had crossed the $18 level and was trading at $18⅛, up 20 percent in less than three months since the news that Western Resources had bought 12 percent of ADT from Laidlaw.

Surprise! Republic Industries Makes a Takeover Bid for ADT

On July 1, 1996, ADT became a superstock, jumping 5½ points in one day, to $24½, on news that ADT had received a takeover bid. That 5½-point one-day gain amounted to a 29 percent gain on the day and a 63 percent gain from the original recommended price of $15 just 4 months earlier.

But the takeover bid for ADT did not come from Western Resources. Instead, it came from Republic Industries, a company run by Wayne Huizenga, who had previously built both Waste Management and Blockbuster Entertainment into major growth companies. Republic Industries had determined that it too wanted to be a leader in the home security business. The takeover bid for ADT was valued at $26, a 73 percent gain over the original recommended price.

Western Resources was strangely silent over the Republic Industries bid from ADT. And the strangest twist in this story was yet to come.

ADT Followers Get Another Chance to Buy at Bargain Prices

During the discussion of the Rexel Inc. takeover, you learned how many opportunities a patient, informed investor can get to buy a genuine takeover candidate at bargain prices, even as additional evidence of an imminent takeover bid accumulates to enormous proportions. *The reason for this apparent defect in the "efficient market" theory is that information is only properly discounted when the Wall Street powerhouses are paying attention.* Mutual funds, pension funds, and other institutional investors do indeed take all new information immediately into account when the information involves the large-cap stocks these institutions, and the analysts who serve them, are following with the precision of an electron microscope.

But when it comes to smaller-cap stocks that are not on the institutional radar screen, you can throw the efficient market theory right out the window.

By July 26, 1996, Western Resources owned 24 percent of ADT and there was a $26 takeover bid on the table from Republic Industries. That $26 bid involved Republic Industries stock, however, which had been weak since the takeover bid was announced.

As a result, on July 26, 1996, an investor following the ADT story could have bought ADT for—would you believe it?—$17¾.

The reason for this price disparity was that Republic shares had begun to slide. As a result, ADT shares fell along with Republic, since the agreement was that Republic would exchange .928 of its shares for each ADT share. Also contributing to weakness in ADT was a general question over whether this deal could ever take place. Why? *Because neither ADT nor Republic thought it important to check with Western Resources, which owned 24 percent of ADT.*

You heard it correctly. Republic Industries and ADT had entered into a takeover agreement without bothering to seek the blessing of Western Resources, owner of 24 percent of ADT. In response to the Republic–ADT agreement, Western said only that it was "exploring its alternatives."

The intent of that statement was probably an indication that Western Resources had intended to ultimately buy the rest of ADT, and its management was angry about not being consulted about the deal. Also, it was highly unlikely that Western Resources would accept shares of Republic Industries for its stake in ADT, because Republic shares carried with them a substantial "personality premium," based on the popularity of Wayne Huizenga.

At this point, most Wall Street commentators were saying it would be impossible for Western Resources to mount a competing bid for ADT. Was it impossible? Not necessarily, but another possibility was that Western Resources would find another buyer for ADT who was willing to pay cash or stock with a more stable or reasonable value than Republic Industries. A third possibility was for Western Resources to force Republic to substantially increase its offer in light of the decline in Republic shares. All three of these scenarios should have resulted in a sharp rise in ADT shares from their trading level of $17 to $18—a price level lower than where ADT traded prior to the Republic bid! Yet another possibility was for Western to simply oppose the merger but do nothing but vote against it—possible but unlikely considering Western's aggressive personality.

Finally, the Republic Industries–ADT agreement carried with it an unusual arrangement that seemed to indicate that both Republic and ADT were actually *expecting* a higher bid: ADT granted Republic a warrant to purchase 15 million ADT shares at $20 if the agreement was terminated for any reason. This, by the way, is another reason why Western Resources was understandably miffed. In effect, it meant that anybody making a competing bid for ADT at any price over $20 had to buy 15 million additional shares and hand Republic Industries an instant profit. Why would ADT and Republic agree to such a warrant unless they both felt that a competing bid from Western Resources or someone else was possible?

Now, a reasonably perceptive superstock observer would have to say that the Republic bid for ADT appeared to be only the opening salvo in a bitter war for control of ADT. Based on what you've observed of Western Resources to this point, you would probably have agreed it was highly unlikely that Western would simply hand ADT over to Republic Industries and simply abandon its plans to become a security alarm powerhouse without at least putting up some semblance of a fight.

And you would expect that a "perfectly efficient stock market" would have processed all of this public information and decided that ADT should be selling perhaps in the low to mid $20 range, especially in light of the fact that Republic had already offered $26 in stock to acquire the company.

Because of the drop in its own stock price by early October 1996, Republic Industries had withdrawn its bid for ADT, and ADT shares had dropped back to $18, following a brief run up toward the $22 area. *This provided yet another opportunity for savvy investors to buy ADT stock at a significant discount to the $19.75 price Western Resources* *had paid for part of its 1.3 million share purchase just a couple of months earlier.* Republic withdrew its bid even though Western had not uttered one public comment on the Republic–ADT takeover deal. But, Western really didn't have to say anything to Republic.

Western's purchase of an additional 1.3 million shares of ADT in August, after the Republic bid was announced, was Western's way of saying: "Get lost."

Sure enough, just 1 month later, Western Resources purchased *another* 1.3 million shares of ADT in the open market, this time paying between $18¼ and $19. ADT shares once again rose above $20, but just barely, trading around $20¾.

Now, those of you who are thinking, "Aha! A creeping takeover!" can go to the head of the class. By saying nothing and continuing to accumulate ADT shares well below $20, Western Resources was creating a situation in which the final price it would pay for ADT would be lower. The more shares Western purchased before making a formal bid, the less it would ultimately have to pay for the entire company. To anyone trained to think like a takeover detective—in other words, trained to think in superstock paradigm terms—it was perfectly obvious what Western Resources was up to as it continued to buy ADT shares on the open market while saying nothing about the Republic bid or its own intentions.

Finally, after buying another 209,500 ADT shares at the end of October at $19¾, Western Resources made its move: Western offered $22.50 per share for ADT, making the offer in a hostile manner (surprise!) directly to ADT shareholders and completely bypassing ADT management. In addition, Western called for a special ADT stockholders meeting to replace the ADT Board of Directors. This move was just what you would have expected from Western Resources in light of the company's hostile takeover bid for Kansas City Power & Light and also in light of the arrogant and cavalier manner in which ADT had disregarded Western's interests when it accepted the Republic takeover bid.

A hostile bid from Western Resources, in other words, should have come as no surprise to any new paradigm thinker who had been following this situation. Western's anger, by the way, was evident in the fact that its $22.50 takeover bid was significantly less than Republic's previous $26 bid. In fact, Western's bid was so stingy that we advised subscribers to hold ADT based on the possibility that Western Resources would raise its bid or that the situation would turn so hostile that ADT would find a competing bidder.

And once again, subscribers were reminded that two other smaller security alarm companies, Protection One and Holmes Protection, could also get caught up in the takeover frenzy in this industry (see Chapter 17).

Tyco International Bids $28 for ADT

On March 17, 1997, the ADT soap opera came to an end. On that day, Tyco International, a diversified company seeking to expand its security alarm operations, offered to buy ADT for $28 in stock.

That $28 takeover bid represented an 86 percent premium over the original recommended price of $15 just 1 year earlier, a recommendation that was touched off by a seemingly innocuous news item about Laidlaw selling a portion of its ADT stake to a midwestern utility company, Western Resources. Although the vast majority of investors and Wall Street analysts completely missed the significance of that news item, new paradigm thinkers would have immediately recognized it and realized that ADT was "in play" as a potential takeover target. And although ADT rose 86 percent over the next year, the handful of investors who followed the ADT story would have had numerous opportunities to add to their ADT stake along the way, sometimes at prices below which Western Resources had paid for the stock on the open market. As more evidence accumulated that ADT would be acquired, a perfectly efficient stock market should have removed such bargain-purchase opportunities from the equation; instead the opposite occurred. As it became more obvious that ADT would be bought by *someone*, the stock market offered additional lower-priced entry points for those who were becoming increasingly convinced that a takeover would occur. ADT eventually rose to $33 as Tyco stock moved higher.

If you look at Figure 9–2, you'll see a picture of a stock that had bursts of strength when new developments occurred and then periods of weakness when the takeover saga cooled off for a while. Wall Street has become obsessed with short-term performance, and traders seem more interested in short-term swings and buying stocks with momentum than they are in positioning themselves for a solid profit over time. As a result, what you will find in these ongoing, drawn-

F i g u r e   9–2

ADT, 1995–1997

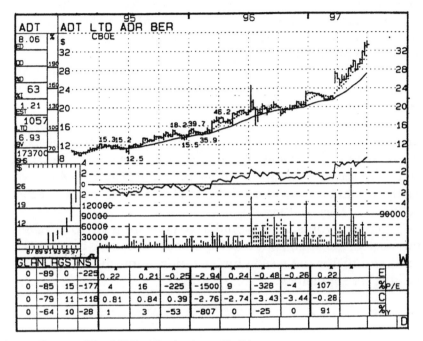

Source: Courtesy of Mansfield Chart Service, Jersey City, NJ.

out takeover situations is that when several weeks or months go by without a new development, interest in these takeover candidates seems to wane. Much like a child with too many toys will quickly lose interest in one toy and move on to the next, for Wall Street there's always a new story, always another stock moving. The "hot" money, obsessed with short-term performance, can quickly lose interest in a takeover situation that temporarily runs out of steam. When the "hot" money sells to move into something temporarily more exciting, it creates buying opportunities in the genuine takeover candidates for those with the insight, foresight, and patience to take advantage of these opportunities.

So it's not just the 120 percent you could have made in ADT if you'd bought the stock at $15 in March 1996 and tendered to Tyco International at $33 a year later that is significant, but also the fact that if you were thinking like a "takeover detective," you would have become increasingly confident along the way that ADT would be bought, and you could have added to your position with confidence at several junctures prior to the final takeover bid. Even if you had paid higher prices than your original $15 purchase price, you would have been doing so based on much more evidence of a probable bid at much higher prices.

And, of course, the best part of the ADT story was that ADT turned out to be a superstock. It would not have mattered what the stock market was doing between March 1996 and March 1997, because ADT was on its way to *finding its proper value as a business*. Instead of being tossed about by the whims of the market, responding to analysts' estimates and interest rate movements, ADT was being *analyzed as a business* by three potential acquirers. And eventually that bid by Tyco forced the stock market to place a realistic value on ADT *as a business*.

In other words, ADT would have gone from $15 to $33 even if the stock market had gone sideways or down during that period of time, and that is the reason for spending so much time and effort looking for superstocks.

CHAPTER TEN

How to Create Your Own "Research Universe" of Takeover Candidates— The Telltale Signs

Two roads diverged in a wood, and I—I took
the road less traveled, and that has made all the difference.

Robert Frost

Now that you have seen how Rexel and ADT became takeover targets, you can probably see the difference between "superstock" analysis and the usual sort of analysis practiced by most investors and analysts. Tracking these two stories from start to finish was sort of like watching a financial soap opera or miniseries, where the plot unfolds excruciatingly slowly over a period of weeks or months. While you might be able to say the same thing about other stocks, the key difference when you're dealing with potential superstocks such as these is that *each plot development along the way points inexorably toward a climax or conclusion to the story, i.e., a takeover bid that forced the stock market to value Rexel's and ADT's stock according to their values as businesses regardless of what the general stock market was doing at the time.*

So how do you find a stock like Rexel or ADT in the first place?

To answer that question I am going to point you down the road less traveled toward an entirely new direction in terms of thought process and analysis.

First, forget about the trendy "momentum" stocks everybody knows and loves. If you want to own some of them, fine—but we're going to explore different territory because we are on the lookout for stocks and information that the mainstream Wall Street analysts are overlooking. I have all the respect in the world for Michael Dell, Bill Gates, Scott McNealy, Jack Welch, and all the rest of the well-known and widely followed business geniuses you can hear and read about every day of the week—but they live on a highly trafficked and overly developed road, and we're headed for a far more barren piece of terrain. These guys and the stocks they're involved with are so widely followed, so idolized and analyzed, that there is absolutely nothing you and I can discover that hasn't already been noted, rehashed a thousand times, and factored into their stock prices.

Instead, *I am going to suggest that you become a browser.*

The definition of *browse* is to look, wander, or meander through something or somewhere in a casual and unfocused manner. When you are browsing, you do not always have a specific goal in mind; you do not always know precisely what you are looking for. You are simply passing through in an unhurried way, noticing whatever it is that happens to cross your path.

This is a very different mindset than setting out to find a specific piece of information.

The Internet is a wonderful tool. It provides a bottomless pit of facts and figures, virtually anything you're looking for. But what if you don't know exactly what you're looking for?

To me, the Internet, which condenses and categorizes information, has eroded the art of browsing, which opens up the playing field for independent-minded investors to notice out-of-the-way bits of information that can lead to great stock ideas and a treasure trove of potential takeover targets. Once you have encountered an interesting idea through browsing, the Internet becomes a valuable tool to gather additional information. But if you're looking for original ideas that have been overlooked by the crowd and that may not even have crossed your own mind yet, the best way to find them is the old-fashioned way—by reading certain publications cover to cover, especially noticing the smaller, out-of-the-way items that would escape the attention of 99 percent of your fellow investors. And *then* dig deeper using the Internet.

Reading every single item in *The Wall Street Journal*, for example—especially the smaller items that may be only a few sentences long—can often lead you to make a mental connection to something else you have seen or read along the way. Browsing through a chart book with no particular stock in mind can often lead you to notice a potential superstock chart pattern belonging to a stock you have never even heard of (more on that later).

Of course, if you're going to browse for antiques, you won't make much progress if you walk into a pet store. If you want to become a browser, browse the following publications on a regular basis because in them you'll encounter information that can lead you to superstock takeover candidates.

Investor's Business Daily

The Mansfield Chart Service

The New York Times

The Vickers Weekly Insider Report

The Wall Street Journal

Create Your Own "Research Universe"

Your goal as you begin your new career as a "superstock browser" will be to create your own "research universe." Every Wall Street analyst has a "research universe" that consists of a group of stocks the analyst follows on a regular basis. Most of the time, these stocks are organized by industry group. A chemical stock analyst, for example, will follow a universe of chemical companies and select one or several as his or her top pick.

As a superstock browser, your goal will be to create your own research universe, a list of potential "superstock" takeover candidates that possess one or more of the characteristics addressed in this chapter. You'll be looking for some of the Telltale Signs that suggest that a sleepy, out-of-favor, and out-of-the-way stock might be about to emerge as a takeover target.

One advantage you will have over the average Wall Street analyst is that your "research universe" will not be confined to a certain industry group. Instead, once you learn to spot specific characteristics of potential takeover targets, you'll find yourself following a diverse group of stocks that span a wide variety of industry groups. And once you've constructed your "research universe," you should look at it as a potential shopping list of investment possibilities.

For example, if you are a conservative investor, you may find that a water or natural gas utility or a supermarket company appears on your list of takeover candidates. Or, if you happen to believe that energy prices are headed higher, you may notice that an oil and gas exploration company is on your shopping list. Or, if you believe energy prices are headed lower, you might note that a trucking company or an airline, or some other company which could benefit from lower energy costs, is on the list.

In other words, once you get the hang of browsing for takeover candidates, you will be able to find stocks that fit almost any investment goal or philosophy. But these stocks will have the added attraction of being genuine takeover possibilities, which means they'll have the potential of rising suddenly and substantially in price, no matter what the stock market is doing.

And here's the best part: This "icing on the cake" comes free of charge. *If you do your homework properly and focus on stocks not widely followed, and therefore undervalued by Wall Street, you will be able to buy stocks that carry this highly charged takeover potential with no takeover premium built into the stock price.* In other words, to the outside world these stocks will look like boring, mild-mannered Clark Kents—but in reality, each will have the potential of slipping into a phone booth at a moment's notice and emerging as a superstock.

WHAT YOU'LL BE LOOKING FOR

I suggest that you read, copy, and post the following list of Telltale Signs that a neglected stock has the potential to become a superstock takeover candidate. You should study this list until it becomes second nature to you because these are the things you'll be looking for as a superstock browser.

Eighteen Telltale Signs

1. An outside company or individual ("beneficial owner") accumulates more than 5 percent of a company's stock

and then files a Form 13-D with the Securities and Exchange Commission.

2. A company that already has one outside "beneficial" owner attracts a second or even a third outside investor who accumulates a position of 5 percent of more.

3. An outside beneficial owner, in its Form 13-D filing, says that it is seeking ways to "enhance shareholder value," "maximize shareholder value," or speak to management or other shareholders about "exploring strategic alternatives"—all code phrases for potentially putting a company up for sale to get the stock price higher.

4. An outside "beneficial" owner pays substantially more than the current market price of the stock in a private transaction with the company to establish an initial position or increase its stake, or agrees to provide services or something else of value to a company in exchange for an option to purchase shares where the option's exercise price is substantially higher than the current market price of the stock. This is often a strong indication that all parties involved see substantially higher values ahead for the company and its stock.

5. An outside beneficial owner adds to its stake in a company through additional open market purchases of its stock.

6. An outside beneficial owner expresses an interest *in selling its stake in a company* and says it will *review strategic alternatives*—often a code phrase for a desire to have the target company acquired by a third party to maximize the value of the beneficial owner's investment.

7. A dispute between an outside beneficial owner and the company in which it owns a stake breaks out into the open—often a signal that a battle for control of the company will take place or that the outside beneficial owner will find a third party to buy its stake as a prelude to a takeover bid.

8. A company in which an outside beneficial owner holds a stake or is accumulating additional shares and/or which operates in an industry where takeovers are proliferating announces a stock buyback program.

9. A company in which an outside beneficial owner holds a stake or is adding to its stake is the subject of insider buying by its own officers and/or directors.

10. A company with an outside beneficial owner and/or operates in an industry where takeovers are proliferating announces a "shareholder rights plan" designed to make a hostile takeover more difficult.

11. A company in a consolidating industry sells or spins off "noncore" assets or operations, thereby turning itself into a "pure play" (see Chapter 14), which is often a signal that the company is preparing to sell itself to a larger company within its core industry.

12. A company in a consolidating industry takes a large "restructuring" charge, in effect putting past mistakes behind it and clearing the decks for future positive earnings reports. Such action can be important to a potential acquirer and is often a sign that a company is preparing to sell itself.

13. A company in a consolidating industry announces a restructuring charge that causes the stock to decline sharply and becomes the subject of significant insider buying and/or announces a stock buyback. This is usually a sign that the stock market is taking a shortsighted, far too negative view of what may actually be an early clue that a takeover is on the horizon.

14. A company in a consolidating industry is partially owned by a "financially oriented" company or investor, such as a brokerage firm or buyout firm, that has a tendency to buy and sell assets and that would be ready, willing, and able to craft a profitable "exit strategy" for itself by engineering a takeover of the company in question, should the opportunity present itself.

15. The founder of a company who owns a major block of stock (10 percent or more) passes away. This type of situation often leads to a desire by the estate to eventually maximize the value of the stock—in other words, a desire to have the company acquired.

16. Two or more bidders try to acquire a company in a certain industry, resulting in a bidding war. Since only one of these bidders can be a winner of the target company, there is a good chance that the losing bidder will look elsewhere for another acquisition target within the industry. In a case like this, you should browse through other companies within the industry looking for one or more of the Telltale Signs on the list.

17. A small-to-medium-size company in a consolidating industry achieves a breakout from a "superstock breakout pattern"; i.e., the stock penetrates a well-defined resistance level at least 12 months in duration following a series of progressively rising bottoms or support levels, which indicates that buyers are willing to pay increasingly higher prices to establish a position. This pattern creates the appearance of a "rising triangle" on the chart. *The best superstock breakout patterns occur when volatility decreases markedly in the weeks or days prior to the breakout.*

18. A company that owns a piece of another company is itself acquired. Many times it can pay dividends to look into a situation where a stake in one company is "inherited" through a takeover of another company. Many times, if Company A acquires Company B, which, in turn, owns a stake in Company C, you will find that Company C becomes a takeover target in one of two ways: (1) Company A may eventually bid for the rest of Company C if this fits its overall business/acquisition strategy or (2) Company A may sell off the inherited stake in Company C to a third party, which then bids for the rest of Company C. A takeover of a company whose stock is "inherited" through another takeover becomes even more likely when there is already a business relationship between Company A and Company C.

For illustrative purposes, let's look at an actual example of Telltale Sign number 18. In June 1999, Weyerhauser, the largest lumber producer in the United States, purchased Canadian timber company MacMillan Bloedel Ltd. As part of that takeover, Weyerhauser

"inherited" a 49 percent stake in Trus Joist, a Boise, Idaho, manufacturer of lumber products, which was partially owned by MacMillan.
The other 51 percent of Trus Joist was owned by TJ International, a
publicly traded company listed on NASDAQ.

There was some speculation at the time of the Weyerhauser
purchase of MacMillan Bloedel as to what would happen to Trus
Joist. Most observers seemed to believe that TJ International would
buy out the 49 percent of Trus Joist that had been inherited by
Weyerhauser. Others seemed to feel that Weyerhauser might make
a takeover bid for TJ International as a way to buy the remaining 51
percent of Trus Joist.

At first TJ International stock rocketed from the low $20s to as
high as $33⅞, based on the second scenario: a potential takeover bid
from Weyerhauser. But TJ shares then fell back sharply, falling as
low as $21⅜, based on the emerging consensus that TJ would prob-
ably buy out the 49 percent Trus Joist stake from Weyerhauser.

A superstock observer who noted that Weyerhauser was the
major distributor for Trus Joist's products and supplied most of the
raw materials for Trus Joist could have concluded that it was highly likely that Weyerhauser, *which was already in acquisition mode*, would
want to own the rest of Trus Joist rather than sell its 49 percent to TJ
International.

On November 23, 1999, just 5 months after it bought MacMillan
Bloedel, Weyerhauser agreed to buy TJ International for $42 per
share. TJ International jumped $9⅜ (or 22 percent) in one day as a
result of the bid, which was nearly 100 percent premium to TJ's stock
price just 4 months before.

OTHER THINGS TO LOOK FOR

In addition to these telltale signs that a formerly sleepy and overlooked stock is about to become a superstock takeover candidate,
you should also pay close attention to any and all merger announcements each and every day, making note of which industries are experiencing consolidation and what the reasoning behind that consolidation may be. You should also read and listen to any interviews of
CEOs of companies that are making acquisitions for clues about
what their future acquisition plans may be. You will be amazed at
how much information you can obtain and how many tantalizing

clues are available by simply listening carefully to companies that are actively acquiring other companies.

USING THE *VICKERS WEEKLY INSIDER REPORT* TO FIND AND TRACK "BENEFICIAL OWNERS"

Browsing through the *Vickers Weekly Insider Report* on a regular basis is a great way to find companies that are already partially owned by outside beneficial owners who are also increasing their stakes by continuing to buy stock on the open market. This type of browsing is what led to discovering Rexel and its outside beneficial owner, Rexel S.A., a browsing coup that led to a 119 percent profit.

The *Vickers Weekly Insider Report* is available by mail and also online. Published by Argus Research, the report is a summary of buy and sell transactions by corporate "insiders" (officers and directors) and also outside "beneficial owners" of 10 percent or more of a company's stock (see Figure 10–1).

Of particular interest is the "beneficial owner" transactions. When an outside investor accumulates 5 percent or more of a company's shares, he or she must file a Form 13-D with the Securities and Exchange Commission. That form will indicate the date and prices paid for the stock and also, in general terms, the purpose of the investment. Some 13-Ds clearly state that the stock has been bought for "investment purposes only," while other 13-D filings leave open the possibility that the outside beneficial owner may seek to influence management in some way, including possibly urging the restructuring or sale of the company as a means of "maximizing" or "enhancing" shareholder value.

In the *Vickers Weekly Insider Report* look for outside beneficial owners that are accumulating additional shares on the open market. When an outside beneficial owner who already owns a stake in a company goes into the open market to buy additional stock it tells you two things. First, at the very least, it indicates that the outside beneficial owner still sees value at a certain price level and is willing to buy more stock at that price. Second, additional open market buying can also be an early clue that the outside beneficial owner intends to eventually take over the entire company and is trying to accumulate as many shares as possible at a bargain price before offering a premium to buy the remainder of the shares owned by the public.

F i g u r e   10–1

Sample of *Vickers Weekly Insider Report*

ISSUER	TRADES	DATES	PRICE	NOW HAS	INSIDER
LUCENT TECHNOLOGIES	S-137,288	MAY 5 '00	60	320,424	DICKSON, JOHN T. CEO
LUCENT TECHNOLOGIES	S-100,000	MAY 5 '00	59 3/8	173,594	RUSSO, PATRICIA CEO
MAGELLAN HEALTH SVCS	B-10,000	MAY 16 '00	2 1/8 - 2 3/16	23,400	WIDER, JOHN J. PR
MAGELLAN HEALTH SVCS	B-10,000	MAY 16 '00	2 1/8 - 2 1/4	14,000	HARBIN, HENRY T. PR
MAIL-WELL INC	S-49,900	MAY 17-18 ' 0	9 3/16 - 9 7/16	816,176	MAHONEY, GERALD F. CB
MARRIOTT INTL INC NEW CL A	S-60,000 X	MAY 12-19 ' 0	34 1/2 - 36 3/4	9,566,616 X	MARRIOTT, J. WILLARD CB
MARRIOTT INTL INC NEW CL A	S-60,000 X	MAY 12-19 ' 0	34 1/2 - 36 3/4	10,248,500 X	MARRIOTT, RICHARD E. DIR
MARRIOTT INTL INC NEW CL A	S-20,000	MAY 15-19 ' 0	36 - 36 15/16	80,097	WIESZ, STEPHEN P. VP
MARSH & MC LENNAN COS INC	S-7,874	MAY 25 '00	109 3/16	9,486	COSTER, PETER DIR
MARSH & MC LENNAN COS INC	S-12,143 X	MAY 30 '00	109 7/16	132,279 X	SIMMONS, ADELE S. DIR
MARSH & MC LENNAN COS INC	S-5,000 X	MAY 22 '00	104 7/8	110,018 X	OLSEN, DAVID A. DIR
MASSMUTUAL CORPORATE INVS INC	B-8,200	MAY 4-12 ' 0	19 11/16 - 20	17,800	HART, MARTIN THOMAS TTEE
MASSMUTUAL PARTN INVS (SBI)	B-30,000	MAY 4-19 ' 0	9 - 9 11/16	44,438	HART, MARTIN THOMAS DIR
MAY DEPT STORES CO	S-1,500	MAY 24 '00	29 5/8	11,490	KNIFFEN, JAN R. SR VP
MAY DEPT STORES CO	S-2,250	MAY 15 '00	29 1/16	5,367	JAY, LONNY J. SR VP
MAY DEPT STORES CO	S-13,000	MAY 25 '00	29 13/16	377,594	LOEB, JEROME T. CB
MBNA CORP	S-50,000	MAY 12 '00	26 7/16	N/A	CAWLEY, CHARLES M. PR
MBNA CORP	S-15,125	MAY 23 '00	27 1/8	188,608	RHODES, MICHAEL G. EX VP
MBNA CORP	S-67,850	MAY 2 '00	26 7/16	N/A	COCHRAN, JOHN R. SREXVP
MCDONALDS CORP	S-26,802	MAY 26 '00	37 3/4	308,612	CANTALUPO, JAMES R. VCB
MCDONALDS CORP	S-260,000	MAY 11 '00	38 5/8	772,554	QUINLAN, MICHAEL R. CB
MERITOR AUTOMOTIVE INC	B-5,000	MAY 2 '00	14 5/8	7,000	MARLEY, JAMES E. DIR
MERITOR AUTOMOTIVE INC	B-675	MAY 19 '00	13 1/16	4,157 X	GOSNELL, THOMAS A. PR
MERITOR AUTOMOTIVE INC	B-28,000	MAY 10-25 ' 0	12 15/16 - 13 3/4	50,500	POLING, HAROLD A. DIR
MERITOR AUTOMOTIVE INC	B-1,000	MAY 9 '00	14 5/16	8,375	STELFOX, DIANE M. VP
MERITOR AUTOMOTIVE INC	B-5,000	MAY 17 '00	13	15,000	SODERSTROM, S. CARL SR VP
MERRILL LYNCH & CO COM	S-160,000	MAY 25 '00	99 11/16 - 102	983,731	STEFFENS, JOHN L. VCB
METRO-GOLDWYN-MAYER	S-31,022	MAY 16-23 ' 0	27 1/8 - 28 7/8	311	BRADA, DONALD R. JR XEXVP
MID AMER APT COMMUNTYS	B-1,000 X	MAY 13 '00	23 5/8	110,544 X	CATES, GEORGE E. CEO
MIDWAY GAMES INC	B-121,100	MAY 5-26 ' 0	6 1/8 - 7 3/4	6,364,765	REDSTONE, SUMNER M. B/O ◄──
MORGAN STANLEY D/W AFRICA INVT	S-45,000	MAY 2-11 ' 0	8 3/8 - 8 1/2	163,112	MORGAN ST DW INV MGMT
MORGAN STANLEY D/W ASIA-PAC FD	S-227,274	MAY 2-11 ' 0	9 7/8 - 10 13/16	117,143	MORGAN ST DW INV MGMT
MORRISON MGMT SPECIALISTS INC	S-13,200	MAY 3-05 ' 0	25 3/8 - 25 9/16	14,567	ROBERSON, RICHARD C. OFF
MORRISON MGMT SPECIALISTS INC	S-55,624	MAY 1 '00	27 1/2 - 27 5/8	16,333	ENGWALL, K. WYATT SR VP
MORRISON MGMT SPECIALISTS INC	S-36,548	MAY 17 '00	27	65,169	DAVENPORT, GLENN A. CB
MUSICLAND STORES CORP	S-23,000	MAY 11 '00	7 11/16	466,892	ROSS, GARY A. OFF
NATCO GRP INC CL A	B-5,000 X	MAY 31 '00	9 9/16	5,000 X	GREGORY, NATHANIEL A. CB
NATIONAL OILWELL INC	S-300,000 X	MAY 25 '00	27 9/16	119,656 X	DUNWOODY, W. MCCOMB DIR
NATIONSRENT INC COM	B-20,000	MAY 24 '00	3 5/8	95,000	PHILIPPIN, CHARLES J. DIR
NELSON (THOMAS) INC	B-10,000	MAY 30-31 ' 0	7 1/16 - 7 1/8	510,111	OAKLEY, MILLARD V. DIR
NEWFIELD EXPL CO	S-2,300	MAY 18 '00	42	38,137	SCHNEIDER, WILLIAM D. VP
NEWFIELD EXPL CO	S-19,860	MAY 4 '00	37 1/2	107,638	WALDRUP, ROBERT W. VP
NEWFIELD EXPL CO	S-50,000	MAY 18-19 ' 0	44	68,961	SCHAIBLE, DAVID F. VP
NOVA CORP GA	S-129,100	MAY 17-31 ' 0	28 1/2 - 30 1/2	559,726	DAILY, GREGORY S. DIR
NU SKIN ENTERPRISES INC CL A	S-20,000	MAY 11-16 ' 0	7 3/16 - 7 1/2	N/A	HALLS, KEITH R. SR VP
OFFICE DEPOT INC	B-60,000	MAY 26-31 ' 0	6 15/16 - 7 1/2	115,120	NELSON, M. BRUCE CEO
OFFICE DEPOT INC	B-65,000	MAY 26 '00	7 1/2 - 7 5/8	3,103,447	HELFORD, IRWIN DIR
OMI CORP NEW	S-1,797,500	MAR.31-MAY 31	3 1/2 - 4 1/8	3,902,500	MEGA TANKERS NWBLDG AS B/O
OMNICARE INC	S-10,000	MAY 11 '00	15 1/2	N/A	KEEFE, PATRICK E. EX VP
OMNICOM GROUP INC	S-2,000	MAY 31 '00	84 1/8	47,015	HEWITT, DENNIS E. TR
ORTHODONTIC CTRS AMER INC	S-9,000	MAY 8-10 ' 0	25 9/16 - 26 13/16	53,390	JOHNSEN, MICHAEL C. COO
ORTHODONTIC CTRS AMER INC	S-2,400 X	MAY 10 '00	25 1/2 - 25 9/16	N/A X	JOHNSEN, MICHAEL C. COO
ORTHODONTIC CTRS AMER INC	S-180,200 X	MAY 15-17 ' 0	26 1/2 - 26 15/16	807,232 X	LAZZARA, GASPER JR CB
PAKISTAN INVT FD INC	S-360,403	MAY 2-11 ' 0	2 1/2 - 2 3/4	7,119	MORGAN ST DW INV MGMT
PATINA OIL & GAS CORP	B-10,000	MAY 22 '00	14 1/16	16,244	LYNCH, ALEXANDER P. DIR
PATINA OIL & GAS CORP	B-10,000	MAY 22 '00	14 1/16	14,483	LANIER, ELIZABETH K. DIR
PATINA OIL & GAS CORP	B-5,270 X	MAY 26 '00	14 1/4	102,254 X	DECKER, JAY W. PR
PATINA OIL & GAS CORP	S-6,500	MAY 2-12 ' 0	14 3/4 - 16 1/4	5,081	RUBY, TERRY L. VP
PERSONNEL GROUP AMER	B-24,000	MAY 12 '00	4 11/16 - 4 13/16	51,000	KING, J. ROGER DIR
PERSONNEL GROUP AMER	B-22,000	MAY 1-09 ' 0	4 1/2 - 5 1/4	81,174	EGAN, KEVIN P. DIR
PERSONNEL GROUP AMER	B-10,000	MAY 9-17 ' 0	4 1/2 - 4 11/16	31,000	NAPIER, JAMES V. DIR
PERSONNEL GROUP AMER	B-2,500	MAY 9 '00	4 7/16	12,484	BRAMLETT, KEN R. JR CFO
PERSONNEL GROUP AMER	B-1,000	MAY 17 '00	4 3/4	3,000	SCITES, JANICE L. DIR
PERSONNEL GROUP AMER	B-10,000	MAY 10 '00	4 3/8	28,220	BARKER, MICHAEL H. OFF

Simply sitting in a comfortable spot with a highlighter and a pen and browsing through the entire *Vickers Report* each week, highlighting those beneficial owner (B/O) transactions that seem interesting and making notations relating to names you have seen before (or never seen before), will often lead to new and profitable ideas you would not have otherwise encountered.

For one thing, you'll notice familiar names popping up in different places. You may find, for example, that an outside beneficial owner you have been tracking in one company also owns a piece of another company in a related industry. Or you may find that an outside beneficial owner is buying shares of one company while selling shares of another. You also may find that an outside beneficial owner owns pieces of several different companies, or that companies are popping up for the first time, which can take your search in an entirely new and different direction, as we shall soon see.

There are other ways to get information on the activities of beneficial owners other than waiting around for the *Vickers Weekly Insider Report* to show up in your mailbox. You can go to the Internet, click on freeedgar.com or any of a number of other sites, and get a list of 13-D filings every day. And once you have developed an interest in a certain stock, you can zero in on all of the relevant SEC filings and develop a wealth of information on your potential target company.

But there are connections that would not show up in a normal 13-D filing or through a search of 13-D's only.

For example, one key reason to use the *Vickers Weekly Insider Report* is that it focuses on "Form 4" filings, which are required to be filed not only by outside shareholders who own 10 percent or more of a company, but also by corporate officers and directors. By grouping all Form 4 filings together, you can get a clearer, more encompassing picture of all the buying and selling activities of "in the know" stockholders than you would get simply by focusing on 13-D filings by outsiders.

You may notice, for example, heavy insider buying by officers and directors in a company where an outside beneficial owner is also accumulating shares—a powerfully bullish signal that a stock is undervalued and that some bullish factor that has not yet been taken into account by the market is lurking beneath the surface. On the other hand, you may also notice heavy insider selling in a stock that is being purchased by an outside beneficial owner, which would raise the question: If a takeover is possible, why would the officers and directors of this company be selling so heavily? In a case like this, you might pass on this particular stock.

You may also notice heavy insider buying by officers and directors in a stock that operates in a takeover lively industry, or you may notice heavy insider buying in several stocks in the same industry, which raises the possibility that something bullish is going on in that particular industry that has not yet been perceived by the market.

Or you may notice heavy insider buying and/or outside beneficial owner buying in a stock where you have previously noticed a potential "superstock breakout pattern" (more on that later).

The point is, by taking the time to browse through this wealth of information and familiarizing yourself with it on a regular basis you will soon find yourself recognizing the names of individuals and companies you have never encountered before. After a while, you'll be making connections between seemingly unrelated bits of information, getting a feel for how some of these outside beneficial owners operate, and you will notice patterns and clues that you could not possibly have noticed in any other way other than taking the time to browse.

Let me give you a real-life example that illustrates the usefulness of this tool.

CASE STUDY: SPOTTING BRYLANE AS A TAKEOVER TARGET

In 1997, *Vickers* reported a purchase of 429,400 shares of a company called Brylane Inc., by an outside beneficial owner, Pinault Printemps-Redoute S.A. The Vickers data indicated that Pinault-Printemps had purchased these Brylane shares between June 3 and June 30, 1998, at prices ranging from $45¾ to $51. Brylane was added to the potential "research universe" of stocks to look into and monitor on a regular basis.

A few weeks later, the following transaction appeared:

```
BLACKROCK INVT  S-1,756     JULY29 '98        8¹/₂         0 SABATH, KAREN H. SEC
BORG WARNER     D-400 X     JULY30 '98       48⁷/₁₆      100 X DRUMMOND, JERE A. DIR
BRYLANE INC     B-128,300 X JULY 1-28 '98  40¹/₄-45³/₄ 8,568,617 PINAULT-PRNTMPS RDT SA B/O
BUCKLE INC      S-20,200    JUNE 5-28 '98  54¹¹/₁₆-55⁷/₈  N/A NELSON, DENNIS H. PR
```

And a few weeks after that, these transactions appeared:

```
BRUSH WELLMAN   B-5.000     AUG. 5-10 '98   16³/₁₆-17¹/₂  10,000 ROBERTSON, WILLIAM R. DIR
BRUSH WELLMAN   B-8.700     Aug. 3-04 '98   15⁷/₁₆-16     17,200 HARNETT, GORDON D. CB
```

BRYLANE INC	B-25,000	AUG.21 '98	25	8,808,017	KRAMER HARTMUT	
BRYLANE INC	B-8,000	AUG.25 '98	26¼	6,000	JOHNSON, WILLIAM C DIR	
BRYLANE INC	B-2,000	AUG.21 '98	24¾	6,000	STARRETT, PETER M DIR	
BRYLANE INC	B-214,400 X	AUG.13-19 '98	24⅝-38¾	8,783,017 X	PINAULT PRNTMPS RDT SA B/O	
BUCKEYE PARTNERS	B-5,000	AUG.25-26 '98	26¹⁵⁄₁₆-27	40,000	BUCKEYE MGMT CO. PART	

Here was a situation where an outside beneficial owner, Pinault-Printemps, was buying huge chunks of a stock that was apparently dropping like a rock. The initial purchases of 429,400 shares in June took place at prices as high as $51. By July, Pinault-Printemps was buying Brylane shares as low as $40¼. By mid-August, Pinault was in the open market buying additional Brylane shares as low as $24⅝—less than half the price they paid just 2 months earlier!

In addition, once Brylane fell to the mid-$20s, several Brylane insiders began to buy shares as well, including two directors, William C. Johnson and Peter M. Starrett, who purchased 6000 shares and 2000 shares, respectively, at $26¾ and $24¾.

The continuing large purchases by Pinault-Printemps, combined with the apparently large decline in Brylane's stock price and the emergence of insider buying, compelled me to literally drop everything and find out just what Brylane and its outside beneficial owner, Pinault-Printemps, were all about. In other words, *experience indicated that Telltale Signs were flashing and that this was a situation worth looking into—right now.*

A chart of Brylane revealed that this stock *had plunged from over $60 down to the $14 area in less than 7 months!* What was particularly astonishing about this price performance was not that Brylane shares had fallen so far so fast—after all, individual stocks are collapsing every day on Wall Street, and it's not all that unusual. What *was* unusual was that an outside beneficial owner had purchased such massive amounts of Brylane stock at very high prices and had been so wrong so quickly.

By tracking the activities of outside beneficial owners, we are operating on the theory that these major shareholders know value when they see it. We assume they are intimately familiar with the operations of a company, they regularly speak with management, and they are therefore well-aware of how things are going and what the company's prospects are.

Usually though, when you see an outside beneficial owner stepping into the open market to buy big blocks of stock, you assume he or she has reached an informed conclusion—i.e., in light of all they know about the company and its prospects, there is compelling value in the stock at this level, and the beneficial owner is willing to invest additional funds to back up their opinion.

When you add insider buying into the mix—i.e., when you see officers and directors buying shares along with the outside beneficial owner at a certain price level—you have a double-barreled vote of confidence that a stock has reached a compelling price point in terms of its value as a business.

Apparently, Pinault-Printemps watched Brylane fall from $61 to $51 and decided that at $51, the stock was a great value. Pinault-Printemps also apparently thought Brylane was a great value at $45, $38, and $24⅝.

Two Brylane directors also thought the stock was a great value at $24¾ and $26¾.

Yet, in a breathtakingly short period of time, Brylane had plunged all the way to the $14 to $15 area.

So, again, here is what was so intriguing about Brylane: How could all of these sophisticated investors be so monumentally wrong in such a short period of time? And, if Pinault-Printemps thought Brylane was a good value all the way down from $51 to $24⅝, why wouldn't it consider buying the rest of the company now that the stock had fallen to $14?

For all of these reasons—and to answer all of these questions, which emerged as a result of browsing through the *Vickers Weekly Insider Report*—we researched Brylane and its outside beneficial owner, Pinault-Printemps. The result of this research can be best summarized by an old adage on Wall Street that you should never try to catch a falling piano. It's always dangerous to try to predict a bottom in a stock that has been falling precipitously. What you want to look for is an easing of the selling pressure, a leveling out of the stock price, and ideally, the formation of a sideways trading range, or base pattern, which indicates that buyers are finally stepping in and that the supply/demand situation is coming back into balance.

So why would you try to catch this falling piano? *Because Brylane was 47.53 percent owned by a French company, Pinault-Printemps-Redoute S.A., the parent company of Rexel S.A.*

That's right—Pinault-Printemps turned out to be the parent company of Rexel S.A. of France, the very same outside beneficial owner that methodically purchased additional shares of Rexel Inc. on the open market prior to making a takeover bid for the entire company!

And Brylane, it turned out, was a very well-known company: a major catalog retailer that published, among others, catalogs for Sears, Lane Bryant (thus the name of the company), Lerner, and Chadwick's. Thirteen months after Brylane's February 1997 public offering, Pinault-Printemps purchased a 43.7 percent stake in Brylane for $51 per share.

Shortly after Pinault-Printemps went into the open market to buy additional shares in June and July 1998, Brylane had plunged in reaction to two separate news developments. First, on August 19, 1998, Brylane dropped 11½ points to $24¾ on news that sales of the company's Lerner catalog were disappointing and below expectations. This news led to several earnings estimate cuts by the small group of analysts who followed Brylane, and the institutional investors who followed these analysts obviously dumped Brylane shares, en masse.

Shortly after Brylane stock plunged 11½ points in one day, the company announced a $40 million stock buyback. This development was especially intriguing because when an outside beneficial owner, company insiders, and the company itself are all buying shares on the open market, it is one of the strongest possible clues that a stock is selling in a great long-term value area and the stock market is overreacting to a short-term problem, creating a compelling buying opportunity value for investors who have the vision and the fortitude to look beyond the hysteria of the moment. (See "Eighteen Telltale Signs," numbers 8 and 9 earlier in this chapter.)

But even though Pinault-Printemps, several Brylane insiders, and Brylane itself all apparently believed that the stock was a great value in the mid-to-high $20s, Brylane shares were blasted *again* on September 24 and 25, 1998, following another analyst downgrade and earnings estimate reduction.

This second price plunge took the stock down to the $14 to $15 area.

Research into Brylane revealed that Pinault-Printemps had agreed to a "standstill agreement," which limited Pinault to owning a maximum of 47.5 percent of Brylane for three years, ending April 3, 2001.

Normally, a "standstill agreement" might be viewed as an impediment to a takeover. However, that's not always the case.

Further research into Pinault-Printemps revealed this company to be Europe's third-largest mail order company. Pinault was a company that generated $14.5 billion per year in revenues. So, paying $300 million or so for the rest of Brylane, which operated a mail order business that obviously fit right into Pinault's business mix, did not seem like a very big deal—especially in view of the fact that Pinault had paid $51 for its original stake, over three times what Brylane was trading for in October 1998.

As a superstock investor, you could have taken a gradual and patient approach with Brylane. Tax-loss selling could have hurt the stock as year-end approached since it is, indeed, tough to catch a "falling piano." But all of Wall Street loved Brylane at $61. Now, close to $15, Brylane looked like a very interesting special situation if you were willing to be patient and take a one-to-two year investment horizon.

In November there was another insider buyer in Brylane, this time at a price of $15¹⁵⁄₁₆. In December, Brylane had once again issued an earnings warning and the stock had retreated to the $10 to $11 area. At these low prices it would be a safe guess that Pinault-Printemps, the French company that owned that 47.5 percent stake, should at least be thinking about a potential takeover bid.

Several weeks later, Brylane soared from $11 to $23, following the news that Pinault-Printemps had made a takeover bid for the company!

Anyone who had bought Brylane at $14 to $15 chalked up a gain of as much as 50 percent in less than 3 months. Any investor who had purchased shares of Brylane following the final plunge to the $10 to $11 area would have made a 100% (or more) profit in just 2 or 3 weeks!

This phenomenally successful recommendation came about for one reason and one reason only: I took the time to browse through the *Vickers Weekly Insider Report* and noticed a couple of names that were completely new to me. Through continued browsing, these names popped up again, which led to further investigation of these companies. This investigation, in turn, led to the discovery that Pinault-Printemps was the parent company of Rexel S.A. of France, a company that had already taken over one of my previous takeover recommendations.

A combination of experience and research, together with the fact that Brylane itself and Brylane insiders were buying stock on the open market right along with Pinault-Printemps—two of the

Telltale Signs I always watch for—created a logical and compelling superstock takeover candidate.

That is how you use the *Vickers Weekly Insider Report*.

CASE STUDY: SAM HEYMAN AND DEXTER CORP.

Experienced observers of thoroughbred horse racing can usually tell halfway through a horse race, with a high degree of accuracy, which horses are likely to be in contention at the finish and which will not. Announcers can usually determine which horses are looking "strong" and which are on the verge of tiring as the race is in progress, and they often use these observations to accentuate certain horses as they call the race. How do they do this? They know the characteristics, through long experience, of horses that are running as fast as they can in the early stages of the race and of horses that are being restrained and have not yet been asked to run at top speed. Once a race is under way and the horses have settled into stride, veteran race watchers can usually tell which horses will be around at the finish and which will be also-rans. They do this by watching the horses' strides, how high the jockeys are riding in the saddle, whether the reins are loose or taut, the position of the jockeys' hands, and other clues that can only be observed by someone who has seen all of this thousands of times before and learned to recognize some of the Telltale Signs to help determine the outcome.

Experience is an invaluable asset when you are browsing for superstock takeover candidates. The more you browse, the more you'll notice, and the more you notice, the more you'll be able to make certain connections that other investors will be unable to make. Given the identical set of circumstances, you'll see something that others do not see and you will be able to see a high probability of a certain outcome, and that's where you gain your edge. Each experience—even those that do not turn out profitably—will lay the groundwork for future experiences. Eventually, you'll find yourself extrapolating a certain set of circumstances all the way to their logical—and profitable—conclusion.

Dan Dorfman, one of the most respected financial reporters on Wall Street and the former author of *The Wall Street Journal*'s "Heard on the Street" column, was writing a column for Jagnotes.com when he called me on November 1, 1999. His request was straightforward enough: He asked me to list my top three takeover candidates in the coming 12 months. I offered the following three stocks. *E'town Corp.*, a New Jersey water utility, *Dexter Corp.*, a specialty chemicals company, and *California Water Service*, another water utility.

Amazingly, within 6 weeks two of those three takeover candidates received takeover bids. E'town jumped 10 points in one day following a bid from Thames Water PLC of Britain. (For more on the E'town takeover and the reasoning that went into it, see Chapter 18.)

The other company to receive a takeover bid was Dexter Corp.

Dexter Corp. proved to be another strong example of the benefits of browsing. While looking through the weekly list of 13-D filings in *Barron's*, I noticed that International Specialty Products (ISP) had purchased 365,200 shares of Dexter at prices ranging from $36.25 to $38.63 per share, giving ISP a total of 1,996,900 shares, or 8.67 percent of Dexter's outstanding shares.

Many, if not most, of the 13-D filings reported in *Barron's* and elsewhere each week involve money managers, and they are of no interest because these are passive investors who are not likely to create a takeover threat.

In browsing through these filings each week, it helps to look for 13-D filers who are either corporations—i.e., real businesses who may want to acquire another business—or individuals who for one reason or another seem to have the ability, the inclination, or both, to mount a takeover bid.

Another tool is to look for names you do not recognize. For instance, when an individual or a company that does not normally acquire a 5 percent interest in another company suddenly files a 13-D, it is often an indication that they are a serious player—i.e., they are thinking in terms of a takeover, or, at the very least, they will use their ownership leverage to prod a company to maximize the value of the stock in some way.

In September 1999, International Specialty Products was not a familiar name. Dexter was, however, because of a company called Life Technologies, which was 53 percent owned by Dexter. Life Technologies was recommended on May 29, 1998, because the "life sciences" industry, where LTEK operated, had seen a wave of takeovers. What really sparked the LTEK recommendation as a takeover target, however, was a simple statement found in a series of Dexter press releases. Press releases are yet another useful tool that can help you get a feel for a company and its thinking in terms of either acquiring companies or selling itself to someone else. *In one of Dexter's releases, the company said that it was actively seeking acquisition candidates.*

Now, this may seem like a ridiculously simple conclusion, and in reality it is. The amazing thing is how few observers managed to reach it. Here was Dexter, a slow-growth chemicals company that owned 53 percent of fast-growing Life Technologies, a company in a popular industry where a series of takeovers had already taken place. Dexter needed something to juice up its growth rate; it already owned 53 percent of LTEK and had just stated that it was looking to acquire a company.

It seemed pretty logical that LTEK might be on Dexter's radar screen as a takeover target, and that Dexter might bid for the 47 percent of LTEK it did not already own.

Soon, LTEK jumped 8 points in one day on news that Dexter had offered $37 per share to acquire the remainder of LTEK. That bid was viewed as too low, and it prompted howls of outrage from LTEK shareholders. Dexter eventually raised its bid to $39⅛. Part of being a superstock investor is knowing when to sell, and that was the recommendation made for this stock at this point in time.

It had been a year since the LTEK takeover, and now somebody had filed a 13-D on Dexter and was raising its stake.

Research revealed *that International Specialty Products was controlled by a man named Samuel Heyman.* This piqued my interest because I had already recommended a Sam Heyman takeover target way back in 1982. The horse race now seemed half over: The outcome was apparent. On Wall Street, just like in horse racing, the past performances can tell you a lot.

I immediately knew that a hostile takeover bid for Dexter was virtually inevitable because history had shown that Samuel Heyman had a burning desire to win every battle he decided to wage.

In 1982, long before the term "hostile takeover" became a familiar part of the Wall Street lexicon, Samuel Heyman was a shareholder in a company called GAF Corp. At some point Heyman reached the conclusion that GAF's assets were worth far more than its stock price and that GAF's management was not running the company in a manner that was making optimal use of those assets.

In other words, to put it bluntly, Samuel Heyman thought that GAF's management was doing a lousy job and that he could do better. Heyman announced that he intended to wage a proxy fight to replace GAF's management and that he would then embark on a program to maximize GAF's value for its shareholders.

Today, this would not be what you would call a startling development. News that a dissident shareholder is urging management to maximize value and is threatening to wage a proxy fight is so commonplace that it would barely raise an eyebrow. But in 1982, Samuel Heyman was a man ahead of his time. He nominated a new slate of directors, headed by himself, and announced that he intended to take over GAF.

Wall Street reacted to Sam Heyman as if Rodney Dangerfield had announced he intended to run for President. It was as though an interloper had decided to get involved in a process where only members of an exclusive club were allowed to operate, and Heyman's battle with GAF was viewed with a combination of amusement and a decided lack of respect in the investment community.

GAF, meanwhile, was not amused, and its management reacted angrily to Sam Heyman's audacity. GAF questioned Heyman's credibility and management abilities and generally scoffed at the idea that Heyman and his inexperienced group of outsiders could unseat GAF's well-entrenched management. Eventually, the scoffing stopped and turned to outright hostility, involving a series of increasingly hostile statements and newspaper advertisements in which the two contestants insulted each other and tried to win the support of GAF stockholders.

Heyman won the proxy fight, ousted GAF management, restructured the company, liquidated some assets, and completely followed through on everything he said he would do. Along the way, he accumulated a 9.9 percent stake in Union Carbide—an especially audacious move, since Union Carbide was many times larger than GAF—and actually threatened to take Union over! GAF made a huge profit on its Union Carbide stock. GAF had soared to $67 a share, a gain of 375 percent in 2½ years. Heyman ultimately took GAF private in 1989, then sold 20 percent of International Specialty Products, a GAF subsidiary, to the public in 1991.

Now, 14 years later, here was Samuel Heyman accumulating a stake in Dexter Corp. on the open market through his new public company, International Specialty Products. On the surface, Dexter seemed an unlikely candidate for an outside beneficial owner to take a major stake: The oldest company listed on the New York Stock Exchange, it was a specialty chemicals company operating in an industry where rising raw material costs and shrinking margins, combined with slowing revenue growth, had put a severe crimp in its earnings growth. This was one of the major reasons Dexter had made the takeover bid for the 47 percent of Life Technologies it did not own—Dexter hoped that LTEK's high-growth business would inject some badly needed excitement into a stock that was being neglected by Wall Street.

There was more to the Dexter situation than met the eye, especially to someone looking at this situation in terms of a potential superstock takeover target. First, the very circumstances causing profit margins to shrink among all chemicals companies had already set off a takeover wave in that industry, as chemicals companies looked for combinations to achieve economies of scale. This has been seen over and over again in recent years: When an industry reaches maturity or when it faces a set of circumstances that makes it appear that growth opportunities will be limited, the larger companies in the industry look to mergers and cost-cutting as a way to grow earnings. In such situations, the smaller and mid-size companies tend to become takeover targets, and suddenly a sleepy company with stagnant or declining earnings, one that is totally ignored by Wall Street, becomes a superstock because it's a takeover target.

These companies will never be on the recommended lists of momentum players, because they have no momentum, either in the earnings or their stock price. They will never show up on a sophisticated "screen" that directs investors' attention to the strongest stock with the most rapid earnings growth. And they will rarely be recommended by mutual fund managers who talk about their most brilliant ideas on television, because what is there to talk about when a company's revenues are flat and its earnings are declining?

And yet, the fact is that some of the most compelling values on Wall Street can be found in sectors where the fundamentals appear to be most unappealing—*provided you can see the potential of some sort of "catalyst" that would force the stock market to recognize the inherent value in these situations.*

Dexter had a catalyst, and his name was Samuel Heyman. Here we had a company operating in a consolidating industry where an outside beneficial owner—Heyman—was accumulating shares on the open market. Even better, the outside beneficial owner had a history of acquiring companies.

But there was even a more interesting twist to the Dexter–Sam Heyman story that convinced me, absolutely and without a doubt, that Heyman and International Specialty Products would soon be making a hostile takeover bid for Dexter Corp.

It turned out that a group led by Sam Heyman and International Specialty Products had been major stockholders of Life Technologies a year earlier, when Dexter angered LTEK's shareholders by making a takeover bid that was perceived to be too low.

The controversy over Dexter's bid still lingered. Actually, I had stopped following Life Technologies after Dexter's takeover bid. Cherrie Mahon went back and pieced together the chain of events that had culminated in Sam Heyman's steady accumulation of Dexter shares on the open market. I discovered that, following Dexter's offer for LTEK, two directors of Life Technologies resigned because they believed that Dexter's bid was too low. Remember, Dexter already owned 53 percent of LTEK, which put it firmly in the driver's seat. Life Technologies formed a special committee to evaluate the Dexter bid; they retained Goldman Sachs, which estimated that LTEK was worth as much as $60 per share, compared to Dexter's upwardly revised bid of $39⅛. Dexter, meanwhile, had retained Merrill Lynch, which said that Dexter's $39⅛ offer was fair and reasonable. The discrepancy between Goldman's estimate of LTEK's value and Merrill Lynch's value estimate proves that value, like beauty, is in the eye of the beholder.

Then again, it may prove something else. Dexter, armed with a "fairness" opinion from Merrill Lynch, and having proved that comparison shopping can save you money on Wall Street, proceeded with its $39⅛ per share tender offer for Life Technologies. The offer attracted another 18 percent of LTEK's shares, giving Dexter a total of 71 percent of the company.

Meanwhile, the rest of LTEK's shareholders refused to tender their shares, a highly unusual situation when the controlling shareholder is issuing a take-it-or-leave-it offer. Dexter allowed the tender offer to expire, issued a statement that it was disappointed that some of LTEK's shareholders refused to take advantage of its takeover bid, and said that it was content to own 71 percent of Life Technologies. Shortly afterward, Life Technologies, which had previously traded on the NASDAQ market, was exiled to the OTC "Bulletin Board" because there were not enough public shareholders left to qualify for NASDAQ listing.

And who were these handful of LTEK shareholders who refused to sell their stock to Dexter at what they considered to be an unfairly low price?
You guessed it—a group led by Samuel Heyman and International Specialty Products.

That's right. Sam Heyman, the man who challenged GAF and took over that company back in the early 1980s because he believed he was being treated unfairly as a GAF shareholder, simply sat on his hands and refused to respond to Dexter's takeover bid for Life Technologies. Not only that, Heyman and ISP actually went into the open market to purchase additional Life Technologies shares just as the Dexter tender offer was expiring—and they paid more for LTEK stock than the value of Dexter's bid, which amounted to one more thumb of the nose at Dexter and a clear signal that Heyman was not going to take this lying down.

During December 1998, the same month that Dexter's bid expired, International Specialty Products went into the open market and bought 1,471,320 LTEK shares, paying as high as $39.28 per share. Other investors associated with Sam Heyman and ISP also went into the open market during December 1998 and bought LTEK shares. As a result, when the Dexter offer expired, Sam Heyman and his group owned a total of 86 percent of LTEK's remaining public "float."

To someone who did not know Sam Heyman's history, the fact that Heyman and ISP were now buying Dexter shares on the open market may have had little or no meaning. In fact, there was no shortage of analysts who dismissed Heyman's purchases of Dexter as nothing more than a ploy to get a higher price for his Life Technologies shares. They felt that Heyman had gotten himself into a box with his LTEK stake and was now seeking to bully Dexter into bailing him out with a higher bid. Others believed Heyman would never make a bid for Dexter because ISP was so highly leveraged that it would not be able to obtain the financing for an offer.

But Sam Heyman did not operate that way. Heyman was not looking for Dexter to "bail him out" and would not have started this fight without the ability to finish it. Heyman would ultimately make a hostile takeover bid for Dexter, with the intention of taking over the company, selling off various Dexter assets for their fair value—including Dexter's stake in Life Technologies—and restructuring Dexter so its true asset value, estimated by analysts to be as much as $55 per share or more, could be realized by its shareholders. Another clue that

Sam Heyman was serious was that ISP had been selling off its "non-core" operations.

The conclusions reached from all of this were that Sam Heyman was trying to put Dexter "in play," and either ISP or a group headed by ISP, or possibly a third party, would soon be making a takeover bid for Dexter. Heyman's intent toward Dexter would be what Wall Street would call hostile, and ISP would attempt to gain control of Dexter, sell off various Dexter operations that it did not want, retain some of Dexter's specialty chemicals operations that fit the ISP business profile, and possibly sell off the LTEK stake to another bidder willing to pay a more reasonable (and much higher) price.

Sam Heyman went into the open market to purchase additional Dexter shares, raising his stake to 9.98 percent of the company, and he filed a notification that he intended to raise his stake to at least 15 percent.

Dexter responded by lowering the threshold of its "shareholder rights" plan from 20 percent to 11 percent. Under the terms of the plan, a "poison pill" would kick in if any outside person or group passed the 11 percent ownership threshold without Dexter's permission. The poison pill would touch off a ridiculously complex series of financial shenanigans that only an investment banker with far too much time on his hands could have dreamed up. But the outcome would be this: The poison pill would make a hostile takeover prohibitively expensive and virtually impossible.

Meanwhile, Dexter shares were drifting slowly but surely down toward that $30 to $33 support area that I advised subscribers to watch for.

This was yet another example of Wall Street's remarkable ability to overlook the obvious in spending its time obsessing over a handful of high-profile "momentum" stocks while ignoring virtually everything else.

On Friday, December 11, 1999, Dexter closed at $32⁹⁄₁₆. On that trading day, Dexter was just another basic industry "value" stock with uninspiring revenue and earnings growth, of little or no interest to trendy "momentum" investors seeking to beat the stock market.

On Monday, December 14, 1999, Dexter was the best-performing stock on the New York Stock Exchange, soaring 8⅝ points, or 26.5 percent in a single day. In other words, Dexter had become a superstock.

Why?

Because Sam Heyman's International Specialty Products announced a hostile $45 per share takeover bid for Dexter—a takeover bid that seemed to come out of the blue for most market watchers but that certainly came as no surprise to anyone who was tuned in to the events that led up to the bid.

And it certainly came as no surprise to anyone who knew anything about Sam Heyman.

You probably think this is the end of the Dexter story. In fact, the most lucrative part of the story was yet to come!

Following Sam Heyman's $45 bid for Dexter, Dexter stock spent the next 4 months trading within a range of $34 and $40. The Wall Street analytical community, you see, still did not take Sam Heyman seriously.

Following the jump in Dexter's stock price to $41\frac{3}{16}$, which was still nearly 4 points below the value of Sam Heyman's takeover bid, Dexter's stock began to erode again because analysts openly questioned: (1) whether Heyman was seriously trying to buy Dexter, and (2) whether Heyman and ISP had access to the financing to actually do the deal.

It took Dexter nearly two weeks to respond to Heyman's takeover bid. Finally, in a letter that literally dripped with sarcasm and insults, Dexter's Chairman and CEO, K. Grahame Walker, rejected Heyman's offer, calling it "inadequate."

But Walker did not stop there. First, to buttress his case that Heyman was not really serious about buying Dexter, Walker quoted a Merrill Lynch analyst who questioned Heyman's true motivation—as though a securities analyst had any insight into what Heyman's actual intentions were.

Walker then laid into Heyman for "opportunistically intervening" to frustrate Dexter's objective of acquiring Life Technologies. He accused Heyman of "inviting himself" to a meeting with Dexter management and "disregarding the interests and welfare" of Dexter's stockholders; an ironic charge when one considers how this situation ultimately turned out.

Walker concluded his letter by suggesting to Heyman that "we fervently hope (and strongly recommend) that you return your managerial focus to your own companies, leaving the stewardship of Dexter . . . where it belongs."

In January 2000 we offered the following analysis of the situation:

The stock market is reacting to this takeover bid with caution. As this is written Dexter is trading around $38¼, quite a discount from the $45 takeover price. This discount reflects apparent skepticism that Mr. Heyman and his group will be able to raise the financing for this bid. *I completely disagree with this skepticism . . . The insulting tone of Dexter's letter to Heyman is only likely to take this battle to another level, and my view is that Dexter will ultimately be bought by ISP or a third party more to Dexter's liking and that the ultimate takeover price will be at least $50/$55 a share.*

At this point Dexter and its genius investment bankers had made two miscalculations: First, by lowering the threshold of its "poison pill" to pointedly single out Heyman and prevent him from increasing his stake in Dexter, they had thrown down the gauntlet to the wrong guy, virtually guaranteeing a hostile bid. Then, by sending such a condescending letter in response to Heyman's $45 takeover bid, they had very likely ticked him off again. Based on everything I knew about Heyman, it was very clear to me that this sort of arrogant response—which was precisely the sort of response Heyman received from GAF back in the 1980s—would only serve to make Heyman more determined to win this fight.

Then on January 20, Dexter made its other blunder by offering to buy the remaining publicly traded shares of Life Technologies at $49 a share—a price $10 higher than it had previously paid the rest of LTEK's shareholders. Since Heyman and his group controlled virtually all of the remaining public float in Life Technologies, and since LTEK was trading around $44 when Dexter announced this $49 offer, the overwhelming interpretation on Wall Street was that Dexter was trying to get Heyman to drop his bid by offering him a premium price on his LTEK shares.

Here is a perfect example of how a superstock investor who understood the history and motivations of Sam Heyman—and who stopped to think about how Heyman could benefit most from this situation—could look at precisely the same set of circumstances as everyone else on Wall Street and come to a diametrically opposed—and absolutely correct—conclusion. If Heyman accepted the Dexter offer for his LTEK shares, the value of Heyman's Dexter stock would undoubtedly drop further once the takeover threat evaporated.

And there was another, more compelling reason for Sam Heyman to reject the Dexter bid: From a public relations point of view, and possibly from a legal and ethical point of view, the Dexter offer had a tainted feel to it from the very beginning because to some veteran stock market observers the Dexter bid for Heyman's Life Technologies shares smelled an awful lot like "greenmail," a term used to describe one of the most outlandish and fundamentally unfair practices that emerged during the heyday of the so-called corporate raiders of the mid-1980s. In those days, investors like T. Boone Pickens, the Bass brothers, Saul Steinberg, and Rupert Murdoch would accumulate a stake in a public company and then announce a hostile takeover bid.

The target company would then essentially bribe the raider to go away by offering the raider—but not the public shareholders—a premium price for his or her shares, in exchange for a promise to drop the takeover bid and refrain from buying any more shares in the target company for a specified period of time. Once the news of a "greenmail" deal was announced, the stock of the target company—which had risen on word of the takeover bid—would plunge, leaving the public shareholders holding the bag. The raider, meanwhile, would pocket a huge profit and move on to the next victim.

Greenmail was so fundamentally obnoxious and unfair that in 1987 it was effectively outlawed when Congress decreed that there would be a 100 percent tax on any profits achieved in this manner. This put an end to greenmail.

If Dexter's offer were actually a form of greenmail, and if Heyman took the bait and dropped his bid for Dexter, that would be bad news for Dexter shareholders. But by knowing Heyman's history, remembering that he had more at stake in Dexter than in LTEK, and realizing that to Heyman this was not only a matter of principle but also a financial question to be decided in a rational manner, a superstock investor would have come to the clear conclusion that the smart move was for Heyman to reject Dexter's bid. Not only could Heyman make more money by plowing ahead with his bid for Dexter, he would also avoid the negative firestorm of publicity and criticism that would have inevitably been directed toward him had he chosen to accept the offer from Dexter.

On January 27, 2000, Sam Heyman sent a letter to Dexter CEO Grahame Walker rejecting the $49 per share offer for Life Technologies. In the letter, Heyman made it clear that he found the Life

Technologies offer inappropriate under the circumstances—which is precisely the response one would have expected from a man like Heyman in a situation like this.

"It is apparent from the timing of Dexter's offer for our Life Technologies shares coming on the heels of ISP's $45 per share offer for Dexter . . . that Dexter is seeking to divert ISP from a course of action designed to maximize shareholder values for all Dexter shareholders," Heyman wrote. "In this connection, we believe that Dexter's attempt to deter us by providing benefits to ISP not available to other shareholders is simply inappropriate."

Heyman also called the Dexter bid for Life Technologies in 1998 "an attempted squeeze-out of LTEK's minority shareholders," which once and for all made Heyman's motivation in this situation crystal clear: He was paying Dexter back, in spades, for what he perceived as Dexter's mistreatment of ISP in the Life Technologies tender offer.

In the letter, Heyman also informed Dexter that ISP would launch a hostile proxy fight in which it would nominate a slate of directors to Dexter's board. He also told Dexter that Chase Securities had agreed to provide the funds for the acquisition, and he noted that ISP's stake in Dexter amounted to "more than five times that held by Dexter's entire board," a pointed reference to the question of which slate of directors had the most incentive to act in the best interests of the shareholders.

Heyman concluded with this zinger:

> Grahame, I just do not think it would be productive at this time to respond to your mischaracterizations and attempts to impugn our motives—which by the way I do not appreciate.
>
> All the best, Samuel J. Heyman

Heyman's rejection of the Dexter bid for Life Technologies resulted in a jump in Dexter shares back to the $38 to $39 area—a nice bounce, to be sure, but still far lower than the $45 takeover bid.

When you get to the point at which a takeover bid has turned into a public mudslinging contest you can be certain of two things: (1) Neither side is going to capitulate and be perceived as the loser without putting up one heck of a fight, and (2) the target company will do everything in its power to find another potential suitor to sell itself to in order to avoid being bought by the hostile bidder. The rule of thumb is simply this: *The more venomous the dialogue in a hostile takeover situation, the more likely that the target company will wind up being acquired, usually by a third party.* Even if the target company started out by making statements that it was determined to remain independent, once it becomes obvious that the hostile bidder is not going to be deterred, the target company is usually left with only one alternative: find another bidder more to its liking willing to pay a higher price than the hostile suitor.

Proving once again that things change, on February 28, 2000, Dexter announced that it would open up its books and records to other third parties and that it had hired Lehman Brothers Holdings to "explore a possible merger, sale or restructuring, or the spinoff or sale of a business unit."

Dexter's shares jumped $4\%_6$, or 12 percent to $42—still well below Sam Heyman's lowball $45 takeover bid.

In March 2000 I noted that Dexter stock could have been purchased at extremely low prices even in the face of mounting evidence that this company would be taken over by *somebody.*

> Even now, following Dexter's announcement that it will entertain potential takeover bids from other buyers, Dexter shares are trading below ISP's $45 per share lowball bid . . . lower than they should be under the circumstances. By the time this soap opera plays itself out, I think Dexter shareholders will receive $55 a share or more for their stock, and that one of three things will happen: (1) Mr. Heyman and ISP will raise their $45 offer significantly, (2) another bidder will emerge for Dexter with a substantially higher offer, or (3) Dexter will decide to liquidate the company and pay out cash and/or stock to shareholders on a tax-free basis, thereby passing through the true value of Life Technologies and Dexter's other assets to the stockholders.

On March 23, 2000, ISP raised its takeover bid to $50 "based on our evaluation to date" of Dexter's books, and said it might raise the offer even further if its continuing evaluation warranted such a price increase.

The continuing hostility between Dexter and ISP made it quite obvious that Dexter would move heaven and earth to avoid being purchased by Sam Heyman's group. Dexter shares jumped to a high of $56¼, then fell back to the low 50s again as the general stock market slumped. At their highs of $56¼, Dexter shares were already up 53 percent from my original recommended price—and the final act in this superstock drama was yet to unfold.

Finally, on September 14, 2000, Dexter shareholders approved the sale of Dexter to Invitrogen. Under the terms of the takeover, Dexter shareholders were offered $62.50 per share.

The Dexter opportunity came about from a 13-D filing in *Barron's* involving Dexter. It came about because my business partner, Cherrie Mahon, sent me a research folder where I spotted the name of Samuel Heyman. This became the road map that clearly pointed to a takeover bid from Samuel Heyman and ISP. This is a far different feeling than holding on to declining stock with nothing more than a vague hope that someday it will reverse course and go back up.

CHAPTER ELEVEN

How to Use the Financial Press

There is a growing tendency for the media to downsize, categorize, analyze, and trivialize the news—a sorry trend that panders to the desire of an American public, suffering from information overload, to have the news prefiltered, explained, and generally oversimplified.

When the media operates in this manner, almost everything becomes either black or white, and the various shades in between tend to disappear. Not only that, when the media begins to think in terms of giving us what we want, rather than simply acting as a conduit for information, it is only a matter of time until our sources of information become nothing more than a reflection of the consensus of majority opinion—a circular, reinforcing mechanism that virtually guarantees that original thinkers will have an increasingly difficult time accessing the sort of information that leads to unique ideas.

The financial media is becoming increasingly infected with this information virus because it has learned that many investors—especially those who have only recently become enamored with the stock market—would prefer to believe their research "homework" can be easily done for them and the process of making money on Wall Street is really not all that difficult.

Certainly any journalist or stock market adviser who chooses to oversimplify the stock picking process will find a receptive audience for this approach. After all, what could be easier than buying the high-profile "momentum" stocks you hear about day in and day out, based on the premise that today's market leaders will be tomorrow's market leaders as well? Besides, there is comfort in buying the stocks everybody else is buying and every analyst on Wall Street is already recommending, even when they go down. Group commiseration is always more comforting that suffering alone.

The fact that Wall Street and the financial press has learned that it pays to play to your audience is one reason why Fund Manager A will appear on television and tell you his three favorite stocks are Dell Computer, General Electric, and Microsoft, followed by Fund Manager B, who will inform you that her three favorite stocks are General Electric, Intel, and Dell Computer. Then Fund Manager C, after exhaustive research, has decided that his three favorite stocks are Intel, General Motors, and Coca-Cola, although he may be challenged by Fund Manager D, who will argue that her three favorite stocks are Coca-Cola, Dell Computer, and IBM.

When it comes to reporting and analyzing the news, financial television reporters understand that there are a lot more viewers who own Time Warner and Warner Lambert than some obscure water utility that has just received a takeover bid. Therefore, they will spend 10 minutes dissecting the latest rumor involving the possibility that Time Warner might buy NBC or some nuance of a 30-day old takeover battle involving Warner Lambert and Pfizer, while completely neglecting the stunning and ongoing takeover wave in the water utility industry that has been pushing sleepy, conservative water stocks up by between 50 and 100 percent all year—an amazing story, especially in terms of risk and reward—which was badly underreported throughout 1999 in large part because it would play to a small audience, and who needs that?

The only way to counteract this tendency of the financial media to narrow its focus to the widely held stocks and to oversimplify things by playing to an audience that seems to prefer things that way is to become a serious browser. But to do that, you cannot rely on just one financial news source because chances are you will not get all of the information you need in just one place.

Some of the best sources to browse are *Investor's Business Daily*, *The Wall Street Journal*, and *The New York Times* Business Day section.

Investor's Business Daily (IBD), published by William O'Neil and Company in Los Angeles, is a pioneer of financial journalism. In

many important ways IBD is a unique and highly useful, sophisticated publication that has made giant inroads into areas where *The
Wall Street Journal* has stubbornly refused to tread, especially technical, momentum, relative strength, and chart analysis.

If you are looking to identify current market leaders or emerging market leaders, stocks with unusual and possibly telltale volume "spikes," stocks that are about to break out on the charts or
stocks that are performing well versus the general market, there is
no substitute in the daily financial press for IBD.

But when it comes to actually reporting the financial news, IBD
is sort of the *USA Today* of financial journalism. Everything is reported in sound bites. What's worse, IBD has become a prime example
of the "Big Brother" approach to financial journalism that is making
it increasingly difficult to find the sort of original ideas that we're
looking for as superstock browsers. Because of this, if you're going
to be looking for off-the-beaten-path stock ideas, you will not be able
to rely solely on IBD for all the information you need.

As I said, IBD has taken it upon itself to become your "Big
Brother" information filter, directing its readers toward the popular, high-profile, relative strength "momentum" stocks, and steer-
ing them firmly away—like a parent with an all-knowing guiding
hand—from the lower-priced, thinly traded stocks that might get
you in trouble. IBD's attitude is that the big winners come from a
certain "gene pool" involving certain industries and stocks with certain characteristics, and it does not want you wasting your time
thinking about losers with low stock prices, low trading volume,
and limited upside potential.

In an incredibly bold move that stands as possibly the ultimate
example of Big Brother financial journalism, on October 19, 1998,
IBD proudly announced that it was taking its stock tables "to the
next level"—IBD did not specify in what direction—by exiling low-
priced, low-volume stocks to the financial netherworld. In a front
page story written by IBD chairman and founder William O'Neil,
IBD announced that these lower-priced and less active NYSE and
NASDAQ stocks would be relegated to their own section in the back
of the newspaper, away from the main stock tables, presumably
where they might contaminate portfolios and impair the performance of unwary investors.

When I first read this story, I thought of Michael Caine and Steve Martin in *Dirty Rotten Scoundrels*, and a scene in which Steve Martin pretends to be Michael Caine's mentally unbalanced younger brother who must be housed in a basement dungeonlike bedroom under lock and key, away from the normal daily activities of the household so that the staff and guests would not be offended or endangered.

To *Investor's Business Daily*, these "Dirty Rotten Stocks," which are lower-priced and not very actively traded, are a danger to your portfolio and financial well-being, so IBD has taken it upon itself to make it just a bit more difficult for you to find them—sort of the way drugstores put the girlie magazines on the top shelf, making it harder for impressionable and naive adolescents to get their grubby little hands on them.

As William O'Neil explained in his articles to IBD readers, "With more than 500 initial public offerings added a year, the tables get longer and get harder to scan for future big winners."

Good Heavens! Too much information!

Therefore: "To save you time, we will separate lower-priced and less active NYSE and NASDAQ stocks from the main tables. These tables show NYSE and NASDAQ stocks priced at $7 or below or trading less than an average of 10,000 shares a day."

Later in the article, Mr. O'Neil gets around to explaining the real reason for IBD's decision to banish lower-priced and less-popular stocks to the financial dungeon. "Studies have shown that most stocks priced below $7 or trading less than 10,000 shares a day have lower quality, less institutional ownership, or weaker recent performance. They usually carry greater risk or offer less long-term potential."

There are several problems with this logic that superstock investors should be aware of. For one thing, the term "lower quality" is an awfully subjective term. For example, throughout 1999, the high-yielding, conservative water utility stocks were undergoing a takeover wave that made this group one of the top performers of the year. Several of them, as I noted before, rose between 50 and 100 percent, or more, following takeover bids , and most of the rest of the water utility stocks rose sharply in response to this takeover trend.

And yet, if you had looked for water utility stocks like Connecticut Water Service (CTWS) in the main NASDAQ stock listings carried in IBD, you wouldn't have found it, because its trading volume fell below the respectability line, which makes this stock riskier and gives it less long-term potential, according to IBD. Nor would you have found a water utility like Middlesex Water (MSEX), another genuine takeover possibility, until the stock jumped over 50 percent and began to trade big volume following a series of water utility takeovers. Once Middlesex went up in price and became more active, it "graduated" to IBD's more respectable neighborhood. But when Middlesex was neglected and a much better value, it was still listed in the dungeon section.

Or take a stock like Pittway (PRYA), a large and well-known manufacturer of alarms and other components used by manufacturers of security and fire alarm systems. Pittway had just sold its publishing business, turning itself into a "pure play" company operating in an industry where takeovers were taking place (see Chapter 14). For this reason Pittway was on my recommended list. The stock traded at a respectable $31 a share. Yet, in November 1999, for the "crime" of having average daily trading volume of less than 10,000 shares, Pittway had been exiled to the IBD "Dirty Rotten Stocks" list. Barely a month later, Pittway soared 16 points in one day to $45 (+55 percent) following a takeover bid from Honeywell (see Figure 11–1). Also in November 1999 the IBD dungeon list was peppered with numerous low-priced energy stocks. Their only "crime" was that they were trading below $7, not because they were low-quality companies but only because energy was out of favor at the moment. But most of these stocks did well in 2000 when oil and gas stocks returned to favor. A number of low-priced health care stocks were also on the list just before this group returned to favor in 2000. In IBD's eyes, all of these stocks were of lesser quality than, say, Stamps.com (STMP), which was trading at $98.50 in November 1999 and had a market cap of $3.5 billion with zero revenues. STMP was right there on the "respectable" mainstream list, even though it was on the verge of making a stunningly swift trip down to $2.50 a share, a decline of 97 percent. Priceline.com (PCLN) was on the "respectable" list, too, before it dropped from $150 to $1.19, along with countless other Internet stocks with out-of-this-world valuations that ultimately crashed. Of course, you can prove anything with 20/20 hindsight, but that is not my point. My point is this: If you are going to use the methods of analysis outlined in this book you cannot restrict yourself to publications that skew their reporting toward stocks and industries which are trendy at the moment, because much

Figure 11–1

Sample of *Investor's Business Daily's* Section "Where the Big Money's Flowing"

Stocks $18 and higher, with at least 1/2 point price change & trades 60,000 shares (if Vol % Chg. is +300% or more, must trade 75,000 shares). For stocks up in price, the EPS + RS must be 110 or more and next year's earnings estimate 17%+. Stocks w/o estimates are included. Stocks rated 80 EPS and 80 Rel Str. or higher are boldfaced.

EPS	Rel Str	Grp Rtg	SMR	Acc Dis	52-Wk High	Stock Name	Stock Symbol	Closing Price	Price Change	PE Ratio	Float (mil)	Volume (1000s)	% Change In Vol.
80	**86**	**B**	**B**	**B**	**37 3/4**	**Pittway**	**PRY**	**44 7/8**	**+15 7/8**	**29**	**3.7**	**352**	**+2648**
85	**85**	**C**	**B**	**C**	**38**	**Pittway Corp Cl A**	**PRYA**	**44 3/4**	**+14 7/8**	**29**	**27**	**1,235**	**+2280**
82	**92**	**B**	**C**	**B**	**38 7/8**	**London Pacific ADR**	**LDP**	**43**	**+15**	**11**	**17**	**1,028**	**+1291**
88	**91**	**A**	**A**	**B**	**15 7/8**	**N F O Worldwide o**	**NFO**	**22 1/4**	**+ 8 1/4**	**30**	**22**	**487**	**+644**
58	78	B	D	B	25 1/2	Broken Hill Proprtry	BHP	25 7/8	+ 1/2	34	817	237	+542
78	63	B	A	B	46 11/16	Aon Corporation o	AOC	39 3/8	+ 1 7/16	18	223	1,823	+100
75	75	A	B	C	70	Electronic Data Sys o	EDS	65 3/8	+ 6 1/8	36	466	3,171	+75
82	**80**	**B**	**A**	**A**	**154 3/4**	**General Electric Co o**	**GE**	**153**	**+ 1 1/2**	**49**	**3.2b**	**7,697**	**+37**
53	77	B	B	B	66 11/16	A E S Corp o	AES	67 1/2	+ 2 1/2	63	144	1,143	+37
81	**87**	**A**	**B**	**D**	**66 1/2**	**Scientific Atlanta o**	**SFA**	**57 1/8**	**+ 2 7/16**	**54**	**76**	**1,018**	**+31**
62	37	A	B	B	66 3/8	Pharmacia & Upjohn o	PNU	47 1/8	− 3 1/8	27	513	12,518	+467
89	50	D	B	C	36 5/8	Canadian Nat Ry o	CNI	29 1/16	− 11/16	8	200	2,348	+454
57	75	B	D	B	68 9/16	Aventis ADS o	AVE	60 3/4	− 9/16	33	359	529	+368
80	81	B	B	A	39 1/2	Manpower o	MAN	36 1/16	− 1 1/16	20	74	1,320	+325
87	47	D	.	B	40	Vornado Realty Trst o	VNO	31 15/16	− 3/4	17	65	741	+300
28	39	C	C	B	50 13/16	Monsanto o	MTC	36 5/8	− 5 1/8	48	616	11,798	+290
58	25	D	B	B	37 15/16	Burlington Nth SFe o	BNI	24 13/16	− 3 9/16	10	452	4,574	+281
85	60	C	B	B	68 5/8	Honeywell Inc o	HON	56 5/8	− 7 1/8	22	784	8,275	+256
73	41	D	.	C	25 3/4	Gables Rsdntl Trust	GBP	21 5/16	− 1 5/16	15	25	256	+253
87	81	A	A	D	79 1/2	Tandy Corp o	TAN	50	− 3	37	189	5,989	+207

Source: *Investor's Business Daily*, December 21, 1999.

of the information you will need to implement this approach will not be easily accessible to you, and some of it may not be available at all.

And since when does "less institutional ownership" translate into the financial version of *The Scarlet Letter*? To a genuine superstock sleuth, that is the whole point. A dearth of institutional ownership is precisely the sort of characteristic in a neglected stock with little or no mainstream sponsorship that we look for. It is precisely that current lack of sponsorship that will translate into a sharply rising stock price later on, when the mutual funds and the mainstream Wall Street analysts finally catch on.

The crime of "weaker recent performance" is also enough to get a stock sent to the IBD doghouse, which is more of the same short-term, lemminglike thinking we are trying to avoid here.

IBD believes that it is just encouraging you to think and act in a manner that is best for your long-range investment performance because everybody knows that the big-name, high-capitalization stocks, with high trading volume and extensive institutional sponsorship, are the best way to outperform the stock market. The trouble is, it has not always been that way (as we have already seen in Chapter 5), and if you are stubborn enough to believe that there is more than one way to skin the proverbial stock market cat, you will need something more than *Investor's Business Daily* to get all of the information you need.

Another problem with *Investor's Business Daily* is that, in its ongoing drive to categorize everything, the newspaper often allows significant news items to fall through the cracks. In contrast, IBD's "To the Point" section, which appears on page 2 of the newspaper, is an excellent summary of the significant news stories of the previous day. This section usually is a great source of merger and deal news and it often points to new and interesting directions in the ongoing search for takeover candidates.

But IBD could not leave well enough alone, apparently, and someone decided that it would be better to make this section more efficient by categorizing all of the news items under such headings as "Computers & Tech," "Telecom," "Internet," "Medical," and other such groupings—in other words, making certain that its readers were seeing the news in a well-organized fashion in the most popular and trendy industry groups of the moment.

The problem with this approach is that when a very interesting item pops up that does not fit in with the trendier industry groups IBD is using on any particular day, it's not available. In November 1999, for example, E'town Corp., a NYSE-listed, New Jersey-based water utility, which we discussed earlier, agreed to be acquired by Britain's Thames Water PLC. E'town soared over $10 a share on this news to just over $62, a 22 percent gain in one day. But the more significant part of this story was not E'town's stock price jump. Rather, it was that the takeover bid for E'town was part of a continuing and astonishingly rapid trend toward takeovers of U.S. water utilities, many of which were being acquired by foreign companies eager to establish a major presence in the U.S. water industry.

The takeover bid for E'town represented the fourth takeover in less than a year from a list of nine water utilities that I had recommended to my subscribers, and it would not be an exaggeration to say that the rapid takeover wave in sleepy, conservative water utility stocks at premiums of 50 to 100 percent, or more, of their recent trading prices—to once again repeat this notable phenomenon—was probably the single most interesting takeover story of 1999, especially considering the excellent risk/reward ratio involved in these conservative, high-yielding stocks and also in light of the limited universe of public water utility stocks to begin with. To those who were tuned into this trend, for most of 1999 it was literally like shooting fish in a barrel.

Immediately preceding the takeover wave in the water utility stocks, five of the nine stocks I recommended in my water utility "Water World" portfolio were listed in IBD's second-class stock listings, presumably too risky and/or uninteresting for the average investor to bother with.

By the time E'town received its takeover bid, the water utility takeover trend was in full force. Yet, the E'town takeover did not manage to make it into the news section of *Investor's Business Daily*. Either it did not fit the cookie-cutter mold of categories that IBD used to present its news items on that particular day, or E'town's market capitalization or industry group was too small and/or uninteresting to present to IBD's readers, who were constantly being schooled in the high-profile follow-the-leader momentum school of investing. (IBD has since abandoned its news "categorization" approach.)

Compare this total lack of analysis in IBD to the way *The Wall Street Journal* reported the E'town story: The *Journal* presented a complete background report not only on the E'town takeover, but also on its larger implications. Anyone reading this story who was schooled in the superstock approach to reading the financial news would immediately recognize the water utility industry to be a fertile hunting ground for takeover candidates, if they hadn't already noticed it months before.

Despite the efforts of *Investor's Business Daily* to portray itself as an alternative to the *The Wall Street Journal*, there is really no comparison between the two—especially if you are on the lookout for overlooked special situations and the background information that will allow you to read between the lines and make connections between seemingly unrelated news items that other observers are not perceiving.

The moral of all of this is that you should not depend on a single source for all of your business/financial information.

If you want to be certain of seeing as many news items as possible that contain the sort of superstock Telltale Signs you will be looking for, you should browse through the page 2 "To the Point" section of *Investor's Business Daily* every day, paying special attention to the smaller, seemingly unimportant items. You should also scan the front page of IBD, particularly the "IBD's Top 10" section, which contains IBD's version of the 10 most important business stories of the previous day.

But that will not be enough, and if you want to cover all the bases, you should also browse the "Company News" column in *The New York Times* Business Day section. "Company News" generally runs the entire length of a page on the left-hand side, and the column focuses on deals and transactions, such as mergers, spinoffs, asset sales, and other news items that would generally be of interest to you as a superstock sleuth.

By browsing through certain sections of certain publications like *Investor's Business Daily* and *The New York Times*, you will assure yourself of encountering important information. Some will be new to you and cause you to move in a new, analytical direction, and some will remind you of something you have seen before that you haven't had the time to investigate or may have seemed an isolated event—until another seemingly isolated event or piece of information places the previous item in a new and more meaningful context.

The Wall Street Journal is the financial "newspaper of record," and it will be a rare occasion when a story of financial significance fails to rate a mention in *The Journal*. However, when it comes to the information we superstock investors are looking for, it may help to look in the more out-of-the-way sections of *The Journal* to find it. Of course, the high-profile takeovers, spinoffs, asset sales, and so on, will often be discussed on the front page of *The Journal* in the "Business & Finance" section of the "What's News" column, which runs the entire length of page one.

The more intriguing information, which can point the way to superstock takeover targets long before they attract the attention of most investors, can be found inside *The Journal*, often at the bottom of the page, in a one- or two-paragraph story.

Another "must read" section of *The Wall Street Journal* for superstock sleuths is the "Corporate Focus" column, which appears in Section

B of that newspaper. This column often deals with mergers and acquisitions news, providing background and insights involving deals in the news. You will often find interviews with CEOs in which they talk about why they have decided to acquire a certain company, what sorts of acquisitions they may still be looking for, and whether they believe their industry will continue to consolidate. You will also find this sort of material from time to time in *The Journal*'s "Industry Focus" column, which also appears in the B Section.

You never know where you will find interesting and useful information. It often won't be on the front page of *The Journal* because the more obscure the information, the more useful it will be to you since it's less likely that the Wall Street "discounting" mechanism will have factored the information into the prices of the stocks involved. (The E'town takeover, for example, did not make the front page.)

For example, our old friend, Pinault-Printemps-Redoute—acquirer of both Rexel Inc. and Brylane—made the news again in October 1999 by buying out the 42.8 percent of French office supply company Guilbert S.A. that PPR did not already own.

You could have learned two things from this story, which appeared in the international section of *The Wall Street Journal*. First, PPR was still out there acquiring companies in which PPR already owned a stake, so this article served as a reminder to keep an eye on Pinault-Printemps—especially if PPR were to go into the open market to buy shares of another company in the future.

But you would also have learned something else by browsing through this story: that PPR is the largest shareholder of Gucci Group NV, the Italian company (NYSE: GUC) that designs and markets luggage, handbags, shoes, watches, and other luxury items.

Since PPR has a history of acquiring companies it already owns a piece of, and since this article indicated that PPR was still making acquisitions of partially owned companies, you would have noted PPR's partial ownership of Gucci, if you did not already know it, and added Gucci to your "research universe" for further study.

Among the other examples presented here, you would have noted that Burns International Services terminated discussions with a potential acquirer, which you would have viewed as a signal that Burns would be interested in selling itself at the right price. The fact that a company has entered into discussions for its sale tells you that the company is receptive to the right buyer offering the right terms; the fact that Burns did not come to terms with a potential buyer was too bad for Burns shareholders over the short run, but would have been an interesting thing to note and remember in the longer run, especially since a number of security firms had been taken over in 1999.

So you might have added Burns International Services to your research universe, keeping an eye on the stock and watching for potential Telltale Signs that a takeover of this company might be on the horizon. And you would not have been shocked when in August 2000, Burns stock soared 62 percent in one day following a takeover bid from Sweden's Securitas AB.

You should have noticed that Abbott Labs (NYSE: ABT) had enacted a "shareholder rights plan" designed to make a hostile takeover more difficult at a time when takeovers of pharmaceutical companies were proliferating. And although Abbott Labs stated, as companies always do, that it had not received any takeover overtures and that it knew of no potential suitors lurking in the wings, you would also know that companies implement shareholder rights plans for one reason and one reason only: They believe their stock is undervalued relative to its true value as a business, and they feel vulnerable to the possibility that an unwanted suitor might make a bid at a premium to the current market price, which would still represent a substantial discount to the company's true worth.

You would also have noticed that an outside shareholder of Dun & Bradstreet (NYSE: DNB) was trying to organize other shareholders in an attempt to prod DNB management to sell the company.

And you would have noticed that Mead Corp. (NYSE: MEA), a company that operates in the consolidating forest products industry, had announced a 10 million share buyback, often a sign that a company believes its stock is undervalued relative to its true worth as a business.

These items, and many others like them, are the sort of things you will be looking for and noticing as you train yourself to think like a superstock sleuth. The more you browse the financial pages, the more you will see and the more connections you'll make to other items you have seen, until slowly but surely pieces of a previously unnoticed puzzle will begin to come together in your mind and a picture will be formed—a picture that only you and others who think as you do will be able to see.

OTHER PLACES TO FIND "TELLTALE SIGNS" OF FUTURE SUPERSTOCK TAKEOVER CANDIDATES

I've noted some of the shortcomings of *Investor's Business Daily*. But, IBD is a unique and innovative publication that provides a great deal of information you will not find in any other daily or weekly financial publication.

So, let's look at some things that IBD does extremely well that can be useful to you as a superstock sleuth.

There are three sections of IBD, in addition to the general news summaries, that are often helpful in the ongoing search for superstock takeover candidates.

Industry Profiles

Investor's Business Daily regularly carries either a profile of a company or an industry that can provide a wealth of information. These profiles are helpful tools in the search for companies and/or industries where consolidation (takeovers) is taking place. Very often you will find that IBD is profiling a company that has been on the acquisition trail itself or that operates in an industry where takeovers are taking place. Since we already know that IBD is partial to the larger, higher-profile companies, you will usually find that the companies profiled in this section are larger companies that have been buying other companies rather than potential takeover targets. But that's fine, because by reading the profiles of companies like this, you can often get a feel for the reasoning behind the takeover trend in a certain industry. Not only that: When IBD profiles a company that has been acquiring other companies, you will often find a detailed explanation of the reasoning behind these takeovers, and on occasion the CEO of an acquiring company will offer a set of clues as to where that company might be looking for future takeover targets.

Another extremely useful aspect of the industry profiles section is a listing of companies that operate within the industry being profiled. Headlined "Who's Who in the Group," this list of companies provides an excellent starting point for superstock sleuths who may be seeking takeover candidates within that particular industry.

This list of industry participants is also useful because IBD will often note various takeover transactions that have recently taken place within the industry. For example, on August 16, 1999, IBD's industry profile was entitled: "Paper Products: Tighter Supplies, Consolidation Fuel Upswing in Long-Suffering Industry." The story talked about the recent trend toward takeovers in the industry and contained a table of 25 companies operating within the paper and paper products industry, including three notations on takeover transactions involving Kimberly Clark, Boise Cascade, and Pope & Talbot.

When I encounter a story like this in IBD, my tendency is to focus on the mid-size and smaller companies in the industry, based on two premises. First, if a consolidation trend is taking place and the larger companies in an industry are getting bigger and more cost-efficient, the mid-size to smaller companies in that industry are likely to be more receptive to being acquired. Second, the smaller companies in any given industry are less likely to be overfollowed and overanalyzed by Wall Street, which increases the probability that there will be bargains among them relative to their takeover potential.

Of course, *Investor's Business Daily*, which focuses on relative strength, earnings momentum, and other characteristics of stocks that are already currently in vogue and in the forefront of the market, cannot simply list the industry participants from top to bottom in terms of size, based on revenues or market capitalization. Instead, IBD lists the companies from top or bottom in terms of stock performance and/or earnings growth. The stocks, says IBD, are "ranked (not 'listed,' mind you, but 'ranked'—this is Big Brother we are talking about, remember) by a combination of their earnings per share and Relative Strength rankings."

So you will have to do a little reshuffling of the list if you want to focus on the smaller companies in the group.

But that's a small price to pay for a very useful presentation, and I have uncovered quite a few takeover targets by reading IBD's industry profiles section on a regular basis.

"Where the Big Money's Flowing"

Another useful section of *Investor's Business Daily* to look at on a regular basis, which can contain clues that may direct you to future superstock takeovers, is "Where the Big Money's Flowing" (see Figure 11–1). This table, which precedes the listings for the NYSE, American Stock Exchange, and NASDAQ listings, is designed to highlight stocks with significant increases in trading volume, both on the upside and downside.

As a superstock investor, you should read this section, focusing on stocks moving higher with significant volume increases, in search of familiar names. When you see a stock that is part of your "research universe" suddenly pop up on IBD's list of upside volume alerts for a fundamental news-related reason, pay close attention. The basic premise is that there is always somebody who knows more than you do, and very often that person will take advantage of that knowledge by buying the stock.

If a stock has already exhibited one or more of the Telltale Signs of a potential superstock and suddenly begins showing up on IBD's list of stocks with unusually high upside volume, this is often a sign that one of the Telltale Signs you have already noted is about to translate into a takeover bid or some other positive corporate development that will boost the stock price.

Characteristically, IBD tends to "filter" this information for you that only stocks trading at $18 or higher ($16 or higher on NASDAQ) and moving at least ½ point will be included in the table. (For the American Stock Exchange, a stock must be trading $12 or higher and move at least ¼ point.) In addition, a stock must trade at least 60,000 shares to pop up on IBD's NYSE volume-alert table, and the stock's Earnings Per Share and Relative Strength Ratings—both assigned by IBD—must exceed a certain number. To top it off, the earnings estimate for a particular stock for the following year must be at least 17 percent higher than the current year. The entire section, in other words, is designed to keep you focused on the strongest, trendiest stocks. What all of this means is that you will not necessarily see a previously underperforming "value" stock with stagnant earnings pop up on this volume-alert section—even if the stock begins acting out of character.

Still, these volume-alert tables are a valuable tool and you should browse them on a regular basis for familiar names that you have already noticed for other reasons. IBD deserves a lot of credit for this innovative way of calling to your attention stocks that are showing unusual volume and activity.

Charts: IBD's "Stocks in the News"

Another area where *Investor's Business Daily* is head and shoulders above *The Wall Street Journal* is in its presentation of stock charts.

IBD correctly recognizes that technical analysis—including chart analysis—is a valuable tool that can be used to your advantage. Again, the whole premise of technical analysis is that there will always be somebody—usually many somebodies—with more information than you have, and this information will usually be put to use either buying or selling the stock involved.

The premise of technical analysis is that while you may not know what the "insiders" know, you know what they do by analyzing charts, volume, and other technical tools designed to spot signs for stock accumulation (buying) or distribution (selling).

You will learn more about chart analysis, including how to spot the Telltale Signs of a "superstock breakout," later in this book. But for now, you should know that if you are going to become a serious browser, one of the places you should be browsing is the "Stocks in the News" sections of *Investor's Business Daily*.

IBD has a "Stocks in the News" chart section for the NYSE, AMEX, and NASDAQ markets. It presents a series of stock charts that carry certain characteristics, including stocks that have just reached new price highs or have recently reached new highs, or stocks that have had an extraordinarily large increase in volume. These charts are designed to call your attention to stocks that are showing signs of becoming market leaders, and as with "Where the Big Money's Flowing," IBD provides valuable information in "Stocks in the News."

And here's another reason to pay particular attention to IBD's stock charts: IBD tries to focus on stocks that are just emerging from a consolidation or basing formation, which, as you will soon see, is one of the key characteristics of a superstock chart breakout. Any stock that is up 15 percent or more from where IBD considers its breakout level to be is omitted from the charts that are presented. *What you are left with is a group of stocks that are acting well relative to the market, showing signs of unusual volume, and are at—or not very far above—key breakout levels on the charts—a valuable combination of characteristics, for our purposes, which you can only find in* Investor's Business Daily.

Again, just as in the IBD volume-alert tables, what you will be watching for are stocks you have already noticed for other reasons which suddenly exhibit the sort of characteristics that qualify them to be presented in the IBD chart sections. The fact that a stock that has already caught your attention as a result of one of the Telltale Signs is now flashing one or more of the technical signals that it may be about to emerge as a market leader is often a tipoff that some good news, such as a takeover, is about to break. This can often be the final catalyst that prods you to take the plunge and buy the stock in question.

E'town Corp., as an example, popped up in IBD's NYSE "Stocks in the News" section just several weeks prior to its takeover bid from Thames Water PLC. So did SJW Corp. (SJW) in the months preceding the announcement that it might put itself up for sale. If you had been a superstock browser at the time, both of these water utilities would already have been very high on your radar screen.

Barron's Financial Weekly

One other financial publication you should browse on a regular basis is *Barron's*. You will often find interviews with industry analysts who discuss industries where consolidation is taking place. *Barron's* very often asks these analysts to zero in on some potential takeover targets. You should use these interviews in the same way we are using most of the rest of the information discussed here: Look for familiar names that have managed to achieve a spot on your "research universe" for other reasons. Often, you will find background information that is new and reinforces a point of view you have held for some time but for a different reason.

Another important section is *Barron's* listing of selected Form 13-D filings, which usually appears in the early pages of *Barron's* "Market Week" section. Many, if not most, of the 13-D filings *Barron's* presents involve mutual funds or pension funds or other institutional investors that are not really a threat to take over a company and which may not even be interested in an "activist" role to urge a company to maximize value. But a new name will occasionally pop up, or you may see a transaction involving a familiar name that you may have overlooked for some reason. Browsing through this one-page section in *Barron's* each week will prove worthwhile on many occasions.

CASE STUDY: THE TRIPLE PLAY AND MIDWAY GAMES

One of the strongest clues that the stock market is severely undervaluing a stock is a combination of outside beneficial owner buying and insider buying on the part of a company's officers or directors.

The reason is that any major outside shareholder with a stake of 10 percent or more would probably be aware of information or developments that would give the beneficial owner a better idea of a company's true value than most outsiders. And it goes without saying that a company's own management would know better than anyone what the underlying fundamentals of a company look like and what its future prospects might be.

When you see a situation where the outside beneficial owner *and* a company's officers and directors are consistently buying stock on the open market, this is the "double play"—a bullish signal that should not be ignored. When you also have the company itself buying back stock, this is the rare "triple play"—one of the closest things you will get to "a sure thing" on Wall Street.

An example of a "triple play," which turned out to be very profitable for those who noticed it, was the dramatic turnaround in Midway Games (MWY) that took place in 1999. Midway Games began its corporate life in late 1996 as a spinoff from WMS Industries. A manufacturer of arcade and home video games, Midway was perceived by Wall Street to have excellent growth prospects, and for most of 1997 and into early 1998 the stock traded between $20 and $27 a share.

Early in 1996, however, analysts began to see signs of an earnings slowdown. Midway's business model was to introduce new games into the coin-operated arcade market, where the games developed consumer awareness, and then to release the games into the home video market. But a delay in introducing certain company-developed games and a shortage of third-party titles available for selling into the home video market created a series of worse-than-expected earnings reports in 1998. Midway's stock collapsed as Wall Street analysts began pulling their buy recommendations.

As you can see in Figure 11–2, Wall Street does not show any mercy when a "growth" stock stops growing. Midway shares plummeted from near $25 in the spring of 1998 to a low of $7⅝ by early 1999. Virtually all the analysts who had been strongly recommending Midway throughout 1997 and into early 1998 stopped recommending the stock as the company reported one earnings disappointment after another. By the time Midway shares had plunged into the $7 to $8 range, the company's support among the mainstream Wall Street analysts had evaporated. A former Wall Street darling in the high $20s, Midway was totally unloved at $8 by January 1999.

F i g u r e   11-2

Midway Games (MWY), 1997-1999

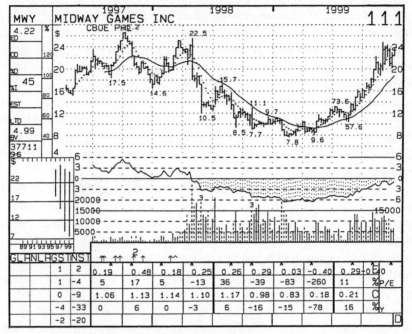

Source: Courtesy of Mansfield Chart Service, Jersey City, NJ.

Well, not exactly totally. Because as one Wall Street analyst after another threw Midway overboard, and the institutional investors who follow their advice dumped Midway shares, two people who knew this company better than anyone else were buying huge blocks of Midway stock on the open market: Sumner Redstone, chairman of Viacom, and Midway's own chairman and CEO, Neil Nicastro.

Several of Midway's conference calls with Wall Street analysts from 1998 to 1999 were real eye-openers for me. In particular, I could sense the frustration in the voice of Midway chairman Neil Nicastro as he attempted to explain that Midway's earnings setbacks were temporary and that the analysts who followed the company should be looking beyond the current shortage of product to a much stronger product lineup that would lead to a strong earnings rebound.

The analysts did not want to hear it. They wanted to know what would happen in the next quarter, which Nicastro had already explained would also be weak because the backlog of product the company had been developing would not appear for another 6 to 9 months. Midway was operating on a June fiscal year, and by late 1998 and early 1999 it was already apparent that the fiscal year ended June 1999 would not be a good one for the company. From the conference calls, it was obvious that Midway had pretty much conceded that fiscal year 1999 was going to be a big disappointment and that there was nothing much to be done about it. It also seemed that Midway was getting all of the bad news out and was stockpiling some new products to make as positive an impact as possible when fiscal 2000 began on July 1, 1999.

But the analysts insisted on talking about what was happening now and what had gone wrong in the latest quarter, and who was to blame for it.

Neil Nicastro and the Wall Street analysts who followed Midway Games were not communicating at all because they were talking about two different things. *Nicastro was talking about business, while the analysts were talking abut the short-term momentum (or lack thereof) of a number that appears in* The Wall Street Journal *every day: Midway's stock price.*

Meanwhile, something very interesting was appearing in *Vickers Weekly Insider Report*, which clearly suggested that Midway shareholders would soon be experiencing better times.

The first clue that Wall Street might have been overreacting to Midway's short-term speed bump appeared in the June 10, 1998, issue of *Vickers Weekly Insider Report*. Midway shares had already plunged from over $25 to below $15 when four Midway insiders went into the open market to purchase a total of 115,500 shares at prices ranging from $13¼ to $13⁷⁄₁₆. The purchase that really stood out was a 100,000-share buy on the part of Midway chairman Nicastro at $13¼, on May 21, 1998.

These insider purchases, combined with an announcement that Midway itself would buy back 1 million shares of its own stock, strongly suggested that Midway's stock price decline was far out of proportion to the short-term earnings problems the company was experiencing. When a company announces a stock buyback, it can be misleading. Though the Board of Directors has "authorized" a buyback "up to 1 million shares," it does not necessarily mean the company will actually buy the shares. In most cases the authorization will say that the timing and/or implementation of the buyback will "depend on the stock price or market conditions," which gives the company wide latitude in deciding when to buy stock or even whether it will buy stock at all.

Immediately following the 1987 stock market crash, a wide range of companies announced authorization for stock buybacks that never took place. In many cases, these announcements were made to create the appearance of support for the stock or to get the message across that the companies themselves believed their stocks were undervalued. When the market bounced back and it was later revealed that many of the announced buybacks never occurred, many companies said it was because their stock prices had recovered sharply from the prices which the buybacks authorized. This was a plausible explanation, of course, but the large number of buybacks announced in 1987 created a lingering skepticism among investors and analysts over the meaning of company "authorizations" to buy back shares.

However, when a company stock buyback is coupled with the news that officers and directors are going into the open market to buy significant amounts of stock with their own money, this a far more meaningful set of circumstances. It's easy for the CEO of a company to use company money to support the stock price, especially if the CEO owns a large number of shares personally, even if the CEO harbors a suspicion that the stock market's negative view on his stock might actually be accurate. But when company officials are in the market buying shares with their own personal funds at the same time the company itself is buying back stock, the company buyback announcement should be taken far more seriously, and it has been my experience that this is usually an accurate indication of an undervalued stock.

So, by the summer of 1998 there was evidence of two-thirds of a "triple play" in Midway Games: The company itself and several of its insiders were buying stocks in the $13 area in the face of disappointing earnings. And yet, Midway stock was destined to fall significantly below that level, providing an amazingly lucrative buying opportunity for superstock browsers who were on the lookout for the rare "triple play!" A few weeks later, Midway insiders purchased 7500 shares at $13⅞₆, another bullish omen.

By mid-1998, Midway had dropped below $10, and the September 16, 1998, issue of *Vickers Weekly Insider Report* noted more insider buying. Once again Midway chairman Neil Nicastro had purchased a large block of stock, this time buying 20,000 shares on August 31, 1998, at $9¾ to $9⅞. Also, on August 31, Midway's VP Byron Cook purchased 5000 shares at $10⅞.

It was in September that the last piece of the"triple play" materialized: Sumner Redstone and his holding company, National Amusements, went into the open market and began adding to their stake in Midway by purchasing large blocks of stock. Redstone bought 107,800 shares at $10½. Then, during the second half of October, Redstone bought a huge block of 573,200 shares at $9¼ to $12⅝. So now, Midway itself, several Midway insiders, and an outside beneficial owner were all buying Midway shares on the open market, following a stock price decline touched off by what Midway was openly calling a short-term earnings setback.

And the open market buying did not stop there: Nicastro purchased another 25,000 shares, bringing his total purchases to 169,000 shares. And in late November, Sumner Redstone bought another 140,000 shares, followed by an additional purchase in early December of 119,800 shares. *This brought Redstone's total purchases since September 1998 to 940,800 shares, a nearly $10 million commitment to Midway stock, which is quite a vote of confidence, even for a man of Sumner Redstone's means.*

It's important to take a step back at this point and examine the thought process that went into my strong recommendation of Midway as the stock fell below $10 late in 1998.

First, the only reason I was following this stock was because 24 percent was owned by Sumner Redstone, an astute businessman who has made a career out of acquiring other companies. That Midway was partially owned by an outside beneficial owner was the catalyst that caused me to focus on it. Then, the fact that Midway had an outside beneficial owner *and* there was heavy insider buying in the stock were the reasons to not bail out along with everyone else on Wall Street. Instead, I became *more* aggressive with the stock as it fell, because these purchases by Redstone, Midway insiders, and Midway itself had provided a **road map**, or a **benchmark of value**, which can be totally lacking in other stocks that have to carry some of the Telltale Signs of a potential superstock.

Here is a classic case of Wall Street focusing on momentum, while Redstone, Midway chairman Nicastro, and other insiders— as well as the company itself—were focusing on Midway's longer-term value *as a business*. The "value" assigned to Midway by the

Wall Street momentum crowd and the analysts who pander to them, compared to the "value" assigned to Midway by Redstone and its own management team, were as different as night and day, providing that value, like beauty, is in the eye of the beholder.

To continue with the clues that made Midway a superstock, in January 1999, Midway chairman Nicastro bought an additional 303,950 shares at $8 and Sumner Redstone bought another 80,000 shares between $8½ and $10. In February, however, Midway shares took another plunge, falling to the $7⅝ to $8 range.

In a Midway conference call reported in March 1999, Nicastro indicated that earnings and revenues for the next two quarters would be lower than expected. But Nicastro and other Midway spokespersons attempted to call analysts' attention to what they believed would happen in the second half of 1999, which would be the first 6 months of Midway's fiscal year 2000. In particular, Nicastro tried to direct the analysts' attention to a strong product lineup as the Christmas 1999 selling season approached, and as I listened I knew exactly what Nicastro was trying to say: If you're smart, you will forget about the next two quarters and focus on the last two quarters of calendar 1999, because they are going to be blockbusters.

When a company has growing earnings, Wall Street will recommend the stock at almost any price. But when earnings are slipping or stagnant, it seems that Wall Street *is not interested at any price.* This creates a large gap between a stock price and the true long-term value of a business, an environment that creates takeover bids at large premiums. In order to participate in this profit potential, however, you must be able to think like a Wall Street insider. In other words, you must be able to buy a stock nobody else is interested in at the moment, and you must be prepared to take a longer-term view of perhaps 12 to 18 months. If you can do these things, neglected stocks flashing Telltale Signs should interest you.

In May 1999 my business partner and research associate, Cherrie Mahon, conducted a most remarkably informative interview with Neil Nicastro in which he explained, in detail and in a refreshingly straightforward manner, why he had been buying so much Midway stock on the open market. That type of interview can serve as a blueprint in illustrating the difference between how a corporate executive views his or her company and how Wall Street analysts view that very same company.

The $64,000 question, or in this case, the $5 million question, was why had Nicastro spent roughly that amount of his own money purchasing 461,450 shares of Midway stock over the preceding 12 months? The Midway chairman said: *"I believe that at some point the market will value our business much differently than it values it today. I just don't think Wall Street is properly anticipating the opportunity for a substantial earnings rebound. That is the great opportunity I see, and that is why I bought the stock."*

You may have noticed that Neil Nicastro used the phrase "value our business." Too often, Wall Street treats a stock as nothing more than a piece of paper. Terry Rudd, author of the book *1929 Again*, makes reference to stocks being treated by Wall Street as nothing more than pieces of playground equipment, with so-called professional investors rushing around from one piece of equipment to another as they quickly became bored with one and frantically looked for something else to amuse themselves. That is about as good a description of "momentum investing" as I have ever seen. The problem with this approach is that it does not take into account that these pieces of paper we call "stocks" represent shares in a business, and business is not always a one-way street. Even a true "momentum" business, a true "growth" company, can hit an occasional pothole or speed bump. To a company's management, this is just how business can be sometimes; to Wall Street, it is interpreted as the end of the world, and the stock involved is treated as though it were infected with some exotic virus to be ditched immediately lest it contaminate the year-end portfolio statement institutional investors send to their clients.

When Cherrie Mahon asked Neil Nicastro, "Why are you buying so much stock?" Nicastro said, in effect, because Midway's profits were going to go back up and Wall Street would be nuts to place such a low valuation on this company.

Despite Nicastro's comments and the outlook for Midway stock, analysts were not focusing on what was ahead. They were more interested in their rearview mirrors. They were turning their backs on Midway just when they should have been issuing buy recommendations in anticipation of an earnings rebound.

The story of Midway Games not only provides an example of the rare "triple play," in which an outside beneficial owner, company insiders, and the company itself are all buying stock at the same time.

It also shows a rare behind-the-scenes glimpse at how company insiders beat the professional Wall Street analysts and investors at their own game by simply taking a step back to take a longer-term point of view. In fact, "longer-term" in this case only meant 6 to 12 months—but to the Wall Street "momentum" crowd, that is an eternity. And that is where the buying opportunities arise for those who are willing to take a step back and use a little perspective.

The ultimate outcome of this little drama: Midway's earnings rebounded strongly in the second half of 1999, just as Neil Nicastro said they would. The rebound resulted from a surge of new product released into the home video market, just as Nicastro said it would. Everything transpired just as he suggested in early 1999—in that same conference call that led to a rash of analyst sell recommendations virtually at the bottom of Midway's stock slump.

By November 1999, Midway had reached $24⅞ as earnings soared to record levels, and the same Wall Street analysts who had been issuing sell recommendations at the bottom reinstated their buy recommendations—at triple the price from Midway's lows in January or February 1999.

So the next time you see a "triple play" think of the Midway Games story. No matter how dismal the news may seem on the surface, if an outside beneficial owner, company insiders, and the company itself are all buying stock on the open market, it's almost always a signal that you have a potential superstock on your hands and that the news is about to get better. A *lot* better.

CHAPTER TWELVE

Family Feuds

Here's another lesson to be learned from the ADT-Western Resources takeover saga we examined in Chapter 9: *When animosity develops between a company and its major outside shareholder, the eventual result is often a takeover bid.* In the case of ADT–Western Resources, the discord that developed between these two companies made it extremely unlikely that Western Resources would simply sit silently on the sidelines as a passive outside investor. The two more likely scenarios: ADT would either attempt to sell itself to a third party (which it did) or Western Resources would attempt to buy ADT and remove its directors and top management (which it tried to do).

Therefore, *a useful rule of thumb is that you should pay close attention when disagreements arise between a company and an outside "beneficial owner," especially when these disagreements break out into a public squabble.*

Consider the following case study as another example.

CASE STUDY: COPLEY PHARMACEUTICALS

On July 27, 1998, two directors of Copley Pharmaceuticals (CPLY), a generic drug manufacturer, resigned. They did not go quietly. One of the directors, Agnes Varis, publicly blasted Hoechst AG, a huge German chemical and pharmaceuticals company that owned 51 percent of Copley. According to Varis, Hoechst had disrupted Copley's operations by continuously changing its mind about what it wanted to do with its Copley stake. Hoechst, said Ms. Varis, "was demoralizing

149

management and depressing shareholder value." She complained that Hoechst "forced Copley to hire investment bankers and spend millions of dollars in fees and time of key Copley personnel who could have been developing new products and expanding Copley's business." She claimed that after forcing Copley to go through the process of hiring an investment banker, Hoechst decided it did not want to sell its stake after all.

In a parting shot Varis added: "I'll serve Copley's shareholders better from outside the company. You can't do anything inside."

Agnes Varis's stinging public criticism of Hoechst AG was highly unusual. From time to time you will see private disagreements between officers or directors of a company and a major shareholder. Usually, these disagreements come in the form of structured letters, written by attorneys, that are "leaked," filed with the SEC as a 13-D amendment, or simply released to the press. In most cases these disagreements arise between mutual fund companies or pension funds that hold sizable stakes in a company and that, for one reason or another, are unhappy about the direction the company has taken.

Investment companies in particular have been taking a more active role in recent years to get corporate managements to take actions that will increase the stock price. It's not unusual for an institutional investor to take a stake in a company, sit with it for a while, and then fire off a letter to management suggesting the company take steps to "enhance shareholder value" or "maximize shareholder value." Sometimes, the institutional investor will release the letter to the press, perhaps do a round of television interviews, and feign outrage over the manner in which the company has been managed or mismanaged.

In reality, in most cases the institutional investor is trying to light a fire under a losing position—i.e., trying to bail out of a mistake by bullying the management into taking short-term actions that could boost the stock price.

For a while these public relations tactics seemed to work, but in recent years corporate management has learned that the best way to deal with institutional saber rattling is to simply ignore it. Institutions like mutual funds or pension funds are, for the most part, not equipped to get down into the trenches and force the management of a company to put itself up for sale to maximize value. An institutional that owns, say, 5 to 10 percent of a company would be more likely to send up a few threatening flares, see what happens, and then quietly liquidate its position on any runup in the stock as a result of the brouhaha.

So, don't take it too seriously when a mutual fund or a pension fund sends a letter to a company criticizing management and demanding that steps be taken to "enhance shareholder value." Any management that has been paying attention to recent trends should respond with a polite letter thanking the institution for its thoughts, and then go back to running the business. This sort of publicity gambit usually won't lead to a takeover bid.

The situation at Copley Pharmaceuticals, as you will see, was quite different. The background of the Copley Pharmaceuticals-Hoechst AG situation following Agnes Varis's public blasting of Hoechst indicated that the bitterness between Copley and its largest shareholder would probably lead to one of two outcomes: Hoechst would bid for the 49 percent of Copley it did not already own and throw out Copley management, or Copley would find a third party to buy the Hoechst stake and then acquire the rest of the company, which would effectively result in Copley throwing out its 51 percent shareholder.

Copley Pharmaceuticals had gone public in October 1992 at $12.67 per share, adjusted for a subsequent 3-for-2 split. Copley stock went straight up, and in the fall of 1993 Hoechst AG arrived on the scene, offering to pay $55 per share for a 51 percent stake in Copley, proving that even a gigantic international pharmaceuticals company can act like a lemming under the right circumstances. It turned out that Hoechst had made its move right at the peak, and Copley shares began a long, downhill slide that took the stock down to the $5 to $6 area by early 1997.

The drop in Copley's stock price was helped along by the recall of one of its products due to contamination problems, and by shrinking profit margins and brutal price competition in the generic drug business. On the way down, Agnes Varis purchased additional Copley shares in the low $30s, proving that even corporate insiders can misjudge a company's prospects and the future direction of its stock price.

In September 1996, Hoechst publicly stated that Copley did not fit its "core" business strategy, and forced Copley to hire an investment banker to look into the possible sale of the company. This move, according to Varis, severely disrupted Copley, its management, and its employees. Nothing came of these efforts, and Copley shares languished in the $5 to $6 area until Varis left the company and issued her public criticism of Hoechst.

In August 1998 we noted that a "standstill agreement," which prevented Hoechst from buying additional Copley shares, would expire in October 1998.

What is a *standstill agreement*?

Sometimes, when one company buys a sizable stake in another company, the purchase is subject to certain conditions. One of the conditions may be a limitation on any future purchases of stock for a specified period of time. Generally, these agreements will say that Company A cannot increase its stake in Company B beyond a certain percentage without expressed permission from Company B. That's a *standstill agreement*.

Whenever a big chunk of one company is owned by another, you should check the terms of the standstill agreement to see what the terms are and, most important, when the standstill agreement expires. You can find this information in a company's 10-K report, which is the annual report filed with the SEC. When the relationship between a company and an outside beneficial owner is turning testy and the standstill agreement is set to expire soon, it indicates that a takeover situation may be about to unfold.

As a result of this research, Copley was recommended in the newsletter as an "additional idea."

In September 1998, Copley Pharmaceuticals was added to the superstock recommended list. The stock price for Copley at the time was $8¾. The news that Hoechst AG had decided to undergo a corporate restructuring was significant. In a situation like this, where a general corporate "housecleaning," such as Hoechst was about to undergo, would take place, a decision was likely to be made about Hoechst's 51 percent stake in Copley.

Now, all of the pieces were in place for a takeover drama to unfold.

Every relationship, even personal relationships, start out with high hopes. But when the relationship sours and both parties begin to get on each other's nerves, it is only a matter of time before a separation has to take place.

When the relationship is personal, it may be a relatively easy matter to dissolve it. But in the corporate world things get a bit more complicated. The next time you see a story in *The Wall Street Journal* similar to this one, where a corporate insider resigns in a huff and criticizes management, the Board of Directors, or a major shareholder, and starts to talk about enhancing shareholder value or doing what's best for the shareholders, you have encountered a Telltale Sign of new paradigm thinking. In situations like this the usual outcome is that someone, somewhere, will make a bid for the company in question because that is usually the only way to settle disputes where two parties that are inextricably linked no longer see eye-to-eye.

It seemed clear to me that Hoechst or some third party would have to make a bid for Copley. Unfortunately—or perhaps fortunately, depending on how you look at it—it wasn't clear to anybody else. Copley shares sank as low as $6 by October 1998, providing new paradigm thinkers, who were focused on the takeover possibilities by recognizing one of the Telltale Signs, an ideal opportunity to buy more Copley shares at what would turn out to be bargain-basement prices. Late in 1998, I appeared on CNBC and predicted that Copley would become a takeover target. The stock ran up briefly, then sagged back and traded listlessly in the $8 to $10 range.

In December 1998, with Copley trading at 8\frac{7}{16}$, there were rumors that Hoechst AG was about to merge with France's Rhone-Poulenc SA. The rumors, if true, would create the world's second-largest pharmaceuticals company. Remember, Hoechst had announced a planned "restructuring," and in fact Hoechst had already sold several of its noncore operations, including its paints business.

Here is how we analyzed this rumor of a potential Hoechst–Rhone-Poulenc linkup in terms of Copley:

> As Hoechst is reinventing itself and moving to focus on pharmaceuticals while divesting itself of unwanted operations, Copley Pharmaceuticals could become an issue to deal with. I would not be surprised to see Hoechst either bid for the rest of Copley and assimilate the company completely, or sell its 51 percent stake in Copley to a third party who might bid for the rest of the company. Given Copley's book value of $5.30 per share, any time this stock drops down to the $6 to $7 area I would rate it as a strong buy. I think Copley has a good risk/reward ratio anywhere in the $6 to $9 range.

In February 1999, with Copley trading at $9^{11}⁄$_{16}$, Hoechst had been selling off some of its smaller, noncore operations and we indicated that "the idea that Hoechst may simply sell its Copley stake to someone else has actually gained the upper hand over the past few weeks, as Hoechst has been selling off one small operation after another. Copley could be part of this trend."

And then we added: "The difficult matter in analyzing Copley is determining what this company might be worth. If you find that hard to believe, remember that Hoechst paid $55 per share for its original Copley stake!"

As things turned out, that last statement was significant.

It's usually a lot easier to figure out that a takeover bid is coming than it is to determine the price at which the takeover bid will take place. In most cases, you will see a takeover bid take place at a premium—sometimes a significant premium—to a stock's 52-week high. In nearly all cases, a takeover bid will a carry a premium to a stock's average trading price over the past 30 or 60 days. Only in rare cases, where word of a takeover bid has leaked and a stock has had a dramatic price advance, will you see a takeover bid at virtually no premium to the previous day's closing price. And once in a blue moon, when word of a takeover has leaked so badly that the target company's stock has really soared, you will witness what is called a *takeunder*—a situation where the takeover price is actually *lower* than the previous day's closing price because advance word of the deal was so widespread that speculators got carried away and simply bid the price of the target company too high.

In the case of Copley Pharmaceuticals, we had a buy limit of $11½ on our recommendation. However, based on some apparent improvement in Copley's earnings, and influenced by the fact that Hoechst had paid an incredible $55 per share for its original stake, it seemed that raising the buy limit on Copley to $13 would be a sound move.

At that point, Copley was trading near $10¼. By April 1999, Copley had crossed $11¾. For the next several months, Copley traded quietly between $8¾ and $10½. Then in June 1999, a news item was the clincher. Copley was trading at $9^{15}⁄$_{16}$ when Hoechst announced that it would spin off its Copley stake as part of Celanese AG, a Hoechst operation containing most of Hoechst's chemical and industrial businesses. This was a curious move, since Copley did not fit the Celanese business model at all. This spinoff made it crystal clear that Hoechst would be willing to part with Copley at the right price. This move, which angered Copley shareholders, made it even more likely that some of Copley's other major shareholders would try to take Copley private or sell it to a third party.

For the next 2 months Copley traded quietly between roughly $8½ and $10½. Then, on August 10, 1999, Copley jumped 21 percent in one day, following news that Teva Pharmaceuticals of Israel had agreed to buy Copley for $11 per share in cash. As part of the deal, Hoechst AG also agreed to sell its 51 percent stake in Copley to Teva for $11 per share.

Anyone who had bought Copley at $8¾ would have made a profit of 25 percent, based on this $11 takeover bid, in 10 months. Anyone who had followed the growing body of evidence that a takeover bid for Copley was brewing and had taken advantage of dips in Copley's stock price to the $6 to $7 level would have done much better in percentage terms.

And, to be perfectly fair and honest about this, anyone who paid $10 to $11 for Copley would have just about broken even as a result of the takeover bid.

To repeat, the toughest part of uncovering takeover targets is not finding the targets themselves. The toughest part, especially when we are dealing with smaller companies, is trying to determine what the ultimate value of the takeover bid might be.

When a certain industry is consolidating and a number of takeovers have already taken place, it is often possible to establish a benchmark value that will give you a general idea of what a company would be worth in a takeover situation. In other industries, however, pegging a value is more difficult.

In the end, Copley proved solidly profitable, although less profitable than anticipated.

But the most important lesson to be learned from the Copley Pharmaceuticals saga is that the *original analysis*, based on the original evidence, *proved to be accurate*.

The next time you see a public disagreement erupt between a company and its largest shareholder—especially if that shareholder is another corporation, and not an investment company—you should think in terms of a potential takeover bid. The next time you see a public disagreement between a director and a company's management—especially if the director resigns and makes statements about protecting shareholder interests or enhancing shareholder value—you should think in terms of a potential takeover bid.

In the world of the stock market, a family feud is often the first sign that a company is going to wind up being acquired.

PART THREE

Takeover Clues

CHAPTER THIRTEEN

"Beneficial Owner" Buying

CASE STUDY: SUMNER REDSTONE AND WMS INDUSTRIES

Knowing how to read a stock chart can be a valuable tool in selecting potential superstocks. A stock that is breaking out above a well-defined multiyear resistance level is usually telling you something, i.e., that something bullish is going on. Here's how chart analysis led to a recommendation of WMS Industries.

In spring 1989, the chart in Figure 13–1 caught my attention. Research indicated that WMS Industries manufactured pinball and video games and owned two hotel/casinos in Puerto Rico. Here was a stock with a terrific long-term chart that was acting like it was about to attempt a superstock chart breakout.

In April 1989, WMS was trading at $7⅝, and the chart indicated a very well-defined resistance area near $8, which had turned back several rally attempts since 1986. The chart also shows a series of rising bottoms in WMS in late 1988 and early 1989, which indicated that buying pressure was coming in at progressively higher levels. This can often be a signal that a stock is about to make a serious attempt at a major breakout—a superstock breakout pattern.

By browsing through a chart book looking for this sort of superstock breakout pattern, an investor might well have noticed WMS and decided to do some further research into this company.

F i g u r e   13–1

WMS Industries (WMS), 1987–1989

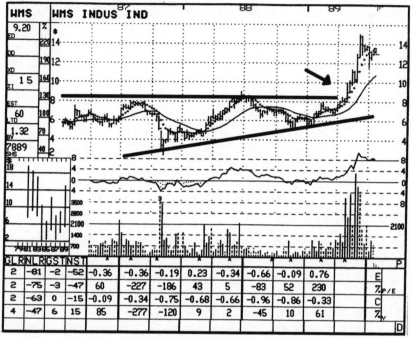

Source: Courtesy of Mansfield Chart Service, Jersey City, NJ.

The first thing I noticed about WMS Industries once I began to research the company was that WMS had an outside beneficial owner: Sumner Redstone, chairman of Viacom, Inc. and National Amusements. Viacom was a well-known media company; National Amusements was a major owner of motion picture theaters. The WMS financials revealed that Redstone had recently been purchasing WMS shares in the open market, buying a total 157,500 shares in early 1989 at prices ranging from $5⅝ to $8.

This was a potentially powerful combination: a little-followed stock with a potentially explosive superstock chart pattern, combined with open market buying by an outside beneficial owner. All that was needed to confirm this explosive combination was a breakout above the $8 to $8¼ area, the multiyear resistance level that had contained WMS since 1986.

When a well-defined multiyear resistance area in a stock is being penetrated, it usually means something has changed significantly for the better. Sometimes it's the overall market environment, but sometimes the bullish development is specific to the company itself. In the case of WMS Industries, a specifically bullish development was already brewing deep within the company that was not apparent to outside observers. But the WMS chart was calling attention to the situation—in effect telling anyone who knew what to look for that something interesting was going on. The consistent buying of WMS shares by Sumner Redstone, a well-known and sophisticated entrepreneur, was also a suggestion that something bullish was brewing.

At the time, WMS Industries was in the early stages of developing a new gaming device, a so-called video lottery terminal that would sell like hotcakes as state governments legalized video gambling in order to generate desperately needed revenues. WMS was also thinking about "spinning off" its hotel/casino as a separate company.

When WMS received its first official order for its video lottery terminals 30 months later, this $7 stock was trading at $42 and had earned the honor of being the best-performing stock on the New York Stock Exchange for 1991!

But the road from $7 to $42 was a tortuous one. As is the case with most superstocks, the WMS saga was dotted with twists and turns that provided a number of bargain-priced buying opportunities but also tested the willpower of those who were attuned to the superstock manner of stock analysis.

In late April 1989 the stock broke out above its multiyear resistance level. This breakout resulted in a focus on two things: the open market purchases of WMS stock by Sumner Redstone, and an apparent earnings turnaround that was taking place at WMS. This earnings turnaround was probably going to be more explosive than Wall Street realized. That would explain why WMS had broken out of a superstock chart pattern and why Sumner Redstone was buying more stock on the open market. But there was a lot more potential lurking beneath the surface of the WMS situation than the research initially indicated. What was the *real* reason WMS would turn out to be such a huge winner?

Undoubtedly, many people were becoming aware of the explosive potential for video lottery terminals and of WMS's desire to maximize the value of its hotel/casino operations. When a company is thinking of getting into a new business, it's hard to keep it under wraps. And WMS was a leading manufacturer and distributor of pinball and video games—with the trade names "Williams," "Midway," and "Bally"—that could be found in restaurants and taverns throughout America. Now, a brand new industry was emerging—video lotteries and video poker—that would enable patrons in these taverns and restaurants to gamble on state-sanctioned machines. What do you do when you want to branch into a new business? You talk to suppliers, talk to your customers, and begin to sound out state officials about becoming licensed in various jurisdictions. Even in the early stages, long before the new business is actually launched, many individuals in all walks of life will get wind of what is going on.

The superstock chart pattern and the major breakout came about as a result of buying pressure in the stock. Who was doing the buying? A good guess would have been that a growing number of people close to WMS and/or its business were beginning to get wind of the potential for the video lottery business. (In addition, by this time WMS was already looking into how to "maximize the value" of its Puerto Rico hotel/casinos, which were carried on WMS Industries' books at far below their actual values.)

These are the sort of "under the surface" developments that create bullish chart patterns and major breakouts. Sometimes the reasons for the major breakouts are apparent—and sometimes they are apparent only in retrospect. Either way, if you know what to look for, a knowledge of chart analysis can often point you toward a situation you would never otherwise have noticed—which is precisely what happened in tracking WMS Industries.

On April 28, 1989, I noted the major breakout in WMS: "This stock seems to have a lot going for it: A solid story, an apparent earnings turnaround; a great long-term chart, and steady accumulation on the open market by a potential acquirer."

By mid-May, WMS had moved up to $11. By this time, any chartist on the lookout for potential superstock breakouts would have had a hard time missing the significance of the WMS chart pattern. Here was a classic multiyear resistance level breakout that had taken place on a clear volume "spike." Again, the chartist may not have known *why* WMS shares were being bought with such urgency, but the chart was clearly suggesting that something very bullish was going on.

By the first week of June, WMS had rocketed to $15, a gain of 96 percent in two months. The stock had performed just as the WMS potential superstock chart pattern indicated it might: Following the breakout above the well-defined multiyear resistance area, WMS powered higher on sharply rising trading volume. By June, Sumner Redstone had once again purchased WMS shares in the open market, this time buying 101,100 shares at prices between $8¼ and $11⅝. Redstone's stake in WMS had now increased to 28.8 percent, and he was not deterred by the rising price of WMS stock at all.

Once again, the sharp advance in stock price was attributed to the substantial earnings recovery taking place at the company, which was certainly accurate. But, it was far from the entire story.

By mid-August 1989, WMS had fallen back below $12 per share. Revenues and earnings continued to rise sharply due to rapid growth in the company's pinball and video arcade games. On September 1, 1989, our recommendation was that "since Sumner Redstone paid as much as $11⅝ for WMS stock, this should serve as somewhat of a benchmark for us—i.e., whenever WMS falls below $12, the stock is in an excellent buying range because Mr. Redstone, who probably knows this company as well as anyone, bought stock at that level."

By late 1989 the stock was getting wobbly as signs of a potential recession rattled Wall Street. Although the major averages were hanging in there, smaller stocks and the advance/decline line were sinking relentlessly. In October, a sharp sinking spell took the Dow down a quick 11 percent, but smaller stocks suffered much more.

Meanwhile, WMS had announced some disappointing news. The company said it would report a loss at the quarter due to a planned shutdown of its manufacturing line, for "retooling." The bullish significance of that announcement would not become apparent until much later. The stock market, which was in no mood to forgive any disappointment involving a small-cap stock, was relentless in punishing WMS. The stock plunged as low as $8.

According to classic chart analysis, that $8 level should have represented a major support level because a well-defined resistance area, once penetrated to the upside, should serve as support on the way down. And for a while $8 did serve as support. WMS bounced back to $11 by late October as the market steadied. Then another disaster struck: this time, a natural disaster. Hurricane Hugo damaged some of the WMS hotel/casino properties in Puerto Rico. The combination of Hugo and the assembly line shutdown caused WMS to report a loss of $0.76 per share for the quarter, and the stock slumped back toward the $8 support area again.

1990: Convictions about WMS Are Put to the Test

What happened during 1990 to WMS stock was a classic example of how superstock investing differs from almost any other method of stock selection. A combination of recession, Iraq's invasion of Kuwait, a crumbling market for small-cap stocks, and a sharply eroding stock price for WMS would have made it difficult, if not impossible, to hang in there, except for one thing: Sumner Redstone, the outside beneficial owner.

Redstone had paid up to $11⅝ for WMS shares on the open market. As WMS declined in price, it was reasonable to assume that if a sophisticated investor like Redstone had paid that much for WMS shares, we should hold tight and even buy more as the share price fell further into the single digits in the midst of increasingly demoralized stock market.

Without those open market purchases by Redstone there would have been no benchmark of value with which to work. But since we did have that benchmark—and since we were betting on Redstone or on something Redstone knew about WMS as a potential catalyst to get the stock price higher—we added to our stake in WMS during nearly all of 1990 at single digit prices.

It was not easy to watch WMS decline as far as it did in 1990, but there was a specific reason for hanging in there and to buy more shares at lower prices. That reason was the presence of Sumner Redstone. WMS had something extra going for it that most other stocks did not—and that, as it turned out, made all the difference.

By late December 1990, WMS Industries' stock had fallen to $3⅞. But two new Telltale Signs emerged during that year to indicate it was still a potential superstock.

The two catalysts were the announcement that WMS would seek to spin off its Puerto Rico hotel/casinos to "enhance shareholder value," and WMS would write off its investment in a company called Divi Hotels, even though the investment still had apparent value.

These two Telltale Sign announcements, along with the continuing 28.8 percent ownership of Sumner Redstone and the fact that Redstone had paid as high as $11⅝ for WMS stock, was a sign that WMS had significant unrecognized values lurking beneath its low stock price. The decision to write off the investment of Divi Hotels was an example of what is called *kitchen sink* accounting—a term used when a company writes off any and all potential losing investments or expenses in a single year to set the stage for a cleaner, more explosive earnings rebound the following year.

As a superstock detective, these telltale signs clearly suggested that something very bullish was lurking beneath the surface at WMS—some development, or some value that the stock market had not yet recognized. Yet WMS shares plunged throughout the year.

To fully appreciate the environment in which WMS shares were falling, it might be instructive to briefly revisit the stock market and economic environment of that turbulent year. WMS was not simply dropping on its own. It was victimized by a horrible market for smaller-cap stocks, rising interest rates, a declining overall stock market, a severe recession, a virtual collapse of the Japanese stock market, and the virtual collapse of most U.S. bank stocks, which were suffering from a rash of bad loans.

In an environment such as this, it is not easy to disregard the general stock market and focus on specific events or potential "catalysts" that will affect the special situation stocks in your portfolio. Nor is it difficult to understand how a low-priced, analytically neglected stock like WMS could suffer dramatically, especially since the company was taking write-offs and had just reported a large loss. Even in the best of times, a company with little or no analytical support would have had difficulty bolstering its stock price while it reported nonrecurring charges, even though revenues and operating earnings remained on track. But these were not the best of times—in fact, they were the worst of times for small stocks, and WMS spent all of 1990 eroding in price.

Sooner or later, it will happen to you. Chances are it has already happened. You buy a stock with high expectations for what you believe are sound reasons. But the stock starts to decline, and you are faced with a difficult decision: Do you hang in there and possibly buy more at lower prices? Or do you cut your losses and move on?

There are no clear-cut answers. "Cutting your losses" is easier said than done. Nobody has perfect timing; you may have bought precisely the right stock for precisely the right reasons, and your scenario for why this stock will double in price may be perfectly valid. But who is to say the stock cannot decline 10 to 20 percent, or even more, before your scenario plays itself out precisely as you expected? Perhaps the stock has declined because the overall market has been weak: Does that make your original analysis invalid? Perhaps some mutual fund is getting out of a position, and the stock is dropping: Does that make you wrong and the mutual fund right?

That's why you should understand *why you bought the stock in the first place.* If you know *why,* and if the reasons for your purchase remain valid, you should hold it and even buy more on the decline. But if you don't really know why you bought a stock—if you bought it for some vague reason (an analyst recommended it on television, it's a "good company," it's a growth stock, etc.)—then you're going to have a difficult time deciding what to do when the stock starts moving in the wrong direction.

Superstock investing, while it is by no means perfect, at least gives you a guidepost. In the case of WMS Industries, the stock took a sickening plunge from $10 to as low as $3¼ between July and December 1990. It was not pleasant: But I knew *why* I had recommended the stock in the first place, and did not see anything that caused me to doubt my original premise.

To reiterate, here are the reasons I stuck with WMS:

1. Sumner Redstone, an outside beneficial owner with a stellar track record, owned 28.8 percent of WMS and had recently bought stock for as much as $11⅝. With WMS trading in the $4 to $5 range, there was a good possibility he would either step in and buy more stock or even offer to buy the entire company.

2. WMS had raised the possibility of spinning off its Puerto Rico hotel/casinos as a separate company to enhance shareholder value. The term "enhance shareholder value" is a *key* phrase and a telltale sign for superstock investors. It means that the management of a company sees hidden value within its corporate structure that the stock market is not taking into account, and management is looking for ways to force the stock market to reflect this value.

3. The earnings disruption at WMS had taken place for a specific reason—a shutdown of the manufacturing facility for

retooling. Yet the stock market—due to a lack of analyst coverage of WMS —was overacting to the temporary loss.

4. The WMS write-off of its investment Divi Hotels, even though the investment still had value, was similar to many situations in the past where a company that is expecting a dramatic earnings turnaround takes every possible write-off to "clear the decks" for better news around the corner—another Telltale Sign.

There is no way around this. If you want to make the right decision when a stock starts moving against you, you *have* to know exactly *why* you bought the stock in the first place. One of the benefits of superstock investing is that you should always buy a stock for a specific reason—you should be looking at a specific "clue" or potential "catalyst" that tells you to buy this stock. Then, if the stock moves the wrong way, you should ask yourself: Is the reasoning still valid? If the outside beneficial owner starts to reduce his or her stake in your stock, for example, the original reasoning is no longer valid. If a company says it is looking into ways to enhance value and then announces that the plan has been scrapped, the original reasoning is no longer valid.

But if the original premise remains sound, you should hang in there—and if you can, you should buy more to take advantage of the lower price.

On December 31, 1990, WMS closed at $3¼. Despite what seemed to be a logical analysis, the stock had now declined 57 percent from my original recommended price of $7⅜.

I did not use a stop loss on the way down and did not recommend a "sell" of WMS for year-end tax loss. In other words, I did not follow any of the simplistic "rules" for intelligent investing.

And it's a good thing too, *because in 1991 WMS Industries turned out to be the best-performing stock on the entire New York Stock Exchange.*

On February 8, 1991, WMS had broken out of a nice base in the $3½ to $4½ area. The stock moved up quickly, trading above $6. Earnings rebounded nicely, following the onetime charges and the retooling, which really was not much of a surprise since WMS Industries' basic business was continuing to grow.

But again, the lack of analytical coverage had caused the market to overreact to the temporary earnings setback. Without analysts explaining the situation to a force of retail brokers, who in turn can reassure investors that a charge or write-off is temporary, a neglected small-cap stock can overreact in a major way, all out of proportion to the earnings setback. This is precisely what happened to WMS late in 1990 on its way from $10 to $3¼.

Once again, Sumner Redstone had paid over $10 for large blocks of stock and there was WMS's desire to enhance shareholder value—one of the key code phrases for superstock investors—spinning off its hotel/casinos operations as a separate company.

Research into this plan led to some interesting information about appraisals of the value of the WMS hotel/casino properties. The Condado Plaza was worth between $105 and $110 million, which meant that the 80 percent owned by WMS was worth about $84 million (about $10/share). Yet WMS carried its 80 percent ownership of the Condado Plaza on its books at a value of $37 million (about $4.35/share). The other property, the El San Juan, was appraised at $100 million. WMS owned 50 percent of the El San Juan, or $50 million (about $6/share). However, this asset was also carried on the WMS books at only $37 million ($4.35/share).

In a situation like this it's important to focus on the difference between "book value" and true "asset value," especially when you're dealing with real estate. A great deal of unrecognized value on the WMS balance sheet could be recognized by the market if this spin-off did take place.

Here was a classic example of how inefficient the stock market can be when you are dealing with lesser-followed small-cap or micro-cap stocks. In order to understand why, you have to understand the term *book value* and how misleading this figure can be in certain circumstances.

When a company carries an asset on its balance sheet, that asset must be assigned a certain value, which is called "book value." Usually, the asset is initially valued at its historical cost, which may or may not reflect the actual value several years down the road.

In the case of a piece of machinery, for example , the value of that machinery will decline over time as the machine's useful life grows shorter. Eventually, the machine will wear out and become virtually worthless. As a result, the accountants came up with the concept of *depreciation*, whereby a company is allowed to deduct a certain portion of that asset's cost each year from its earnings. The depreciation "expense" is not really a cash expense; it is just a bookkeeping entry that allows the company to reduce its tax bill somewhat and also reduces the carrying value, or "book value," of the asset each year.

For example, a $1 million piece of machinery with a 10-year useful life would be carried on the books at its $1 million cost for the first year. In the second year the company would take a $100,000 depreciation charge (one-tenth of the machine's cost), that is deducted from earnings. If the company earned $2 million that year, it would only report $1.9 million after the $100,00 depreciation "expense." The "expense" did not involve a cash outlay, but saved perhaps $40,000 in taxes because it reduced reported earnings. That $40,000 saving is supposed to allow the company to accumulate cash to replace the machine when its useful life wears out in 10 years. That is the purpose of the depreciation allowance.

The other effect of that $100,000 depreciation "expense" is to reduce the carrying value, or "book value," of the machine on the company's balance sheet. At the end of the first year that $1 million machine will be carried on the books at its newly depreciated value of $900,000. The book value of that machine will decline each year by $100,000 until the machine wears out and a new one must be purchased.

Of course, if the company has a really good mechanic or if the machine is particularly well-constructed it may last 15 years, or possibly 20 years. In that case the machine will actually be worth more than its carrying value, and therefore the "book value" of the company will understate the actual value of its assets.

It can also work the other way. If a company buys a piece of land for $1 million, based on a bet that this land will soon be directly in the path of a brand new highway, but then the Highway Department decides to build the highway someplace else, the land may not be worth $1 million anymore. But the company may keep the land on the books at its historical cost. Or a company may purchase inventory and find that it cannot be sold at anywhere near cost. Or a company might buy drilling rights on a piece of property and spend a number of fruitless years trying to find oil. In cases like this, the "book value" may overstate the actual value of the asset.

On the other hand, let's say you buy some oil and it turns out your geologist had an eagle eye. You hit pay dirt, the oil and gas start flowing from the wells, and you are rolling in clover. The properties are still carried on your books at historical cost, but that was before you found oil. Now these properties are worth many multiples of what you paid—but their true worth is not reflected in your company's "book value."

Book Value and Kirby Industries

The term "book value" can be very misleading. In 1974, in the midst of a crushing bear market, a small oil and gas company called Kirby Industries announced that it would sell off its assets and pay out cash to its shareholders. This type of self-liquidation is fairly common today; it usually occurs when a company believes its assets are worth far more than its stock price and when the stockholders would be better served by selling the assets and paying the proceeds directly to the stockholders.

In 1974, however, the concept of voluntary liquidation was novel—so novel, in fact, that nobody seemed to know how to analyze the situation. I was still a junior analyst at Merrill Lynch when Kirby announced it would liquidate itself, and the only reason I noticed the announcement was that I had a friend who owned a substantial number of Kirby shares. I called him and asked him what the announcement meant.

"The assets of this company," he told me, "are worth way more than the stock is selling for. They have properties with proven oil and gas reserves that are worth far more than book value. They have other properties that are adjacent to major discoveries where they haven't even started drilling yet, but they know the oil and gas are there. They even have a small auto insurance company in Puerto Rico that's worth way more than its book value. They think selling the company off piece by piece will create a better value for the stockholders."

This was intriguing. The idea of selling assets and paying out cash to stockholders seemed a very efficient way to force the stock market to reflect the true value of your company. I called Kirby Industries and asked them to send all of their financials. I talked to a Kirby spokesperson and tried to get a feel for the reasoning behind the liquidation plan.

The oil and gas analysts were hopelessly confused. They had never come across a voluntary liquidation and they did not know now to handle it. Besides, Kirby was not on their radar screen; the company was too small. Their advice was to stay away from the situation because it appeared "too risky."

Too risky? What is risky about a management knowing that the value of its assets is substantially higher than the stock price and setting out to deliver that value to stockholders? Actually, the term "too risky" means: "It doesn't fit the paradigm in which I am used to operating." Everybody is used to a certain way of doing things, both personally and professionally. When a situation arises that breaks the mold, the initial reaction is to *not deal with it. Ignore it. Pretend it does not exist.* Just go on doing what you're used to doing while an opportunity sits there, outside the box, waiting to be experienced and profited from.

In the case of Kirby Industries, a voluntary liquidation was outside the familiar paradigms of most securities analysts. So, instead of "thinking outside the box," the oil and gas analysts just didn't think about Kirby at all. They ignored it because it did not fit their preferred and preconceived manner of thinking.

The stock market did not know what to do about Kirby Industries because the analysts who followed oil and gas stocks did not know what to do about it. Kirby had announced in November 1974 that it would self-liquidate; the stock, which had previously traded at $15⅛, did not trade for several days as the specialist (market maker) on the floor of the American Stock Exchange tried to figure out where to open the stock in light of this new and confusing information. *When Kirby finally opened, the price was $28—up nearly $13 or 86 percent in a single trade!*

This opening price was very interesting because the stock had opened almost precisely at its book value figure of $28.28! In other words, what the stock market seemed to be saying was that, when Kirby finished selling its assets, it would be worth what the balance sheet said it was worth. But this seemed far too simplistic based on what I knew about "book value" and "historical cost" in relation to oil and gas properties.

More research on Kirby Industries indicated the stock market was overlooking a huge opportunity. I became so convinced that Wall Street was missing the boat on Kirby Industries that I resigned from Merrill Lynch to start my own stock market advisory letter— and decided to make Kirby Industries my very first recommendation!

And how did my December 1974 recommendation of Kirby Industries at $24 turn out?

By the time the dust settled, Kirby shareholders had received a series of cash and stock distributions with a combined value of over $450 per share!

The experience with Kirby Industries brought to mind WMS Industries and its plan to unlock the value of its Puerto Rico hotel/casinos. Because the hotel/casinos had been depreciated on WMS's books, they were therefore undoubtedly worth more than "book value." There was a high possibility, then, that these properties were worth more than the stock market was giving WMS credit for. Not only that, for WMS to even consider a plan to unlock the value of these properties could mean only one thing: WMS management believed they were worth more than the stock price was reflecting and were looking for ways to force the stock market to reflect that value.

Then there was the Sumner Redstone factor. Here was an astute businessman who had proven time and time again that he had an eye for value. Redstone had made a career out of seeing what others failed to see, making a bet on his vision and proving to be correct. He had paid far in excess of WMS's current market price for stock, and he must have seen something that the market was missing. Could it have been the value of the hotel/casinos? Or something else that was not on Wall Street's radar screen?

Looking at the WMS situation through the eyes of its management and outside investor Sumner Redstone, it seemed clear that something valuable was lurking beneath the surface of this neglected, low-priced stock. My experience with the way Wall Street can overlook situations like this for extended periods of time explained the weakness in WMS stock.

By early February 1991, however, WMS had doubled in price from its 1990 close of $3¼. One reason for this was that earnings per share were rising again. As already noted, the earnings problems WMS experienced in the second half of 1990 had been the result of unusual charges that had nothing to do with the company's basic business, but since there was no analytical support to interpret this information for investors, the stock had reacted badly to lower earnings that had not truly reflected what was going on at the company.

Now, the true earnings power of WMS was becoming apparent once again, and the stock was moving higher.

By March 1991, WMS was trading between $6 and $7, and Sumner Redstone had just filed another report with the SEC, indicating additional purchases of WMS shares on the open market at prices between $3⅜ and $6⅛. This was a major reinforcement to hang in there and continue to follow Redstone's lead by buying more of WMS at these low levels. Again, this is the difference between panicking out of a stock that is declining (because you have no "road map" to guide you) and adding to your stake in a declining stock. *Knowing* why you bought the stock in the first place—in this case, because we were following a sophisticated outside beneficial owner—tells you what to do if the stock starts going against you. Redstone, by adding to his stake in WMS at these lower prices, had just updated the road map. WMS was still a buy.

At the same time, there were also some interesting "technical" or chart patterns in WMS. Take a look at this chart in Figure 13–2 and you will see that WMS, on the way up from its low at $3¼, was actually sketching out a series of very short-term superstock chart patterns: a series of well-defined resistance levels, combined with rising support levels, followed by a breakout, and then a new short-term superstock consolidating pattern.

What was the importance of this? Demand was coming in at progressively higher levels, chewing through supply, and the demand for WMS shares, wherever it was coming from, was perfectly willing to keep buying at progressively higher price points. By April 1991 it became apparent where at least part of this demand for WMS had been coming from: Sumner Redstone reported that he had been buying more WMS shares in the open market.

In May 1991, Redstone purchased an additional 193,100 WMS shares at prices between $8⅝ and $11. This was extremely important news because it demonstrated his willingness to buy more WMS shares even as the stock rose to new short-term highs. This could only mean that he knew or suspected something very bullish was brewing beneath the surface at WMS that was not yet reflected in its stock price.

Now, think about what this would mean to you, as an investor. Suppose you had been a WMS shareholder at the time. You bought stock at $8 and watched it slump to a low of $3¼. "Old paradigm"

Figure 13-2

WMS Industries (WMS), 1989-1991

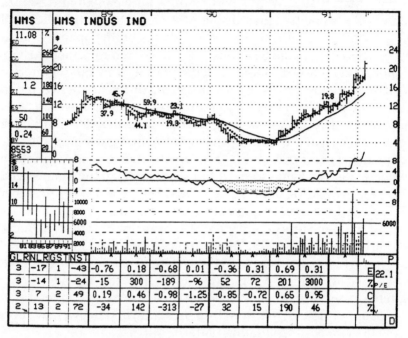

Source: Courtesy of Mansfield Chart Service, Jersey City, NJ.

investors would have been discouraged and confused—but as a superstock investor, you would not because you'd be following two road maps: Sumner Redstone's continuing purchases of WMS, and the WMS plan to unlock the value of its hotel/casino properties. While old paradigm thinkers who get into a losing situation like this might think of throwing in the towel, a superstock investor would be thinking in precisely the opposite terms. You'd be looking at the slump in WMS stock price as *an opportunity to add to your stake,* so that if your original analysis was correct, your ultimate profit would be even greater.

Compare this confident attitude to the plight of someone who buys a stock for some vague reason—let's say because it is a "growth" stock. You buy the stock and it starts to decline. What do you do? You hang in there because you have been told it is a "growth" stock. Pretty soon the stock is down 25 percent. Now what do you do?

Cutting Your Losses

Do you follow the simplistic "cut your losses" routine, or do you buy more? Well, it's hard to say because you really don't have a handle on why you bought the stock in the first place. Even if it's a "growth stock," what is it worth? Are interest rates rising? If they are, your growth stock might be growing nicely but the stock price is going to be worth progressively less as interest rates rise because its price/earnings ratio will decline, as we have already learned. Then one day the company announces that its earnings are still growing all right, but they will be growing at a rate that is somewhat less than Wall Street expected. This "new business," which is immediately taken into account by the market, results in your "growth stock" opening another 25 percent lower in a single trade, which means you should have followed the "cut your losses rule."

On the other hand, maybe you did follow the "cut your losses" rule and sold your growth stock after it had declined 25 percent. No harm there, right? You live to fight another day. Except that the growth stock you just sold bottoms out and doubles after you sold it, and it turns out that what you have done is dump your shares at the bottom of a perfectly normal short-term correction within the context of a major uptrend. Now you feel really stupid.

But should you? How could you have possibly known what to do? You were operating without a road map, without guidelines—without a guiding principle, if you want to put it in those terms.

Compare this feeling of being lost in the Wall Street wilderness to the feeling you would have had as an investor in WMS. You *knew* the company had assets on the books that were worth far in excess of book value. You *knew* that WMS management was aware of this and that they were looking for ways to force the stock market to reflect this value. You *knew* that Sumner Redstone, a busy man who is running Viacom and has better things to do than speculate in low-priced stocks had somehow found the time to accumulate WMS shares on the open market and was still buying, even as WMS shares were in the doldrums. He must be doing this for a reason, so if you followed his lead in the first place by buying WMS shares, you should also follow his lead by hanging in there and buying more after the stock has dropped.

This mind-set is the major difference between superstock investing and any other approach to the stock market. It won't always lead to profitable investments—but it will lead to peace of mind, a coherent strategy, and the ability to make decisions for rational reasons. And there is a lot to be said for that.

In June 1991, I received a letter from a subscriber who asked whether WMS might eventually become a manufacturer of video lottery terminals.

Video lottery terminals? Some research revealed that video lottery terminals were actually video poker games, sanctioned and sponsored by state governments, that were popping up in restaurants and taverns in the handful of states that had legalized this kind of gaming. A small item in *Replay Magazine*, a magazine devoted to pinball and video game manufacturing, reported a rumor that Williams Electronics, a WMS subsidiary, had been secretly designing its own video lottery terminals for some time and that WMS was about to enter the market for these machines.

Further research indicated that a number of states were seriously considering legalizing video poker, which meant that this was potentially a brand new growth industry.

And there was another burgeoning market for video poker machines: Native American casinos. These casinos were popping up in various regions of the country, and every new casino required hundreds, if not thousands, of slot machines and video gaming devices. For a long time Wall Street had looked at manufacturers of casino gaming devices as a stagnant, slow-growth industry because they viewed gambling as an industry confined to Las Vegas and Atlantic City. With the number of casinos relatively fixed, where would the major growth in demand for gaming machines come from? Suddenly, there was an answer to this question: The growth in demand would come from state-run video lottery/poker terminals and the proliferation of Native American casinos across the country.

Some further research led to the stock price performance of International Game Technology (NYSE: IGT), the industry leader for casino games. IGT had vaulted from below $10 in October 1990 to nearly $50 a share by June 1991, a gain of 400 percent—all because of the growing excitement over video lottery terminals and the potential new source of demand for casino-style machines from state governments and Native American casinos.

Would WMS Industries enter the market for video lottery terminals? If so, the effect on its stock price could be huge.

WMS was not commenting. But Dow Jones News Service had talked to a distributor of WMS's pinball/video games, which as I said were ubiquitous in restaurants and taverns all over the country. *The distributor confirmed to Dow Jones that WMS had told him it would soon be unveiling a video lottery terminal—possibly within the next 60 to 90 days.* This report suggested WMS would have advantages over a competitor like International Game Technology. While IGT had been selling its gaming machines to casinos for decades, WMS had been selling its pinball and video arcade games to bars and restaurants for equally as long. And the potential demand for state-run video lottery terminals would put WMS at a distinct advantage should it enter this market. Why? Because the WMS sales force (distributors) were already placing WMS products in these establishments. It was, and still is, literally impossible to walk into any establishment with a pinball and video game and not see one of WMS's products— Williams, Bally, and Midway. Now, if WMS were about to unveil a video lottery terminal—which in manufacturing terms was not all that different from what WMS was already producing—the relationships of WMS distributors with bar and restaurant owners across the country could mean that WMS would be in the drivers' seat versus IGT when it came to placing these machines.

The stock market had taken the WMS announcement during the past summer that it would temporarily close its manufacturing facilities to retool as a major negative. But did this retooling have something to do with the fact that WMS was planning to add video lottery terminals to its product line?

By June 1991, WMS had already advanced from $3¼ to $12 since year-end 1990. Sumner Redstone had added significantly to his stake along the way, and other buyers were bidding for WMS stock at progressively higher levels, something the chart had indicated months earlier as WMS chewed through successively higher resistance levels with the greatest of ease.

In retrospect, it's easy to see why WMS was performing so well, and this strong price performance is a good lesson in what drives stock prices. Even though WMS had made no official statement, the word about manufacturing video lottery terminals was already leaking out, most notably in the Dow Jones report. How could it not? WMS had to retool it's manufacturing facilities, it had to conduct market research, it had to bring in teams of designers, and it had to prepare its distributors around the country for the introduction of this new product. The increasing awareness of WMS's upcoming entry into this exciting new growth industry was undoubtedly one of the major factors in the bullish patterns being created on the company's stock price. The increasing demand for WMS shares, the easy penetration of resistance levels, and the willingness of informed buyers to bid for stock at progressively higher prices were Telltale Signs of something bullish brewing at WMS.

This is another example of how charts can help point you toward potential stock market winners. It's not that charts can predict the future, but that when informed investors who know more than you do are buying or selling, they are in effect leaving "footprints" on the chart. By recognizing the signs of informed and confident demand, you can pretty much know what the smart money is doing—even if you do not know what the smart money knows.

By the end of June, WMS confirmed that it would enter the market for video lottery terminals.

Of all the portents that WMS was going to turn into a huge winner, to me the most significant was the performance of International Game Technology, whose stock soared between late 1990 and mid-1991. Here is a rule of thumb that works nearly 100 percent of the time: *When the stock of an industry leader takes off to the upside, virtually every other stock in that industry will eventually move up in its wake.* The reason for this tendency makes perfect sense. Whatever bullish developments are inducing investors to buy the industry leader should also apply to other companies doing business in that industry. Sometimes, there will be no "lag time" at all, and all of the stocks in the industry group will move together. Other times there will be a brief lag—days or a week or two at the most—before the other stocks in the industry group start to move up in sympathy with the leader.

In recent years the lag time has grown longer, a phenomenon that has to do with the increased institutionalization of the stock market and the narrowing of analytical coverage discussed earlier. Since institutional investors are focused mainly on liquid, large-cap stocks, they will pour their money into the biggest companies if they see something that leads them to believe they should be weighted in a certain industry group. The mid-size companies will usually follow along quickly if the industry leaders are breaking out to new highs. But, the smaller companies with no analytical coverage and no institutional interest will often sit there for weeks on end, not participating at all in the general strength of other stocks in their industry group.

Eventually, the realization that other stocks in the industry are making new highs will filter down to even the smallest stocks in the group—but the lag time having grown significantly longer, presents an opportunity to individual investors who are willing to go off the beaten path to look for stocks that are being neglected. What finally causes investors to focus on the small-cap and microcap stocks, which have not yet moved along with their larger counterparts, usually involves individual newsletter analysts, small-cap or microcap funds that are looking for bargains, and individuals—just like you— who are willing to put two and two together and come up with four—a simple enough task, it would seem, that is beyond the capability of many institutional money managers and brokerage firm analysts who are forced to operate in a completely different paradigm than the rest of us.

The guiding principle here is that what is superbullish for the industry leader is probably going to be superbullish for everybody else in the industry. It was a good reason to remain ultrabullish on WMS, even though its stock had already tripled from its year-end 1990 low. Here was International Game Technology, soaring from $9 to $50 based mainly on the implications of an emerging new market for video lottery terminals. And here was WMS, which was already experiencing a major earnings turnaround even without video lottery terminals (VLTs), completely neglected by the Wall Street analytical community. *In mid-1991 not one brokerage firm analyst followed WMS Industries.* It was no wonder that WMS was not participating in the excitement over VLTs. In fact, WMS stock responded to the announcement of the company's entrance into the VLT market by dropping from $13 to $10, providing yet another buying opportunity for those who were keeping their eye on the ball.

Finally, in late July 1991, a brokerage firm analyst noticed WMS and published a report recommending it as a buy.

Take a look at the chart in Figure 13–3 and you will see the power of a brokerage firm analysis. WMS immediately jumped to a new high of $15 as a result of this report, and the stock had taken on a new and powerful ally—brokerage firm sponsorship. This was the final ingredient necessary for WMS to follow in the footsteps of

F i g u r e   13–3

WMS Industries (WMS), 1990–1992

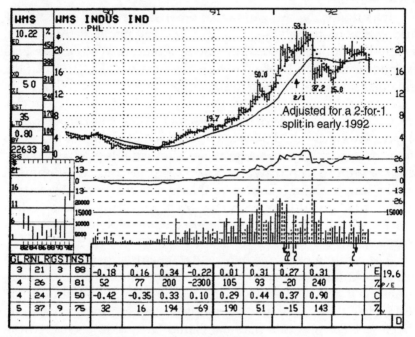

Source: Courtesy of Mansfield Chart Service, Jersey City, NJ.

International Game Technology. WMS was now on the radar screen of Wall Street analysts and institutional investors who monitored their recommendations. The report made it more likely that any bullish development for the VLT market would have a positive impact on WMS. In August 1991 our recommendation was:

> In the final analysis what will drive WMS stock higher will be the perception that state legislatures which face mounting budget deficits will see the legalization of VLTs as a politically painless way to generate desperately needed revenues...each time another state decides to legalize VLTs we think the handful of stocks involved in VLTs will get a boost.

WMS was unveiling its first video lottery terminal on September 12, 1991. In an interview with a confident WMS president Neil Nicastro, he said he believed WMS would do very well competing with International Game Technologies and others in terms of placing its machines into any state that legalized VLTs. Nicastro confirmed that WMS had strong distributor relationships in both Louisiana and Oregon, the two states that had already legalized VLTs, and that the same people who were placing WMS pinball and video games in bars and restaurants would also be representing WMS's new VLT. He told me that "Williams Electronics is the strongest name in the coin operated amusement game business, and our distributors know that we will be able to satisfy demand quickly and with a reliable product." Nicastro also confirmed that "if this business develops as we hope it will, and if we can be an effective competitor, the additional VLT revenues will mean a dramatic spike in income for WMS."

Meanwhile, back on the chart, WMS was sketching out that familiar superstock chart pattern once again. A short-term resistance area near $15 to $15½ was being attacked over and over again by buyers, with demand coming in at progressively higher levels—a strong signal that WMS stock would be moving higher.

By late September 1991, WMS had broken out above its resistance area at $15 to $15⅜ to a clear new high in the $18 to $19 area. In the superstock concept, a stock like WMS Industries should do very well regardless of what the overall economy and the stock market were doing. Our recommendation suggested "concentrating on stocks which will not depend entirely on an economic recovery to do well. Such stocks would include takeover candidates and companies which may be involved in an industry which could actually *benefit* from a sluggish economy. An example would be WMS Industries, which reached another new high and which is up an astonishing 85 percent since late June!"

In October–November 1991 the news started coming fast and furious. WMS reported that revenues and earnings were rising sharply; a judge in Oregon threw out a lawsuit designed to block the introduction of video lottery terminals in that state, which was viewed as a strong signal that anti-VLT forces in other states would have a difficult time as well. Other state governments, strapped for cash, were announcing that they too would consider video lottery terminals as a new source of badly needed revenues. Landenburg Thalmann, the only brokerage firm willing to stick out its neck in recommending WMS, offered the view that a burgeoning market for WMS's pinball games could be developing in Eastern Europe, where communism was giving way to democracy, and also in South America, where pinball games were catching on with young people.

Only on Wall Street does the demand for an item increase as the price rises. As WMS stock price moved higher, analytical coverage increased and the WMS story suddenly became interesting to institutional investors and the analysts who provide the research that influences their investment decisions. Proving that to some people there is nothing that makes as much investment sense as a rising stock, suddenly there were lots of reasons to love WMS Industries. All of the Telltale Signs that had suddenly turned WMS into a Wall Street darling had been in plain sight for months. But now WMS was moving in a more "respectable" price range and the stock had morphed into a "momentum" stock.

Wall Street research departments jumped onboard, mainly because WMS had moved into the price range that would interest their institutional clients.

I had been speaking on a regular basis to one analyst who covered the "leisure" industry, which included gaming stocks. He had loved WMS all along and had actually provided some guidance to me along the way based on his view that video lottery terminals would soon be proliferating. But when I asked him why he wouldn't officially recommend WMS, he told me it was "not an institutional sort of stock," whatever that meant.

Finally, one day I heard that my friend had officially recommended WMS. I called him to find out what thrilling new piece of information he had uncovered that had finally tipped the scales.

"Now that it's a $20 stock, I can get our institutional clients interested," the analyst said.

"Excuse me?"

"Look," he said, "these guys aren't going to buy a $7 stock with no research coverage that nobody's ever heard of. It's too risky. If it goes down you'll get all sorts of heat, and who needs that? Now that WMS is a $20 stock and it's moving, and it's a relative strength leader—see, I can sell that story. They'll listen to me at this price level. The stock is more recommendable at these levels."

"Are you telling me," I said, "that even though you knew the same things about WMS at $7 or $10 that you know now that you didn't recommend the stock simply because it was too cheap?"

"Yes."

"And now that WMS is more expensive you are willing to stick your neck out because you won't get criticized as much as if it doesn't work out?"

The analyst sighed. "I know it sounds ridiculous," he said. "But yes, that is what I'm telling you."

Do you think things have changed since then?

On November 19, 1998, a mutual fund portfolio manager appeared on CNBC. In response to a viewer question, the fund manager launched into an informed and enthusiastic analysis of what you would call a "value stock," which carried a rich dividend yield, sold at a low price/earnings ratio, and seemed like an undiscovered gem.

"Would you buy the stock here?" the host asked.

"Well," the portfolio manager said, "I would if I didn't have so much short-term performance pressure on me. It would be a great stock to buy and tuck away. But, you know, I can't do that . . . it's tough."

The portfolio manager's voice trailed away and the host went on to the next question. But his comments spoke volumes about the "lemming" instinct of mainstream portfolio management and the analysts who provide their research. More often than not there is safety in numbers. It is better to be wrong betting on a stock that everybody else owns than to go off the beaten path and take a chance on losing money on something that nobody has ever heard of. Thus, the trendy momentum stocks are overbought and overpriced, and the neglected gems are unloved and underpriced—until something happens to pluck them out of obscurity and thrust them into the limelight. This portfolio manager had made a sound and bullish case for an undervalued stock that he would have *loved* to buy and "tuck away" in his fund's portfolio, but he didn't have the nerve to do it because short-term performance pressure made it necessary for him to stick with the stocks his peers were buying, just so he could keep up with the lemmings.

On December 31, 1991, WMS Industries closed at $27⅞, up 669 percent from its 1990 closing price of $3¼. *That performance made WMS the best-performing stock on the New York Stock Exchange for 1991.*

By the time WMS received its first order for video lottery terminals from the Oregon Lottery Commission in January 1992, WMS had soared to $41 a share—an incredible gain of 1161 percent from its closing level at year-end 1990!

What is the lesson to be learned from the WMS story?

Actually, there are several.

WMS Industries had three of the Telltale Signs for identifying future superstocks: (1) a potential superstock chart pattern, with a well-defined long-term resistance level being penetrated; (2) an outside beneficial owner (Sumner Redstone) who was buying stock on the open market and who had demonstrated the ability in the past to identify winning investments ahead of the crowd; and (3) management that seemed convinced there was an unrecognized underlying value within the company and appeared determined to take steps to "unlock" that value.

These were the three elements that made WMS attractive and provided the willpower to hang on even though WMS performed poorly at first. Before the evidence emerged and it became apparent what all the excitement was about, the Telltale Signs of a potential superstock were apparent. In retrospect, it seems WMS's bullish chart pattern was created by persistent buying among those who were becoming aware of the company's impending entry into the video lottery terminal industry. It's possible that Sumner Redstone's buying was related to this insight as well—or perhaps Sumner Redstone was buying because he knew that the WMS hotel/casinos were worth far more than WMS's stock price was reflecting.

Who knows?

The point is this: The signs were there, even if the information that created those Telltale Signs did not emerge until later.

WMS Industries is a textbook example of how a superstock chart pattern, together with outside beneficial owner buying, can lead you to a huge winner—even if you don't know *why* that stock is going to be a winner!

Postscript to the WMS Story:

Eventually, WMS Industries got around to spinning off its hotel/casino properties. In early 1997, WMS created a new company, WHG Resorts, which was spun off from WMS and began trading on the NYSE in the $5 to $6 range (adjusted for a 2-for-1 split in WMS stock). Within 6 months WHG Resorts received a takeover bid that valued WHG at more than $20 per share.

The takeover bid for WHG Resorts valued the company at around $130 million. Based on the fact that WMS Industries had around 10.4 million shares outstanding when the company first announced that it was seeking to "unlock the value" of its hotel/casinos, WMS's hotels/casino properties turned out to be worth nearly $13 per share on the presplit WMS share.

No wonder WMS management was looking for ways to unlock the value of these properties.

Which is why you should always take a close look at "spinoffs" as potential superstock candidates.

CHAPTER FOURTEEN

The "Pure Play" and the Drugstore Industry

There is always a disposition in people's minds to think that existing conditions will be permanent. While the market is down and dull, it is hard to make people believe that this is the prelude to a period of activity and advance. When prices are up and the country is prosperous, it is always said that while preceding booms have not lasted, there are circumstances connected with this which make it unlike its predecessors and give assurance of permanency.

Charles H. Dow, Journalist
June 8, 1901, *The Wall Street Journal*

Things change.

Don Ameche, Actor
Things Change

Charles Dow, founder of Dow Jones & Company, and Don Ameche, a great actor, were both saying pretty much the same thing when they uttered these words, only Don Ameche put it more succinctly. In the stock market, as in life, you should never extrapolate current circumstances too far into the future because—well, because things change.

On Wall Street the tendency to assume that current conditions will remain in force indefinitely, if not forever, is a common form of mass delusion that must be experienced the hard way by every generation of investors that comes down the pike. What these investors do not understand about Wall Street is that trends come and go, fads appear and disappear, and the pendulum swings from one extreme to the other, over and over and again, inevitably and without fail. And as difficult as it is to believe that the pendulum can ever swing the other way when you're riding the final, glorious upward arc—it always reverses course, and you had better learn to either get off or turn around and prepare yourself for the return trip because riding a pendulum backwards is no fun, financially or otherwise.

In this chapter you will learn about "pure plays" and spinoffs and how they can lead you to superstocks and superstock takeovers. But first let's go back to the 1960s, when "conglomerates" were all the rage and Wall Street was discovering the meaning of the latest buzzword—a fad called "synergy."

The technical definition of *synergy* is "the joint action of agents, such as drugs, that when taken together increase each other's effectiveness." Two people, for example, can create synergy. Or two muscles. Or, in the case of Wall Street, two businesses. Or three, or maybe five, or ten.

In the 1960s, the concept of "synergy" took hold as the key of conquering business cycles and creating stocks that could continue to go up, in good markets and bad, in recessions and in boom times. The idea was to create multi-industry companies through acquisitions so that when one industry was in the doldrums, the slack would be taken up by another. If the synergist were clever and calculating enough, the resulting company—called a "conglomerate"—would report ever-rising earnings through any and all economic cycles. If the homebuilding division was going bad, for example, this would be offset by a very good year in the rocket fuel business, the bowling alleys, the funeral homes—or whatever else you owned that might be doing well while something else was performing poorly.

That was the theory, at least, and for a while conglomerates were all the rage, until the inflationary recession spirals of the 1970s hit and all of the businesses went bad at the same time. To make matters worse, it became apparent that it was a lot harder than it looked to oversee a company with 27 different divisions, all operating in totally unrelated industries, not to mention how difficult it was for Wall Street analysts to cover these companies in any coherent manner.

So synergy and the conglomerate craze slowly petered out—proving once again that Charles Dow and Don Ameche knew what they were talking about. (Of course, some "synergies" are too powerful and obvious to be denied. In an obviously well-thought-out strategy, Netherlands-based Unilever PLC announced two takeovers on the same day in April 2000. First, Unilever said it would buy ice cream maker Ben & Jerry's Homemade, whose products include the notoriously calorie-laden "Chubby Hubby" brand for $326 million. Also on that day, Unilever announced the $2.3 billion acquisition of diet products company Slim Fast Foods, thus putting Unilever in the business of both causing and curing obesity—a synergistic win-win situation if ever there was one.)

Interestingly, however, there are some vestiges around of the trend toward synergy even today—and when these vestiges begin to jettison operations that do not fit their core businesses—in other words, when a company decides it wants to be more of a "pure play" in a well-defined industry—it can lead you to potential superstocks.

In recent years a growing number of companies have decided that they—and their stockholders—would be better off as "pure plays"—i.e., companies that operate in a single, well-defined industry. The major reason is because Wall Street analysts are industry specialists, and since analytical coverage is the key to a widely held and fairly priced stock, many companies have come to the conclusion that an easily understood corporate identity is crucial for a strong stock price. For example, a mutual fund looking for exposure in the auto parts industry would be more likely to buy shares in a company with 100 percent of its revenues coming from auto parts than it would a company with, say, 60 percent of its revenues coming from auto parts and the other 40 percent from radio stations.

In order to become a pure play, a company needs to remove noncore businesses from the mix. There are two ways to do this: sell the businesses outright, or spin them off to shareholders as a separate company.

In a pure spinoff, 100 percent of the stock of the noncore business is distributed to shareholders of the parent company, and the spinoff starts a new life as an independent, publicly traded company. There are a number of theoretical benefits to spinoffs, including the probability that the management of the new company will be better able to manage the spinoff's business once it is separated from the parent.

Another theoretical advantage to owning shares in a spinoff is that the value of a fast-growing subsidiary hidden within a larger corporate structure may have been overlooked by Wall Street. By separating the fast-growing subsidiary and turning it into a separately trading company, the growth rate that had been previously obscured will become more apparent, which could lead to a higher price/earnings multiple for the spinoff's stock.

A third possibility is that by spinning off a company in an industry where there is a lot of takeover activity, the spinoff could become a takeover target. This is what happened to WHG Resorts, the hotel/casino spinoff of WMS Industries which, following its separation from the parent company in 1997, more than doubled in price within 6 months.

Most Wall Street analysts recommend investing in spinoffs for all of these reasons, but there is a different way to look at spinoffs. As a superstock investor, you should look at every announced spinoff and ask yourself : Which company operates in an industry where there is a great deal of takeover activity, the parent company or the company being spun off?

The answer to that question may surprise you. In fact, in many cases you would be better off buying the parent company—especially if that company operates in a takeover-lively industry. The reason is because a number of instances have occurred over the years where a company in a takeover-lively industry decides to sell or spin off noncore businesses as the initial step in ultimately putting itself up for sale.

A rule of thumb, therefore: *Whenever you see an announcement involving a spinoff, analyze the parent company. Check to see if there has been any recent takeover activity in the parent company's industry.*

If the answer is yes, and if the parent company is a mid-size or smaller company within that consolidating industry, you should seriously consider the possibility that the parent company is turning itself into a pure play as a prelude to selling itself to the highest bidder.

CASE STUDY: FAY'S AND GENOVESE

In fall 1995, I noticed an interview with the chairman of Rite Aid, a drugstore company that had just made a takeover bid for Revco, one of its largest competitors. That merger, which would have created the nation's largest drugstore company, was never consummated because of regulatory opposition. But in commenting on the reasoning for

Rite Aid's bid for Revco, Rite Aid's chairman, Martin Grass, compared the fragmented drugstore industry to the banking industry, which was then undergoing a frantic wave of consolidation. The drugstore industry, said the Rite Aid executive, was very similar to the banking industry in that significant cost savings through economies of scale were possible by combining companies. He went on to predict that the same reasoning being applied to the wave of bank mergers could be applied to the drugstore industry, and that this was the driving rationale behind his company's bid for Revco.

Although the Rite Aid–Revco merger never took place, this interview was the "road map" for finding superstock takeover candidates.

As a starting point, I compiled a list of the 15 publicly traded drugstore companies and ranked them from top to bottom, based on the value of their outstanding stock, or market capitalization:

1. Rite Aid (see Chapter 17)
2. Revco
3. Walgreens
4. Eckerd
5. Melville Corp. (which owned CVS Drugs, which was eventually spun off and acquired)
6. Cardinal Health (which owned Medicine Shoppes)
7. Thrifty-Payless
8. American Stores (which owned Osco and Sav-On Drugs)
9. JCPenney (which owned Thrift Drugs) (see Chapter 17)
10. Longs Drug Stores
11. Big B
12. Fay's
13. Drug Emporium
14. Arbor Drugs
15. Genovese Drug Stores

If you eliminated JCPenney, which was far too large to be acquired and was more likely to be an acquirer itself, 14 drugstore companies were on this list. Amazingly, in less than 2 years, 9 of these 14 companies were taken over! And it all started because of an interview with the chairman of Rite Aid, who described the reasoning behind his bid for Revco—which only goes to prove that Yogi Berra knew what he was talking about when he said: "You can observe a lot just by watching." Or, in this case, browsing.

The takeover wave in the drugstore industry ran its course breathtakingly quickly. One by one the mid-size and smaller drugstore chains were acquired by their larger competitors. Along the way, this takeover wave served as a case study on how to spot various telltale signs of impending superstock takeovers.

My first successful drugstore takeover candidate recommendation was Fay's Inc., and it was recommended for one reason—this small drugstore company was selling off noncore assets, making itself a "pure play" drugstore company. By December 1995, Fay's had just sold its Wheel's Discount Auto Supply stores for $37 million in cash and announced that its Paper Cutter retail stores would also be put up for sale. These announcements, combined with the view that a takeover trend was about to engulf the drugstore industry, made Fay's an obvious takeover candidate. Fay's was readying itself for sale by getting rid of "noncore" operations, a move that would make it more attractive to a larger drugstore company seeking acquisitions. At the time, Fay's was trading at $6¾.

In January 1996 another small drugstore company was added to my list of takeover recommendations. Genovese, the nineteenth largest drugstore company—with 113 stores in the New York City/Long Island area—had also recently become a pure play by selling off its nondrugstore operations.

I quoted Rite Aid chairman Martin Grass on the rationale of potential drugstore industry mergers being "very analogous to what's going on in the banking industry. We're able to absorb stores, eliminate tremendous overhead, and take costs off the system."

Our view was that the managements of Fay's and Genovese, by deciding to become pure drugstore companies through the sale of noncore businesses, already saw the handwriting on the wall and were preparing themselves to be acquired.

In March 1996, I reported another Telltale Sign appeared, indicating that Fay's management might be preparing to sell the company:

> "As I previously reported, Fay's has been selling off its nondrugstore retail operations. Now, Fay's has announced the elimination of 90 administrative jobs, which would save $3 million per year, or about

$0.14 per share. *These are the moves you should expect to see from a company that might be readying itself for sale in a rapidly consolidating industry.*

Fay's stock continued to languish at $7¾. As part of its cost-cutting move, Fay's had taken a "restructuring" charge, and the stock market reacted by pushing Fay's shares briefly down to the $6½ area. *Here was another situation where a complete lack of analytical coverage resulted in the stock market putting the wrong interpretation on this news.* Experience in noticing the Telltale Signs of an impending superstock takeover target—i.e., any company selling off noncore assets and cutting costs in an industry where a takeover trend was in force—was practically hanging a "For Sale" sign on the front door. But when Fay's took its restructuring charge—which would yield future benefits to cash flow and earnings—all the stock market saw was a loss for the quarter. There was no room for nuance: A low-priced stock with no analytical following had reported a loss, and down went the stock. But to the trained eye of a superstock analyst, the very news that was sending Fay's shares lower was another clue that Fay's would soon become a takeover target.

In April 1996 the Rite Aid–Revco merger agreement fell apart when the Federal Trade Commission decided that the resulting combination would be anticompetitive and would dominate the drugstore industry in a way that would be detrimental to consumers. However, the FTC left the door open for other drugstore industry mergers, which would be smaller in scale. By May 1996, Fay's stock was moving higher—ever since the Rite Aid–Revco deal was terminated.

By July 1996, Fay's had finally sold its Paper Cutter office supply stores for $14 million, which meant it was now a pure drugstore company.

Anyone concentrating on the "pure play" concept and the fact that Fay's was operating in an industry which was about to experience a takeover wave would by this time have seen crystal-clear signals that Fay's was a genuine takeover candidate. And yet, despite the fact that Fay's had finally sold off its last nondrugstore operation and taken a "clear the decks" restructuring charge—and despite the fact that the Federal Trade Commission had pretty much publicly stated that it would encourage smaller drugstore mergers—despite all of this, Fay's shares were trading at $7⅝, only slightly higher than the original recommended price of $6¾ six months earlier.

Suddenly, just 8 days later, on July 11, 1996, Fay's announced that it had received a takeover bid from JCPenney, which owned the Thrift Drug Store chain. The stock market reacted as though it was shocked—shocked—at the news. Fay's shares jumped to $10⅞ on this news. Fay's did not specify a takeover price, saying only that it had received a proposal from JCPenney and that it would have no further comment until a deal was consummated or the talks ended.

In July 1996, discussing the Fay's takeover proposal, I again raised the possibility that Genovese Drug Stores could become a takeover target for precisely the same reason that Fay's had. Genovese had sold off its nursing home division in the previous year, a move similar to Fay's selling off its nondrugstore operations in 1995–1996 prior to selling itself to JCPenney.

Also, the Genovese chain of drugstores was located almost precisely in the middle of the geographic areas that would be served by Penney's Thrift Drugs chain and a newly acquired Fay's chain. At that time, Genovese Drug Stores was trading near $8, adjusted for two subsequent 10 percent stock dividends.

Within two weeks Fay's announced that it had agreed to be acquired by JCPenney for $12.75 per share—an 85 percent gain from the recommended price of $6¾ in just 7 months, and *all because Fay's had tipped its hand by selling off its noncore operations and becoming a pure play in an industry where a takeover wave was under way.*

The Fay's recommendation had turned out to be on target, so we next turned our attention to Genovese, a very similar company. In addition to operating in the same general area of the country as Fay's and, like Fay's, recently becoming a pure play by selling off noncore assets—in its case, a nursing home division—Genovese had something else going for it: a potential superstock chart pattern. The chart showed a well-defined, multiyear resistance area at $11 to $12— precisely the sort of major, long-term resistance level that if broken to the upside, can create a superstock. This chart pattern, together with the fact that Genovese was becoming a pure play in a consolidating industry, were strong clues that Genovese Drug Stores was probably on its way to superstock status.

Research showed that 43 percent of Genovese's stock was owned by the family who founded the company. Now, you might logically think that would be a roadblock to a takeover. But in fact, the opposite is true. Around a third of Fay's outstanding stock was owned by the founding family, yet Fay's decided to sell itself to JCPenney. Why? *Because when you have a large block of stock in a small company in a consolidating industry controlled by the founders of the company, you will very often find that these stockholders recognize the proper moment to "cash out" and become part of a larger company.*

Look at it from this point of view: You start a small company, build it up over the years, compete and prosper, and wind up with a large chunk of a small, profitable company. Suddenly, you find that the industry you operate in is consolidating rapidly, and you begin to realize that it will soon be dominated by a handful of giant companies that will be consolidating operations, cutting costs, and squeezing the profit margins of its smaller competitors.

What do you do? Do you stubbornly hold on to your independence and take the risk that your company's profits will be squeezed by increasingly large competitors, leaving you on the outside looking in when the takeover wave finally runs its course? Or do you recognize the handwriting on the wall and take this opportunity to cash out at a huge premium to your stock's recent market price?

In such situations, there are tax ramifications to consider and we reported in *Superstock Investor*:

> When a public company is so heavily owned by a founding family, tax considerations come into play. Take a look at the JCPenney–Fay's deal: this buyout was structured as a *tax-free transaction* under which Fay's shareholders receive $12.75 worth of JCPenney stock. For the Panasci family, which founded Fay's, they were sitting with a $7 stock with the realization that the company they founded was worth almost twice that amount. A cash buyout would result in a huge tax liability; but in this tax-free swap with JCPenney, they receive a huge premium for their shares, they have no tax liability unless and until they sell their JCPenney shares, and they have received a far more liquid security to boot. *The Genovese family is in virtually the same position.*

So, here is another superstock clue to keep in mind: When a takeover trend engulfs a certain industry, take a close look at smaller companies in that industry in which the founding family still owns a large stake. More often than you might think, these major stockholders recognize the optimal moment to cash out—and you will find that many of these family-controlled companies will become willing takeover targets rather than run the risk of being left by the wayside as minor players in an industry dominated by a handful of giant competitors.

On July 2, 1997, a news item appeared on the Dow Jones Newswire that reported that two Genovese family members had agreed to act in concert in terms of their stock holdings.

According to SEC regulations, when two or more stockholders who own 5 percent or more of a public company agree to act in concert, they must notify the SEC that they are acting together. This agreement by Leonard Genovese, chairman and CEO of Genovese Drug Stores, and his sister Frances Genovese Wangberg, a director of Genovese, was characterized in the press as an "anti-takeover" agreement.

But our view was that the press had it all wrong, and it was misleading to characterize this as an "anti-takeover pact." The Genovese family members had made an agreement that required mutual consent before either of these two Genovese stockholders could sell. You could look at this agreement this way: these two majority Genovese shareholders—who control 57.4 percent of Genovese stock—recognized that they owned a very attractive property in an environment of rapid consolidation in the drugstore industry and had discussed how they would deal with any potential takeover bid that might take place in the future.

As a rule of thumb: Whenever you see any indication that two or more large stockholders of a company have made any sort of pact to act in concert, to require mutual approval, or in any way have indicated that they have discussed how they will sell their shares, you should take this as an indication that these stockholders are at least considering the possibility that the company will be sold at some point in the future.

In the case of Genovese Drug Stores, this pact between the two largest shareholders of the company indicated—in no uncertain terms—that they were discussing what they would do in the event of a takeover bid.

In November 1998, Genovese agreed to be acquired for $30 per share by none other than JCPenney—precisely the company targeted as the logical buyer. That $30 takeover price represented a 229 percent gain from my original recommended price, adjusted for stock dividends, of $9.11/share.

So, Genovese Drug Stores went from $9 to $30 in just over 2 years and the company received a takeover bid from JCPenney, just as predicted. Except that it wasn't quite that easy to hang in there with Genovese over that 2-year period, and therein lies another lesson in terms of what it takes to stick to your guns during periods in which the stock market completely ignores what might be blindingly obvious to a superstock investor.

When it comes to stocks that are not widely followed by analysts, or sometimes not followed by *any* analyst, news items and industry trends that seem to have clearly bullish implications for a smaller, off-the-beaten-path company have no effect on the stock. You see news, you make the connection, you buy the stock, and— nothing happens. The stock just sits there, or even moves lower, as if nothing significant has occurred. During periods like this (as with the WMS situation discussed in the previous chapter) there is no alternative to keeping your eye on the "road map"—i.e., remembering *why* you bought the stock, making certain that the initial reasoning remains in force, and, if you have the means, buying more at a lower price so that your ultimate profit will be greater once Wall Street catches on to what you have already deduced.

Take a look at the chart of Genovese Drug Stores (Figure 14–1). Within seven weeks of this chart being published, Genovese soared to $30 a share on the JCPenney takeover bid yet, between April and August 1998, as the ultimate takeover bid was fast approaching, Genovese stock plunged from $25½ to $15!

Genovese had also had a sinking spell a year earlier, after the company announced a "strategic restructuring" in which it cut costs and closed underperforming stores—precisely the sort of moves Fay's implemented prior to its takeover, and exactly what you would expect from a company preparing to sell itself. It was a classic Telltale Sign. And yet, the stock market did not react to this restructuring announcement positively and as a harbinger of a potential takeover. Instead, Genovese was punished.

In September 1996 a subscriber informed me that while my Genovese takeover recommendation obviously made sense, I was obviously wrong. Why? Because if Genovese were truly a takeover candidate in light of the Fay's acquisition the stock should be doing better—and it wasn't.

Here was my response:

Figure 14-1

Genovese Drug Stores (GDXA), 1996–1998

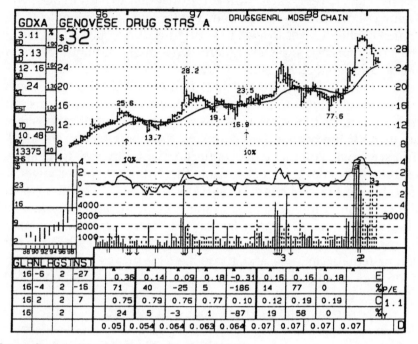

Source: Courtesy of Mansfield Chart Service, Jersey City, NJ.

This is a fact of life on Wall Street: Unless a widely followed establishment analyst with a connection to a strong retail sales force (i.e., lots of stockbrokers) is delivering a certain story, that story—no matter how logical—will not be fully reflected in the stock price. This is a major problem with small-cap and microcap stocks, and I can't tell you how many times I have heard this refrain from a frustrated CEO of a small company who cannot understand why Wall Street does not properly value his or her company.

When I first recommended Rehabcare Group, I asked an officer of the company why his stock was trading at a measily 11 times earnings while most specialty health care stocks were trading at 25 times earnings or more. The answer, of course, was that other than a couple of regional brokerage firms, no major analyst was following the company. Rehabcare was politely informed that research coverage might be forthcoming if Rehabcare were to do a stock or bond offering; i.e., generate fees as an investment banking client.

It used to bother me when I saw something that seemed obviously bullish to me which was not reflected in the stock price, because I felt I must be missing something. But not anymore. Today, with giant mutual funds and other institutional investors calling the shots on Wall Street, most research is directed toward servicing these mammoth clients. Since most of these large funds cannot traffic in small and microcap stocks, there is no mileage for most research departments in following the smaller companies—therefore, some terrific stories go unreported.

When Fay's was selling off its nondrugstore operations, closing unprofitable stores, taking write-offs, and reducing expenses, these were the classic moves of a company that might be preparing itself for sale—especially in view of the fact that the drugstore industry was rapidly consolidating. But Fay's stock did nothing for a long time, despite the fact that it was trading far below its takeover value, until the company finally announced that it was talking to JCPenney about a possible buyout.

Getting back to Genovese Drug Stores, after a smattering of drugstore takeovers over the past year and a half, the drugstore takeover bell was rung earlier this year when Rite Aid announced that it would acquire Revco, a merger that would create the largest drugstore company in the United States. In an interview shortly after announcing the agreement, Rite Aid's chairman carefully spelled out the reasoning behind the agreement, noting that competition and economies of scale would create a powerful incentive for drugstore companies to merge. He compared the coming drugstore merger wave to what was already happening in the banking industry, and said that costs and overhead could be dramatically reduced through mergers.

Although the Rite Aid–Revco merger was not consummated because the Federal Trade Commission believed it was too big a merger, the handwriting was on the wall. Even the FTC said it would look favorably on smaller drugstore mergers because they would theoretically reduce health care costs by reducing overall costs. Therefore, it seemed reasonable to assume that some of the smaller drugstore companies could become buyout targets, and Fay's turned out to be a major winner for us.

In my last letter, I noted that there were a number of drugstore companies who are believed to be shopping for acquisitions. Rite Aid has to be on the list, since they tried to acquire Revco. JCPenney is probably also on the list, since the takeover of Fay's indicates that JCPenney is looking to build its Thrift Drug unit into a major player. A recent Tucker Anthony research report on Arbor Drugs suggests that Arbor has the cash and the infrastructure to handle an acquisition. *Melville Corp. will soon be spinning off its CVS Drug Store chain as a separate company, and analysts believe CVS will attempt to get bigger through acquisitions.* Other potential buyers include Walgreens, Eckerd, and Longs.

Also, in another interesting development, the chairman of Revco recently told Dow Jones that he expects drugstore industry consolidation to continue. Now that the Rite Aid–Revco merger is off, *Revco's chairman told Dow Jones that Revco now plans to be an aggressive buyer itself of smaller drugstore chains.*

So, we have a very large list of potential buyers out there, and it seems obvious that some of the smaller drugstore companies will be receiving takeover bids. Other than Genovese Drug Stores, who are some of the other candidates?

If you want to look further afield, consider Big B, a 383-store chain. After the Fay's takeover, Big B's executive vice president said that Big B has "no interest in entertaining acquisition offers" and that the company is trying to expand on its own. That could mean that Big B is also on the list of possible buyers of smaller chains, but analysts still consider Big B to be a potential target itself.

This lengthy quote illustrates what is meant by the term "road map." Here was the analysis, from beginning to end. Any investor who read this analysis had two choices: It either made sense or it didn't. If it made sense, the logical move was to buy Genovese and some of the smaller drugstore chains. If it did not make sense, the logical move was to take a pass on the whole idea.

Genovese stock languished for 2 years after this report before tripling on the JCPenney takeover bid. And it is not as though the Genovese story did not receive any public attention. During 1996, *BusinessWeek's* "Inside Wall Street" column had two articles on the prospects of a buyout of Genovese Drug Stores by JCPenney and the takeover of Fay's. Here was the complete story on Genovese Drug Stores—the road map, if you will—in an international magazine read by millions of people, brought to you by an analyst who had just predicted the takeover of Fay's in the very same publication—and yet, Genovese stock continued to languish for 2 years, *right up until the takeover bid forced the stock to triple.*

It once again proves that you can be 100 percent correct and the stock market can be 100 percent wrong when it comes to analyzing the prospects of small-cap and microcap stock with no analytical coverage. If you are going to operate in this sector of the stock market, you will have to learn to trust your instincts, learn to maintain the courage of your convictions, and believe that in this sector of the market there is no such thing as an "efficient stock market," which means you'll be able to see things that the Wall Street pros are completely overlooking.

As I've noted more than once, though it is worth repeating: It's difficult to sit with a stock doing nothing or drifting lower—especially when you see evidence that this stock should be selling at a substantially higher price. But when this happens, you have to stick to your guns—as long as the original "road map" is intact.

There is no other way to do it.

A few weeks later Big B—the drugstore company that had publicly stated that it would remain independent—accepted a takeover bid from none other than Revco, the company that had publicly stated that it would start shopping for smaller drugstore companies.

Big B was still controlled by the founding Bruno family, a sign to look around for another small drugstore company with a large block of stock owned by the founding family. If the founders of Fay's and Big B were willing to sell the companies they had built, the same reasoning should apply to other small drugstore companies with large blocks of stock still owned by their founders. Genovese was definitely in this category, which only served to flesh out the Genovese road map. A brokerage firm report had mentioned Arbor Drugs, a Michigan-based drugstore chain, as a potential buyer of other companies. *But based on Arbor's small size and on the fact that the founding family controlled a large stake in this company, Arbor Drugs was likely to be acquired itself.*

In September 1996, following the Big B takeover, Arbor Drugs was added to my recommended list at $8¾. And in February 1998, Arbor Drugs accepted a $23 per share takeover bid from CVS.

CASE STUDY: SMITH FOOD & DRUG CENTERS

In November 1996, browsing through a list of 13-D "beneficial owner" filings in *Barron's* revealed that Transamerica Corp., the giant insurance company, was accumulating shares of Smith Food & Drug Centers (SFD) on the open market. Research indicated that SFD was a potential superstock takeover candidate.

SFD operated in two industries where takeover activity was rampant: supermarkets and drugstores. The company operated 147 food and drug centers mostly in the southwestern United States. Interestingly, SFD had just closed down its 34-store California operations, which resulted in a large restructuring charge. Does that sound familiar? Here was a company that looked like it might be getting its house in order in preparation for selling itself. At the same time, SFD was buying back large chunks of its own stock on the open market—another Telltale Sign, and a strong signal that a company believes its stock is undervalued.

What initially drew my attention to SFD was the open market buying by Transamerica, which had recently raised its stake to 16.42 percent of the company, paying as high as $28.25 for SFD shares. But further research revealed something far more interesting. About 14 percent of SFD was owned by the investment/buyout firm of Yucaipa Cos., which had already been involved in several supermarket deals. Yucaipa owned a controlling interest in supermarket giant Fred Meyer Inc. and also owned stakes in publicly traded Dominick's Foods, a Chicago-based supermarket chain, and Ralph's, a private supermarket company. Clearly, Yucaipa was the sort of sophisticated outside investor who would have the ability to "cash out" of its stake in SFD at the right time and the right price if it chose to do so. Since SFD was operating in two takeover-lively industries, Yucaipa Cos. would certainly be aware of the fact that SFD might be sold at a very rich price should the company be put up for sale.

A look at SFD's long-term chart was also encouraging: SFD had been locked in a fairly well-defined price range with an upper resistance level of $30 for nearly 2 years. Now, with takeover activity picking up in both the supermarket and drugstore industries, SFD looked like it was about to finally break out above that $30 resistance area. In other words, SFD's chart had the look of a pending superstock breakout. This fact, combined with the open market buying by Transamerica, the 14 percent ownership of Yucaipa Cos., and the recent restructuring and elimination of unprofitable operations, all indicated that SFD was a takeover candidate.

In November 1996, SFD was added to my recommended list at $29½.

Less than 6 months later, in May 1997, SFD soared to $49 per share, following a takeover bid from none other than Fred Meyer Inc., which was controlled by Yucaipa Cos.

Ultimately, Dominick's Foods—the other publicly traded super-market company, which was partially owned by Yucaipa Cos.—also received a takeover bid. Remember, I began browsing through those 13-D filings in *Barron's*, which resulted in a single piece of information involving Transamerica's purchases, and that touched off some research. That research yielded additional clues, which eventually led to information about Yucaipa Cos.

That's an example of why it pays to browse.

LESSONS LEARNED

Lesson number one is this: If you believe a takeover wave is about to strike a particular industry, and if you're on the lookout for potential takeover targets, you should concentrate on smaller to mid-sized companies because they will be the most vulnerable to takeovers. This stands to reason because the economies of scale being achieved through takeovers will tend to make it more difficult for smaller companies to compete—and this is one reason why these small companies may decide to link up with a larger company.

The second lesson is to look for companies in a takeover-lively industry that appear to be transforming themselves into "pure plays." Fay's was a perfect example of this approach; so was Genovese Drug Stores. You should pay particular attention to companies that are selling off noncore assets, since this is often a sign that a company is preparing to sell itself.

The third lesson is that any company that operates in a takeover-lively industry and is taking restructuring charges or implementing cost-cutting measures or closing down marginal or unprofitable operations is also a candidate for putting a "For Sale" sign on the door. Think of restructuring, cost-cutting, and other measures in the same way you would think of a property owner doing some cosmetic work on a home or building that is about to go on the market.

The fourth lesson, all things being equal, is that you should take special note of companies in which a large block of stock (say, 10 percent or more) is held by a single shareholder—especially an outside shareholder who would recognize when the time is right to maximize the value of an investment. Try to put yourself in the place of the large shareholder—try to think as that shareholder would think. If that shareholder, even if he or she is a founder of the company, has been sitting with a stagnant stock for a long period of time and suddenly finds that a takeover wave is sweeping the industry and large premiums are being paid for buyout candidates, there will be a strong temptation for that large shareholder to "seize the moment" by cashing out.

Finally, look for superstock chart patterns. Pay particular attention to smaller companies that are bumping up against well-defined, multiyear resistance levels. Any stock that is about to break out above a resistance level that has contained the price for 1 year or more is trying to tell you that circumstances have changed for the better. When you see a chart pattern like this, combined with one or more of these other characteristics in a stock whose industry is undergoing consolidation through takeovers, chances are you have a live superstock candidate on your hands.

Keep in mind that it may be one isolated observation that leads you into a treasure trove of superstocks. In the case of the drugstore industry, the single catalyst was noticing comments of the Rite Aid chairman when he explained why he was making a bid for Revco. After considering his reasoning, the conclusion was that more drugstore takeovers were likely. That observation led to Fay's, a pure play in the making, which led to Genovese Drug Stores—and so on.

One observation will lead you to the next; one clue will lead you to another. As long as you know what characteristics to look for, you will find that this sort of new paradigm thinking will open new doors and lead you down paths where you will encounter your share of superstocks and takeover candidates.

CHAPTER FIFTEEN

Using Charts

The market feels what cannot be observed. It is continually alerting us to those things which are not readily foreseeable.

A.J. Frost

The benefits of stock charts is that they can often lead you into territory you did not suspect. If you recognize the sort of chart patterns that often precede significant moves in stocks, and if you spend some time browsing through chart books, you will find your attention drawn to companies you did not even know existed—often with highly profitable results.

The late A. J. Frost, a veteran stock market analyst, had it exactly right when he said that the collective wisdom of the market is usually ahead of the curve. The reason for this is that whenever new information emerges, it is axiomatic that someone, somewhere, will get around to acting on that information by buying or selling stocks. If an industry is in the doldrums and harbingers of a new, positive trend begin to emerge, someone will be the first to get wind of it. And, as the information becomes more widely disseminated, a light-bulb will go on in somebody's head and a bullish bet will be placed on this trend through the purchase of stock that will benefit from this trend. Long before the analysts get wind of the change for the better—and certainly long before individual investors become aware of it—the stocks that will benefit will be bid higher, and Telltale Signs will emerge to be noticed and interpreted by investors who are familiar with chart analysis. *This is the most important thing charts can do for you:* They can draw your attention to a great stock that you would otherwise never have noticed.

This chapter will describe to you the specific chart pattern called a "superstock breakout" pattern. This chart pattern involves a stock that is breaking out to the upside above a very well-defined, multiyear resistance level. *Resistance level* is a price level that has contained at least three previous attempts to move higher over a period of at least 1 year. Each time a stock attacks the resistance level, sellers step in and offer stock for sale, causing the stock to retreat. The stock falls back, regroups, and moves up toward the resistance level again. Selling reappears, overwhelms demand, and the stock falls back again.

The more often a stock attacks this resistance level and fails to penetrate it, the more significant it becomes when the resistance level is finally penetrated. Once this breakout occurs, it is a sign that demand has overwhelmed supply and the stock should be able to move significantly higher.

The significance of a breakout from a "superstock breakout" pattern is that it usually means something has changed significantly for the better. For some reason, demand has increased to the point at which it is finally able to penetrate the supply of stock for sale at the resistance level. Either the sellers have backed off or have been exhausted, or the buyers are so certain that something bullish is taking place that they are undaunted by the fact that they're buying stock at levels that have contained every previous rally attempt.

Either way, a breakout above a multiyear resistance level is usually a sign that a stock is going to move significantly higher.

The best way to introduce you to this type of chart pattern is to start with an actual example.

In late 1993 and early 1994 there was an emerging trend toward health care takeovers. In January 1994 we wrote that "if there is one clear trend developing in the takeover area right now, it is this: Hospital companies are looking to get bigger by acquiring smaller hospital companies, and they are also looking to broaden their health care services by 'vertically integrating,' or acquiring companies that provide other types of health care."

CASE STUDY: SALICK HEALTH CARE

Browsing through charts of every small hospital and "specialty health care" company in search of the "superstock breakout" pattern just described, a stock called Salick Health Care (SHCI) popped up. Its chart pattern had that of a potentially powerful superstock breakout pattern (Figure 15–1).

Based on its chart pattern, Salick Health Care was exactly the sort of specialty health care company that could get caught up in the trend toward health care takeovers. A close look at this chart illustrates the classic superstock breakout formation: In early 1992 Salick moved up to the $17 area, then fell back to around $9. From there Salick launched another attack on the $17 resistance area, getting as high as $16¼ in January 1993. Sellers won that battle once again, and Salick dropped back down to the $10 area. By summer 1993, Salick was

Figure   15–1

Salick Health Care (SHCI), 1992–1994

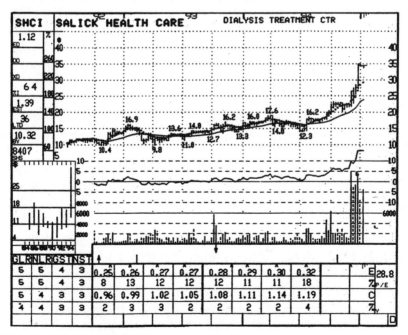

Source: Courtesy of Mansfield Chart Service, Jersey City, NJ.

attacking that $17 resistance area again, and once again the stock retreated—but this time the buyers stepped in just below the $14 area. In early 1994 the stock was in the process of making its fifth attempt at a breakout in the multiyear resistance area near $17.

The strong suspicion was that eventually Salick would be able to break through the resistance level. Why? *Because something fundamental had changed.* Takeovers of "specialty health care" companies were picking up steam, and a company like Salick, which provided cancer treatment and kidney dialysis services, was in the right place at the right time. This chart was indicating that buyers "in the know"—i.e., buyers who either knew or strongly suspected that Salick would ultimately become a takeover target as part of this ongoing trend, were stepping up to the plate and bidding more aggressively for the stock.

When you have this sort of chart pattern in a stock that is part of an industry group where takeovers are proliferating, there is a very strong probability that you have an emerging superstock takeover target on your hands.

As 1994 progressed and a number of specialty health care takeovers took place, it seemed apparent that Salick Health Care was precisely the sort of company that could attract a takeover bid. Yet, after breaking out above the key resistance area near $17, Salick reversed course and fell back to the $14 area once again. In April Salick had strong support in the $14 to $16 area on any decline. It was not expected that Salick would drop back below the breakout area—but it did, providing one last buying opportunity to those who believed in the message of the chart and also in the premise that specialty health care companies like Salick had an excellent chance of becoming takeover targets.

There is no problem so vexing, to an investor, as a stock that seems to have everything going for it that suddenly turns against you. It would be neat to be able to invest according to a set of rules that would enable you to limit your losses. The cold reality is that no such rules exist, and anyone who purports to provide you with them is selling you a bill of goods. No matter how careful you are, no matter how accurate your original analysis, no matter how talented a chart analyst you may be, there will always be times when you are 100 percent correct and you have just purchased a stock that will make you a lot of money. But before that scenario plays itself out, you may have to endure a 20 percent, 30 percent, or even a 50 percent decline in the stock price.

If you insist on limiting your losses to 10 percent, you will be "stopped out" of ultimate winners. Even limiting your losses to 20 percent is dangerous because when you are dealing with relatively thinly traded small-cap stocks, you can experience a 20 percent move for no reason other than general market weakness or perhaps the fact that a single investor is selling a position. In other words, the weakness may have nothing to do with the company and the premise on which you have made the investment.

There is no easy answer to this problem. The bottom line is this: If a stock starts going against you, you should know two things. First, is the original premise on which you based your decision to buy still intact? And second, where is the support level on the chart— i.e., where can this stock reasonably be expected to meet buying support so you can add to your position at an intelligent level? And if your original premise was correct, you will ultimately increase your profits down the line.

In the case of Salick Health Care, the logical support zone was $14 to $16. In July 1994, Salick Health rose sharply from its support zone near $14 on news that the company had signed an agreement to provide cancer treatment services to a large Health Maintenance Organization in Miami.

By August 1994, Salick Health was once again threatening to break out above that long-term resistance area, and in September the stock finally did break out, in a major way.

The ultimate outcome of this recommendation: In December 1994, Salick Health Care soared to $35 per share on news that British pharmaceutical giant Zeneca Group had offered to acquire Salick at $37.35 per share. That takeover bid resulted in a gain of 118 percent in less than a year for those who purchased Salick at the original recommended price of $16.

And how did I manage to unearth a little-known company like Salick Health Care as a takeover target? Was I an expert in the health care industry? Did I have spreadsheets and computer analysis of the latest trends in specialty health care? Was I some sort of expert on cancer treatment or kidney dialysis? The answer to all of these questions, obviously, is no. This stock had a potential superstock breakout pattern that was instantly recognizable because it had worked a hundred times before. By determining that there were likely to be takeovers in the specialty health care stocks, I searched for a super-stock breakout pattern and found it.

That's how I did it—and that's how you can do it too.

CASE STUDY: ROHR, INC.

Investors are like children on a playground. They rotate from one ride to another: from slides and swings to teeter totters. Every piece of market "equipment" gets its use.

Terry R. Rudd
1929 Again

Every dog has its day, and any momentum player can tell you which dog is having its day in the sun at any given time.

But the trick, at least in terms of superstock investing, is to fig-ure out which lucky dog will be next.

The "superstock breakout" chart pattern signifies that some-thing has changed in the fortunes or prospects of a company. This pat-tern involves a well-defined resistance level that has stopped every price advance for at least the past year, and preferably longer. Finally, when a stock is able to break through this long-term resistance level, a sustained and significant price advance becomes highly likely.

The fact that a formerly formidable resistance level has been broken to the upside usually signifies that something has changed for the better; i.e., a paradigm shift is taking place.

When Salick Health Care finally broke out above its long-term resistance area near $17 to $17¼, that breakout was a clue that this stock was responding to a new and very positive development, a development that was able to push Salick Health Care above a wall of selling (resistance) that had contained every rally attempt over a period of 2 years. In the case of Salick, that positive development was this: A takeover wave was unfolding among specialty health care stocks, just like Salick, and the stock market was taking this new reality into account. Prior to this takeover wave, Salick had been a little-known health care company whose stock had been locked in a wide trading range between $9 and $17 for nearly 3 years.

Sellers were quite content to sell Salick every time the stock approached the $17 area, and buyers were very confident in buying Salick each time the stock fell toward the $9 to $10 area. The stock was trading on its earnings, growth prospects, the outlook for its industry, and the general stock market environment, just like every other stock.

But the emerging takeover wave in the specialty health care stocks changed the paradigm for Salick. That takeover wave transformed Salick from an obscure cancer treatment/kidney dialysis provider into a potential takeover target. And when Salick became a potential takeover target, its stock price was removed from the straightjacket of analyst coverage and earnings estimates and placed into a new paradigm: the superstock paradigm. In this paradigm, the question was no longer what Salick might earn in the next quarter. The question was: What would Salick Health Care be worth as a business to a potential buyer? And based on this new paradigm, Salick's supply/demand equation shifted.

That breakout above the $17 to $17¼ resistance area was a clear signal that Salick was being perceived in a different light by Wall Street.

Here is another example of how a superstock chart breakout— and nothing but a superstock breakout—led me to the takeover bid for Rohr, Inc.

In June 1995 an emerging takeover trend was taking place in the defense/aerospace industry. Scanning through the charts in the Mansfield Chart Service, which are arranged by industry groups, indicated that multiyear breakout pattern. Rohr, Inc., a company that manufactured and supplied parts used by most of the major aircraft manufacturers, had a chart pattern that showed a classic superstock breakout pattern. The charts (Figures 15–2 and 15–3) showed a well-defined, multiyear resistance area near $13 and a clear breakout above that level. That long-term resistance area first manifested itself in late 1992 and early 1993, and again in 1994 and early 1995. Beginning in late 1993, Rohr also showed a series of rising bottoms, indicating that buying was coming in at progressively higher levels. For the past few years Rohr had been a stock market "dog," trying on five separate occasions to break out above the $11 to $13 area and failing every time. But the stock had finally managed to break out, *strongly suggesting that this was a dog about to have its day.*

F i g u r e   15-2

Rohr Inc. (RHR), 1991–1993

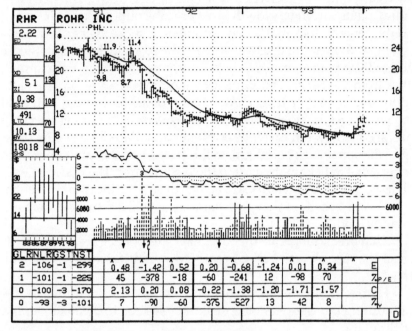

Source: Courtesy of Mansfield Chart Service, Jersey City, NJ.

Rohr was added to my recommended list. Much like an electrocardiogram can tell an experienced physician what is going on inside a patient's chest, there are certain chart patterns that can tell an experienced chart analyst that there is something important going on beneath the surface of an apparently uninteresting stock.

Just a few weeks after the initial recommendation, an outside beneficial owner—an investor named Paul Newton of North Carolina—had accumulated a 5.2 percent stake in Rohr.

Within a year of the original recommendation, based on its superstock breakout pattern, Rohr had soared from $13 to $23¾. Then something interesting happened: Rohr reported an unexpected quarterly loss, the result of *restructuring charges*. This was one of the Telltale Signs of a developing takeover situation in a company that operates in a consolidating industry that decides to write off its past mistakes, "clearing the decks," so to speak, for future positive earnings reports. If you are

F i g u r e   15–3

Rohr Inc. (RHR), 1993–1995

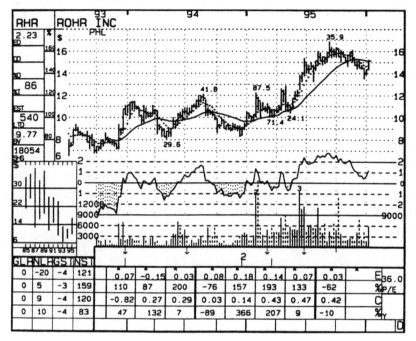

Source: Courtesy of Mansfield Chart Service, Jersey City, NJ.

running a company that you perceive to be a takeover candidate, and you want top dollar for your shareholders, one strategy to make your company more appealing is to get the disappointments that may be lurking beneath the surface out of the way and safely behind you.

As Fay's, Genovese Drug Stores, and others demonstrated, the stock market usually takes news of an unexpected restructuring charge at a sparsely followed company as a negative—but the market's initial reaction is often completely mistaken.

Rohr shares dropped from around $22 to as low as $16 on this news, then bounced back to the $18 to $19 area. Within a few weeks Rohr insiders had gone into the open market to purchase shares on this price decline, another Telltale Sign.

As a rule of thumb: When corporate officers and directors purchase shares in their own company on the open market immediately following a negative surprise that seems like a one-time, nonrecurring item, it is usually a sign that the stock market has overreacted in a negative way and that the news from there on will be considerably better.

In the case of Rohr, this combination of restructuring charge and the insider buying that took place on the dip in the stock price were two excellent omens that the original "road map" remained intact.

Rohr shares eventually fell as low as $14 following the restructuring write-offs and the quarterly loss. Just several months later, though, Rohr roared back to $21 following a better-than-expected earnings report—which is precisely what you would have expected in light of the insider buying following the previous earnings report. That insider buying provided a road map to Rohr's value—in other words, the insider buying provided the confidence to hang in there and not give up the ship simply because Wall Street was taking a panicky short-term view of the situation.

The ultimate outcome of this recommendation, which all began with a superstock chart breakout: *In September 1997, Rohr soared to $33 a share following word that the company had received a takeover bid.*

CHAPTER SIXTEEN

The Domino Effect

Back in the 1960s, when the United States was gradually immersing itself into the morass that became the Vietnam War, there was a lot of talk about the "Domino Effect." This was a geopolitical theory under which a Communist takeover of one country in Southeast Asia would eventually lead to other countries in that region falling under Communist domination, one by one, like a series of falling dominoes.

The Domino Effect may or may not be valid in geopolitical terms, but it can work on Wall Street. And one way to uncover future superstocks is to pay close attention to industries where merger activity is picking up, especially among the smaller players in the industry.

The Domino Effect works best in industries dominated by three or four large players, followed by perhaps 5 to 10 smaller companies that are dwarfed in size by the industry leaders. The drugstore industry (see Chapter 14) was an excellent example of the Domino Effect in action.

CASE STUDY: VIVRA AND REN-CORP. USA

Another example was the kidney dialysis industry, an industry that led to three superstock takeovers over a period of 2 years. *And once again, it all started with a superstock breakout pattern.*

By now you will probably see familiar signs in the chart of Vivra (Figure 16–1). Here is that superstock breakout pattern again: a well-

Figure 16–1

Vivra (V), 1992–1994

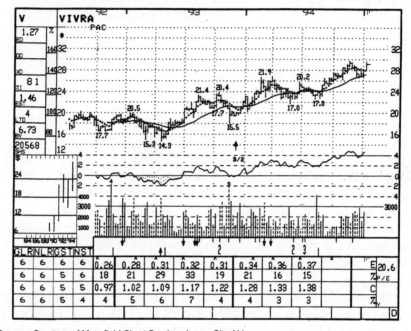

Source: Courtesy of Mansfield Chart Service, Jersey City, NJ.

defined, multiyear resistance level with a recent series of rising bottoms, indicating that buying pressure is coming in at progressively higher levels. In Vivra's case, the key price level was around $24–$26. As a kidney dialysis company, Vivra fell into the general category of specialty health care—an area where takeover activity was very lively.

Vivra was added to my list of recommended stocks at $24. Fourteen months after that initial recommendation, it was trading at $36. Vivra had completed its superstock breakout and forged relentlessly higher. By this time Salick Health Care—which also operated some kidney dialysis facilities, you will recall—had received its takeover bid. The Salick bid, combined with the bullish performance of Vivra following the superstock breakout, led me to review the chart patterns of every other small kidney dialysis company. This research led to Ren-Corp. USA.

Ren-Corp. had a "baby superstock" breakout pattern. The major breakout took place when the stock moved above $14½. Had I focused earlier on the kidney dialysis industry in particular, I might have caught Ren-Corp. sooner. But I was a bit late. Still, Ren-Corp.'s chart did show a long-term breakout crossing $14½ and another potential short-term breakout crossing $16⅜.

But Ren-Corp. had something else going for it: *an outside beneficial owner.*

By this time you're probably beginning to understand how you feel when you find a small, analyst-starved company in a consolidating industry with a superstock breakout pattern and an outside beneficial owner. Your heart beats a bit faster and you absolutely know that you have uncovered a genuine superstock candidate! Fifty-four percent of Ren-Corp. it turned out was owned by Gambro AB of Sweden.

By April 1995, Vivra, a larger dialysis company, had seen it stock soar from $26 to $36 during the past five months, but Ren-Corp. had not followed suit. We reported that the reason might have been "due to underexposure in the financial community . . . but if Vivra continues to be one of the best-performing stocks on the NYSE, they'll get around to Ren-Corp. eventually."

This is another example of a phenomenon discussed earlier: The lag time between a major movement in the stock price of an industry leader and other, smaller stocks in that industry has grown longer as the stock market has become more institutionalized. Do you remember Pavlov's dogs? Ivan Petrovich Pavlov was a Russian psychologist who conducted a series of experiments that studied the relationship between stimuli and rewards. Pavlov demonstrated that dogs could be trained in terms of conditioned reflexes, and that they would respond to certain external stimuli by behaving in a certain way.

In the old days (say, prior to the advent of the Index Fund) when an industry leader like Vivra took off to the upside and became one of the top relative strength stocks on the NYSE, the investment community, like Pavlov's dogs, were conditioned to react by marking up the stock prices of every other company operating in that industry, no matter how small, with very little lag time.

These days, if you think of Pavlov's dogs on Valium, it will give you an idea of how Wall Street reacts to the same stimuli. It's almost as though the connecting mechanism is inoperative. The reason is that the markets are so dominated by large, lumbering institutional behemoths that can only deal in large, liquid securities. Therefore, you do not get the same instant reactions you used to get in the smaller-cap stocks. This is all to the good for our purposes because it means individual investors who can see these connections can uncover all sorts of interesting opportunities and also have the time to act on what they have discovered.

And what did Ren-Corp. USA do next? It dropped from $16 to $12, that's what it did. Despite the fact that specialty health care stocks were being taken over left and right, despite the fact that 54 percent of Ren-Corp. USA was owned by a Swedish health care company—despite all of this, Ren-Corp. dropped 25 percent almost immediately after we recommended it.

We continued to recommend Ren-Corp. because the "road map" was intact. Not only was it intact—it had been enhanced. As Ren-Corp. was dropping 25 percent, a news development involving Vivra sent a clear signal that more takeovers were coming in the kidney dialysis industry.

A leveraged buyout group had proposed a merger between Vivra and National Medical Care, a unit of W. R. Grace, which Grace was about to spin off as a separate company. Grace said it was not interested in such a merger, but this proposal is one of those early clues to look for when trying to peg an industry where a takeover wave is about to strike. *It's not just the deals that get done; it's also the proposals or trial balloons that do not get done that can lead you to future superstocks.* (Remember, the frantic takeover wave in the drugstore industry was foreshadowed by the Rite Aid–Revco merger that was never consummated.)

Here we had an announcement that a major leveraged buyout firm wanted to merge the two largest dialysis companies. The idea was rebuffed, but the fuse had been lit. Under these circumstances, "Pavlov's dogs" should have started buying shares in all of the smaller dialysis companies, based on the prospects of a takeover wave in this industry. But as we have seen, Pavlov's dogs were now zoned out on Valium, and from the way they missed this signal on the dialysis companies, they might have been out drinking or munching hash brownies.

In addition to the rumors swirling around Vivra, Dow Jones Service had reported on June 14 that National Medical, in a defensive move, would seek to buy Ren-Corp. USA. In response, Gambro AB, the Swedish company that owned 54 percent of Ren-Corp., issued a denial that it was seeking to sell its stake in Ren-Corp.

Obviously, takeover clouds were rolling in on the dialysis industry.

Meanwhile, Pavlov's dogs had apparently passed out.

The July 3, 1995, issue of *BusinessWeek* ran a story by Amy Dunkin entitled "Plugging Into Merger Mania Without Burning Your Fingers." In that story, I recommended Ren-Corp. USA as a takeover candidate.

On Friday, July 14, 1995, just 2 weeks later, Ren-Corp. USA soared from $4⅛ to $19⅞, or 26 percent in 1 day, following a takeover bid from—what a surprise!—Gambro AB of Sweden!

Ren-Corp., a formerly sleepy and virtually unfollowed dialysis company, had soared from $12 to nearly $20 in a period of 6 weeks—in other words, it had turned into a superstock.

To reiterate how this successful superstock takeover came to my attention in the first place: I had noticed a potential superstock breakout pattern in Vivra, another dialysis company, and that led to further research into this industry. Eventually, that research led to a smaller company that was already partially owned by an outside beneficial owner.

And *that* is how charts can help lead you to exciting new superstock ideas.

CASE STUDY: RENAL TREATMENT CENTERS

What do you do when you suspect that you are about to witness the "Domino Effect" in a particular industry, where one company after another becomes the target of a takeover bid and a new batch of superstocks are in gestation?

The answer: You immediately look around for additional potential "superstock breakout" patterns. Renal Treatment Centers was another company I had never heard of, but by now I'm sure all you need to do is glance at the chart (Figure 16–2) to understand why I recommended this stock.

There it was: A well-defined long-term resistance area near $25 to $26 in a little followed company in a rapidly consolidating industry. A series of rising bottoms, indicating rising demand.

F i g u r e   16–2

Renal Treatment Centers (RXTC), 1993–1995

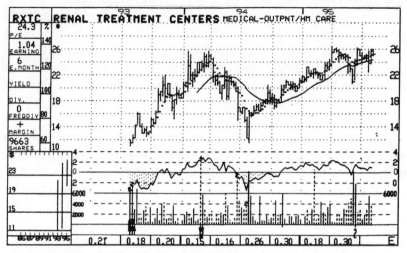

Source: Courtesy of Mansfield Chart Service, Jersey City, NJ.

In July 1995, we recommended Renal Treatment Centers at $23.

The chart in Figure 16–2 emphasizes the significance of a long-term perspective. If the investor had only reviewed the 6-month period from January 1995 to July 1995, which simply shows that Renal Treatment Centers had recently dropped back from $26¼ to around $23—an amazing thing, when you think about it, in light of the fact that Ren-Corp. USA had just received a takeover bid, and that Renal Treatment Centers and Ren-Corp. were nearly identical in size in terms of revenues. It's surprising that this short-term chart of Renal Treatment Centers looked as uninspiring as it did. Again, in the old days when Wall Street's "connecting mechanism" was working properly, a takeover bid for Ren-Corp. would have resulted in strong money flows into a nearly identical company like Renal Treatment Centers. Today, the cause-and-effect process has a much longer lag time, and sometimes the process breaks down completely. This can produce extreme frustration when you see something others don't—but it can also give you time to accumulate more stock, and at lower prices, before the payoff arrives.

Even though the short-term view of Renal Treatment Centers looked like nothing special was going on, the longer-term view clearly showed that this stock was sketching out a potential superstock breakout pattern—you can see the advantage that a longer-term perspective can give you.

In May 1997, Vivra soared to $35 following a takeover bid. The stock had split 3-for-2, so the original recommended price of $24 was adjusted down to $16.

In November 1997, Renal Treatment Centers, which had split 2-for-1 since our recommendation, received a $41.55 per share takeover bid. Take a look at the chart of Renal Treatment Centers in Figure 16–3 and you will see that the original superstock breakout pattern in mid-1995 that prompted the initial recommendation at a split-adjusted $11½ looks like just a distant memory on this long-term

F i g u r e   16–3

Renal Treatment Centers (RXTC), 1995–1997

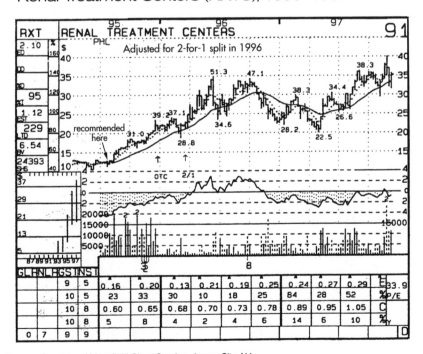

Source: Courtesy of Mansfield Chart Service, Jersey City, NJ.

chart. Again, the importance of having just the right perspective cannot be overestimated.

We recommended three kidney dialysis companies between 1994 and 1997, all of which were taken over and all of which generated huge profits for my subscribers.

How did it happen?

It happened by recognizing a potential superstock breakout pattern in Vivra, which led to focusing on the dialysis industry. A leveraged buyout fund had proposed a merger of Vivra and National Medical Care, and even though that merger never took place, it was a harbinger of merger activity within this industry. And it happened due to anticipation of the "Domino Effect" in this industry: I went on the lookout for other potential candidates with superstock breakout patterns (Renal Treatment Centers) and/or outside beneficial owners (Ren-Corp. USA).

In other words, it happened by using several of the tools described in this book—in particular, with a chart pattern that directed my attention to this industry in the first place.

CHAPTER SEVENTEEN

Merger Mania: Take the Money and Run

*My son, my son, if you knew with what little wisdom
the world is ruled.*

Oxenstierna

What causes the "Domino Effect"? What are the forces that can unleash a takeover wave that literally causes an entire industry to implode, where most of the smaller to mid-size companies are gobbled up by their larger competitors, transforming an industry from a fragmented hotbed of competition to one controlled by a handful of giants?

They are the same forces that have always driven the financial markets, and always will: fear and greed.

When one or two large takeovers in any given industry take place, the fear factor kicks in among other companies within that industry. After a couple of strategic acquisitions occur—sometimes it only takes one—other players within the industry become fearful. Fearful of what? Well, they may be fearful that their competitors, through acquisitions, will achieve economies of scale or greater market share, and that they will become more efficient, competitive, and powerful. Or they may be fearful that their competitors have figured out a strategic approach that they themselves have not thought of yet. Even if they cannot figure out what the heck the reasoning may be behind any given acquisition, they may be fearful that once they *do* figure out the rationale, there may not be any attractive acquisition candidates left to be purchased at a reasonable price.

And, then they become fearful that if they do not play "follow the leader" by acting *now* and buying *somebody*, they will be left out of the parade when the reasoning becomes apparent to everyone, or they'll be forced to pay too much even if they do identify a takeover candidate. And sometimes it is simply *the fear of being acquired itself* that leads a company to take over another company, as an act of self-defense, the reasoning being that if you make yourself bigger, you're less likely to become a target and more likely to be one of the survivors once the consolidation trend runs its course.

I can guess what you are thinking: How can astute business executives making momentous decisions regarding multibillion dollar mergers act on nothing more than emotional reactions to what a competitor is doing? These decisions, you're thinking, must be made in a sober, intelligent, and businesslike manner by serious people who have sound, logical, and well-thought-out reasons for offering to acquire another company.

Well, sometimes that is exactly how these decisions come about.

And sometimes not.

Back in the 1980s, the chief executive officer of a company operating in an industry where takeovers were proliferating made a comment that I will never forget. I had called him to ask if his company had been approached about a possible takeover; I considered the company to be a potential takeover target and I was thinking of adding the stock to my recommended list.

The CEO told me that "we are actually more likely to be an acquirer of other companies; in light of what is going on in our industry, we feel we should be making acquisitions, although, frankly, we are not entirely convinced of the rationale behind those acquisitions. . . . " His voice trailed off, and then he added: "That was off the record, by the way. Don't quote me on that, okay?"

I never did quote that CEO, and his company actually wound up being acquired before it was able to buy someone else. But his comment stuck because he was saying: Everybody else is taking over companies, and if we want to keep up with them and remain independent and not become a target, I suppose we will have to buy somebody, but we're not at all sure why we're doing this and whether these details make any business sense. But what the hell.

In 1993, Merck & Co., the giant pharmaceutical company, decided it would be a good strategic move to acquire a pharmacy benefits manager (PBM). PBMs were obscure businesses at the time. Basically, they acted as agents for employers and their job was to process prescription claims, make deals with drug suppliers, and generally control the costs and manage the health care process for those who didn't want to bother with it. Merck's bright idea was to buy one of these PBMs and to use it to direct business toward Merck products.

Nobody knew at the time whether this would turn out to be a fantastic idea or an absurd idea—but after Merck made its move, other pharmaceutical companies simply had to own a PBM, and PBM stock prices took off because they were perceived to be takeover targets. Shortly after Merck bought its PBM, SmithKline Beecham followed suit, buying Diversified Pharmaceutical Services for $2.3 billion. "Over the past year," SmithKline declared in announcing the takeover, "we have conducted an exhaustive analysis . . . and concluded that the unique alliance announced today positions us to win."

Less than 5 years later, SmithKline would unload its $2.3 billion "unique alliance" for $700 million. But of course, nobody knew this at the time.

Meanwhile, Eli Lilly & Co. was watching its competitors scramble to get into the pharmacy benefits business. At the time of the Merck acquisition, Eli Lilly had not yet even dreamed of buying a PBM. In fact, in a burst of candor, Eli Lilly's chief financial officer said at the time,"We looked at Merck's move and said, 'What the hell is a pharmacy benefits manager?'"

In other words, it was not as though Eli Lilly's strategic thinkers had been sitting around for months, studying their computers and their spreadsheets and musing over the wisdom of strategic diversification through the purchase of a PBM, only to finally feel impelled to make its move following Merck's entry into that business.

The truth was that Lilly was not even thinking along those lines, and the PBM business was not even on the Lilly radar screen.

But that did not stop Eli Lilly from paying $4 billion, or 130 times earnings, for PCS Health Systems on July 11, 1994.

Hot on the heels of Merck and SmithKline, Eli Lilly & Co. had snagged its very own pharmacy benefits manager. Once these two competitors had made their moves, Lilly decided it simply had to get into the PBM business. And so it did.

"We believe," said Lilly, "it's the jewel of those that are out there, and we believe we acquired that jewel at a very attractive price."

Barely 4 years later, Lilly wound up selling its $4 billion "jewel" to Rite Aid for $1.5 billion.

"Our experience," said Lilly as it exited the PBM business, "has been that certain businesses can benefit from new ownership arrangements."

In November 1999, Rite Aid announced that it would attempt to sell PCS Health Systems for a price in the neighborhood of $1.3 billion, which was $200 million less than it paid for the company a year earlier.

There were no takers.

On February 25, 2000, a Rite Aid spokesperson told TheStreet.com that the company had "multiple bidders" for PCS Health Systems. "We need to sell it because we need to pay debt," said the spokesperson. Rite Aid, you will recall, had gone on an acquisition spree during the drugstore takeover mania. The company's overly ambitious expansion strategy combined with accounting irregularities had pummeled its stock, which had plunged from a high of $51⅛ in January 1999 to as low as $4½, a decline of 91 percent—one of the all-time great examples of a respected, predictable company in a stable industry self-destructing by turning into a serial acquirer.

Also on February 25, 2000, *The Wall Street Journal* reported that rival drugstore company CVS was interested in buying PCS Health Systems from Rite Aid for between $800 million and $1 billion—a price that would have been 33 to 46 percent less than Rite Aid had paid a year earlier.

CVS denied that it was interested in buying PCS Health.

Finally, on April 11, 2000, Rite Aid announced that it was unable to sell PCS Health Systems at a reasonable price. "While we will continue to explore opportunities to sell PCS at some point," said Rite Aid's new CEO, Bob Miller, he conceded that the price Rite Aid could get for PCS at the current time was "very depressed."

Rite Aid also announced that it had reached an agreement to restructure a portion of its massive debt load, much of it relating to its purchase of PCS Health Systems. As part of the agreement, J.P. Morgan agreed to convert $200 million of debt into Rite Aid common stock valued at $5.50 per share.

PCS Health Systems would be part of the collateral to secure this new debt restructuring, said Rite Aid.

The saga of PCS Health Systems by this point was beginning to resemble a Wall Street version of "Old Maid"—only this time Rite Aid was finding no takers. And it was all touched off by Merck's decision back in 1993 to diversify into the pharmacy benefits business, which led Merck's rivals to follow suit in a lemminglike stampede that eventually took Rite Aid to the brink of disaster and lopped 91 percent off its stock price.

These stories will help you understand one of the major reasons why the "Domino Effect" occurs: Corporate managers can act like lemmings, just like anyone else. Sometimes a merger wave in an industry is touched off for logical and perceptive reasons, and everybody else in the industry can be jolted into awareness by the brilliance of the initial takeover transaction, which forces them to get into the act before it is too late. And sometimes everything turns out just dandy.

Other times, however, the mad rush to imitate and consolidate is based on less perceptive reasoning—such as the fear that one of your competitors has figured out something you haven't even thought of yet, which means you had better do the same thing, fast, and you can figure it all out later.

So, that is how "fear" can touch off the "Domino Effect."

Then there is the "greed" factor.

It will probably not surprise you to learn that corporate CEOs can have large egos, and it will also not come as much of a shock that some takeovers take place simply because the number two or number three company in an industry had just become the largest company through an acquisition, and therefore the former industry leader decides that it too will have to take somebody over just to regain its status as the top dog. Or it may simply be a case of an executive with a personal whim to get into a certain business.

In September 1989, Sony, the Japanese electronics and entertainment giant, purchased Columbia Pictures for $3.4 billion plus $1.6 billion in assumed debt. The deal stunned both Hollywood and Wall Street, which felt that Sony had staggeringly overpaid for the motion picture studio, a transaction that represented the highest price a Japanese company had ever paid for an American business. Sony, in fact, had paid $27 a share for Columbia—3.6 times the value of Columbia's stock after the shares were spun off from their former owner, Coca-Cola company, just 2 years before.

When the deal was announced, most observers believed the price to be preposterous. *Vanity Fair* magazine called the acquisition "a comic epic." Forbes magazine called it an example of "unprecedented naiveté."

A source on Columbia's side of the negotiations told authors Nancy Griffin and Kim Masters, who chronicled Sony's Hollywood misadventure in *Hit & Run*, that the price Sony paid for Columbia "had no relationship to the worth of the entity."

But that was only the beginning. Sony also paid $200 million for Guber-Peters Entertainment, a production company that had lost $19.2 million on revenues of $23.7 million in its most recent fiscal year because it wanted the expertise and management services of its owners, producers Peter Guber and Jon Peters.

Under their guidance, Sony/Columbia proceeded to embark on a spending and production spree that culminated in a November 1994 write-off of *$3.2 billion*—a gargantuan loss even by the standards of Hollywood, which knows a thing or two about losing the money of outsiders.

For years afterward, Hollywood insiders, Wall Street analysts, and others who witnessed Sony's colossal miscalculation, have wondered: How could a respected, well-run and experienced company like Sony have made such an error in business judgment?

Finally, in 2000, we got the answer. In a book entitled *Sony: The Private Life*, author John Nathan described how the ultimate decision to buy Columbia Pictures came about. According to Nathan, who was granted access and cooperation by Sony in the writing of his book, Sony's CEO Norio Ohga—who had been the leading proponent of the Columbia takeover—told a meeting of Sony executives in August 1989 that he had a change of heart. Sony's founder and chairman, the revered Akio Morita, responded that he, too, was having second thoughts about the wisdom of buying Columbia.

According to the minutes of that board meeting, the decision was made to withdraw the takeover bid. The minutes read: "Per Chairman, Columbia acquisition abandoned."

But later that evening the Sony executives changed their decision and agreed to go ahead with the takeover of Columbia.

Why?

While Sony executives were having a dinner break, some of the board members overheard Sony's chairman Morita say, softly, "It's really too bad. I've always dreamed of owning a Hollywood studio."

When the board meeting resumed, Sony's CEO—apparently in deference to the emotional desire of his beloved and respected chairman, *who had already concurred with the cancellation of the deal*—told the executives that he had reconsidered the situation during dinner, and now believed that Sony should buy Columbia Pictures after all—assuming, of course, the Sony chairman Morita concurred with his change of heart. Which, of course, he did.

And that is how Sony blundered into the Godzilla of all write-offs.

Size, power, industry leadership, status—even childhood dreams—these are all potential driving forces for corporate takeovers, probably more so than many corporate executives would care to admit.

In September 1995 the *New York Daily News* ran a tiny item that quoted Michael Dornemann, CEO of Bertelsmann AG, the largest media company in Germany and the third-largest media company in the world. The brief quote, which was attributed to the German weekly news magazine *Der Spiegel*, was highly critical of the recent wave of megamergers in the media and entertainment businesses. "From a businessman's point of view," Dornemann told *Der Spiegel*, "I can only say the Americans are crazy to pay such prices."

In the interview, Dornemann said that prices being paid for U.S. media properties were, in the immortal words of Crazy Eddie, insane. He said that the megamergers being crafted were not being engineered for sound business reasons, but because of the huge egos of the media moguls involved and the desire of Wall Street investment bankers to generate feels.

"The big media companies are in a kind of race to see who will have the biggest operation," he said, "and the prices are simply hyped up. This sort of thing will never pay off. I predict that many of these mergers will not last.

"The desire for size and power can be a dangerous secondary motive" for many mergers, Dornemann went on to say. He said that Wall Street investment bankers had learned to use the egos of CEOs to their advantage, prodding them to do deals by playing on a CEO's desire to be the biggest or to simply keep up with a rival. "Do not be fooled," he said. "Wall Street has big interest in having big deals like this. The investment bankers earn good money on such takeovers, *and for that reason they make sure that the necessary euphoria exists.*" That last comment can be taken as as implication that Wall Street's euphoric reaction to certain megamergers, even so-called mergers of equals where no premiums are involved, can be more contrived than real, and that it only serves to encourage the next round of megamergers.

Dornemann also scoffed at the idea that "synergy" (see Chapter 14) can justify sky-high buyout prices—i.e., that producers of programming must absolutely own a network or other distribution outlets, and that cross-promotion among various media properties would enhance the value of the entire enterprise. "History has shown," he told *Der Spiegel*, "that a lot can be justified on the basis of synergy, with very little ultimately achieved."

Which brings us to the investment bankers.

Of all of the forces that can touch off a Domino Effect–type takeover wave in any given industry, the Wall Street investment banking community's insatiable desire for fees must top the list. As soon as any new industry is hit with a significant takeover, investment bankers all over the country start burning the midnight oil in an attempt to play matchmaker, trying to find the perfect target for the perfect buyer. Once they find a potential match, they barrage the potential buyer with unsolicited advice, trying to convince the management of the potential buyer that they must make this or that acquisition, before somebody else does and they are left on the outside of the consolidation window, looking in.

Some of the deals these investments bankers pitch to potential clients will turn out to be winners, and some will turn out to be disastrous mistakes, and it is not always easy to determine at the time which will be which.

But to you, as a superstock takeover sleuth the ultimate outcome of these takeovers is irrelevant: All you will care about is that you own shares in the target company and that someone is offering to pay you a premium for those shares.

Over the years, a curious "spin" on the takeover scene has developed among mainstream Wall Street analysts and institutional money managers: They claim investors are better off owning shares in the acquiring companies rather than the target companies.

I have always suspected that much of Wall Street's support and enthusiasm for the acquiring companies was designed to (1) create buy recommendations for institutions that were more inclined to buy higher-priced, liquid high-capitalization stocks anyway, and (2) keep the stock prices of the acquiring companies going higher so they could continue to use their stock to acquire more companies, and so their rising stock prices would serve as examples and inducements for other companies to do the same, thereby keeping the takeover assembly line humming and keeping those huge investment banking fees rolling in.

In December 1999 a study by the accounting and consulting firm KPMG confirmed that after studying the 700 largest cross-border mergers between 1996 and 1998, 83 percent of these deals failed to produce any benefits to shareholders. "Even more alarming," said KPMG, "over half actually destroyed value."

The shareholders KPMG was talking about, of course, were the shareholders of the acquiring company—the "gobbler" that was supposedly going to manage the assets of the target company better, achieving economies of scale and other miracle efficiencies that would enhance value for their shareholders. KPMG was also talking about the shareholders of companies involved in so-called mergers of equals, where two huge companies simply combine operations, with no premiums being paid to anybody. Based on this, the stock prices of both companies often rise sharply at first, as though something new is about to be created. Remember: "synergy," as in two plus two equals five.

What KPMG demonstrated, however, was that much of the ballyhoo surrounding many of these deals was just a lot of hot air—not a scarce commodity on Wall Street, certainly, but surprising perhaps in this light since so many institutional money managers have bought into the 1960s retread concept of "synergy" hook, line, and sinker. (On the other hand, when you consider that many of today's money managers were not even born in the 1960s, perhaps not so surprising.)

The lesson is this: *The way to make money investing in takeovers is to own shares in a company that becomes a takeover target of another company willing to pay a premium for the target company's stock.*

The big pharmaceutical companies that acted like lemmings and scooped up the pharmacy benefits managers were losers as a result of this strategy, and so were their shareholders. The winners were those investors prescient (or lucky) enough to own shares in the PBMs, which soared in price as a result of the takeover bids.

Some examples of "synergistic" losers:

- Quaker Oats was a loser when it bought Snapple for $1.7 billion in November 1994, and so were its shareholders: Quaker Oats unloaded Snapple for $300 million 2½ years later. The big winners were the Snapple shareholders, who took the money from Quaker Oats and moved on.
- Novell shareholders were losers following that company's purchase of WordPerfect for $1.4 billion in stock in March 1994. Less than 2 years later Novell unloaded WordPerfect for $124 million, but the original WordPerfect stockholders who took the money and ran made out just fine.
- Albertsons stockholders saw the value of their stock plunge when it proved far more difficult than expected to integrate itself with American Stores.

What's the best thing to do when one of your stocks is the subject of a takeover bid and the acquiring company is offering you shares of its own stock and the opportunity to participate in some grand vision of the future as the combined companies create ever greater value in the years to come?

The following rule of thumb has served investors well over the years: If you buy a stock because you believe it is a takeover candidate, and you are fortunate enough to receive that takeover bid, *take the money and run*. Leave the "synergies" and the "economies of scale" and all of the future growth prospects to the Wall Street analysts and institutions who invest on this basis—they may turn out to be right or wrong, but most of the time that will *not* be the reason you bought the target company in the first place, and you should not stick around to find out.

Read on to see what can go wrong after the takeover occurs and the happy bloom of marriage has faded into the reality of everyday business. These are cautionary tales of why it may not pay to buy into the grand strategic vision that often accompanies the press release announcing a takeover bid, and why you are usually better off taking the profit from the takeover and walking away.

CASE STUDY: JCPENNEY AND RITE AID

JCPenney was one of the major acquirers of drugstore companies during one of the greatest examples of the Domino Effect that Wall Street has ever seen. Penney acquired two of my drugstore takeover candidates: Fay's Inc. in July 1996 and Genovese Drug Stores in December 1998. In each case, these target companies chalked up big gains for my subscribers, who were then faced with a choice: Should they simply take their profits and move on, or should they accept shares in JCPenney as a long-term play on the benefits of consolidation in the drugstore industry?

At the time it seemed to make sense to go along for the ride, hoping that JCPenney would continue to be a growth stock as it wrung new profits out of its growing collection of drugstores and used those stores to complement its department store operations. Remember, when drugstore consolidation was sweeping Wall Street, it seemed to make all the sense in the world to everyone involved, and there was little reason to doubt that the strategy of combining smaller chains would reap major benefits.

The "guru" of this line of thinking was Martin L. Grass, chairman and CEO of Rite Aid, who never missed an opportunity to explain to the media and to Wall Street the reasoning behind drugstore takeovers. Indeed, it was an interview with Mr. Grass and his vision of drugstore consolidation that led to my recommendation of several small drugstore stocks as takeover candidates in the first place.

"Drugstore consolidation is going to continue," Grass told *The Wall Street Journal* on September 12, 1996, "because the economies are overwhelming. The smaller chains can't survive as independent companies. The independent operators are doomed."

Shortly before his own company was acquired by JCPenney, a district manager of the Eckerd drugstore chain waxed enthusiastic about the new avenues of marketing that would be available to chains with larger data banks of customers: "Say a brand new medicine comes out that is just far superior to anything that is on the market," he said. "We could be able to look at our customer base and see who might be better served by this new medication. We would inform those people, 'Hey, there's a new change on the horizon. Ask your physician about it.'" Larger customer bases would provide the drugstore consolidators more information on medical histories and therefore create new and innovative marketing possibilities. "If one store serves a large number of diabetics," *The Journal* said in 1996, "the chain can establish special services at the location." In January 1997, *The Journal* ran another story on the logic behind drugstore consolidation, explaining that "mergers provide big chains with strong market share, and thus clout, in negotiating more beneficial prescription prices with managed care companies. Acquisitions can also bring attractive lists of prescription customers to whom other products can be marketed. They also permit buyers to slash operating costs in the chains they pick up, thereby increasing their own efficiency."

A warning signal—and a prescient one, at that—was also sounded in *The Wall Street Journal's* January 2, 1997, story on the merger mania in the drugstore industry. The mergers, it was noted, "do not address a range of endemic problems for drugstores, from their general laziness about marketing to their typically lackluster service and staff."

So, here was the choice faced by Fay's and Genovese stockholders when JCPenney offered to exchange Penney shares for these companies: Should I sell and take the profit? Or should I take JCPenney stock and become a part of Penney's growth strategy in the drugstore industry?

There were two ways to look at it. If you owned both Fay's and Genovese because you wanted a long-term investment in the drugstore industry, and you had been pleasantly surprised by takeover bids, perhaps you would have decided to accept JCPenney shares and hold for the long term so your portfolio would continue to be exposed to the drugstore industry. That would have been a sensible point of view, although it probably would have made more sense to own a "pure play" drugstore company rather than a company weighed down by slower-growing department stores.

On the other hand, if you had purchased Fay's and Genovese Drug Stores strictly because you believed they were superstock takeover candidates—and if you turned out to be correct—why would you want to exchange these stocks for shares in JCPenney? The original premise had proven correct, both companies became takeover targets and substantial profits had been made. Why take a leap of faith and become a long-term investor in JCPenney?

The outcome of this story can be seen on a JCPenney stock price chart: Penney shares performed miserably, falling from a high near $70 in early 1998 to below $20 by year-end 1999. Along the way JCPenney cut its dividend nearly in half.

On February 24, 2000, JCPenney announced that it would close 289 of the Eckerd drugstores it had acquired, along with 45 department stores, resulting in $325 million in charges.

By mid-April, JCPenney shares were trading under $13—down 81 percent from their high in early 1998. In September 2000, JCPenney cut its dividend again. It also announced that it would close 270 Eckerd drugstores and that it would report a quarterly loss due in large part to its underperforming drugstore operations. By that time its stock had fallen to $9.

Meanwhile, as we have just seen, Rite Aid, the drugstore addict that had led the way toward the industry's consolidation, had become a basket case and investors were beginning to wonder whether the entire premise of the takeover wave that had engulfed the industry was flawed. (Keep in mind that you would not have needed to even ponder this question had you simply taken the profits on your drugstore takeover targets and used it to buy a cottage on the lake, where you could have sat and pondered something more pleasant.)

Rite Aid's problems, you see, were not confined to PCS Health Systems.

Rite Aid discovered that cost-cutting and"efficiencies" sometimes impacted customer service—often with disastrous results. Customers of drugstore chains acquired by larger companies began to notice a distinct reduction in the quality of service, and many began to shop elsewhere. (Some of the big banks discovered the same thing following acquisition sprees in the mid-1990s: Sharply reducing customer service at acquired banks was a quick way to cut costs and improve profit margins, but poor service and customer dissatisfaction eventually took their toll and many of these acquisitions turned out badly.)

Rite Aid also discovered that it is not always the easiest thing to integrate drugstore chains from various sectors of the country into a seamless and efficient operation because it can be difficult to combine operations that bring different business philosophies, different operating heritages, and a distinctly different mix of people along with them.

In particular, Rite Aid ran into trouble with its acquisition of Thrifty-Payless, a 1000-store chain it bought in 1996 for $1.4 billion in Rite Aid stock. Thrifty-Payless was the largest drugstore chain on the West Coast, and its merchandising mix was far different from anything Rite Aid was used to operating. In addition, the Thrifty-Payless chain required extensive remodeling. Rite Aid responded by changing the stores' merchandising offerings, sharply reducing advertising, and generally trying to turn Thrifty-Payless into what Rite Aid wanted—which was Rite Aid stores.

The only problem with this was that Thrifty-Payless customers shopped at Thrifty-Payless because they *liked* Thrifty-Payless and its unique mix of merchandise and style, which had grown to reflect the communities in which the company operated. The result: As Rite Aid changed the stores, sales began to decline.

As the chart in Figure 17–1 illustrates, Rite Aid stockholders— including those who owned the drugstore companies Rite Aid acquired and took Rite Aid shares in return—suffered through a nightmare in 1999, the year in which grand strategy of growth through acquisition so eloquently (and often) expressed by Rite Aid chairman Martin E. Grass began to unravel. Throughout 1999, Rite Aid issued one earnings warning after another, including one infamous announcement that rescinded an earnings forecast that had just been made by its own chairman. Rite Aid told Wall Street that it "should not rely on forward-looking profitability and cash flow information" the company had just recently given to analysts at an October 11, 1999, meeting. Shortly thereafter, Grass resigned, and so did Rite Aid's accountants.

At year-end 1999, the Motley Fool summed up the sorry saga of Rite Aid this way: "The root of the company's problems stems from an aggressive acquisition play that has failed miserably, leaving Rite Aid mired in debt."

Meanwhile, JCPenney's stock price continued to feel the fallout of the Rite Aid debacle. Penney, after all, had been one of the biggest drugstore "gobblers"—and Wall Street, which had cheered on the drugstore merger wave while it was happening, now began to recoil from the entire premise.

Figure   17–1

Rite Aid (RAD), 1998–2000

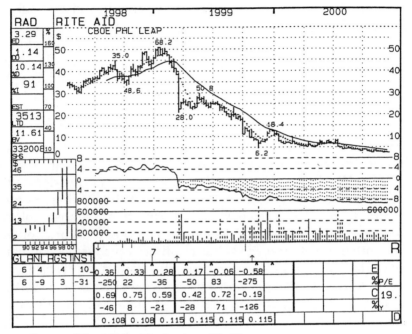

Source: Courtesy of Mansfield Chart Service, Jersey City, NJ.

As a result, *a Fay's stockholder who took JCPenney stock in the fall of 1996 would have seen the value of that stock fall from the $45 to $50 area to below $20 by the end of 1999, a decline of up to 60 percent during one of the greatest bull markets in history, which would have wiped out the bulk of the takeover premium Fay's stockholders received in the first place!*

And a Genovese Drug Stores stockholder who took JCPenney stock in early 1999 would have seen an equally vicious decline, which would have wiped out the bulk of the takeover premium offered to Genovese stockholders in a breathtakingly short period of time.

Meanwhile, those who simply sold their Fay's and Genovese shares following the takeover bids received full value for their stock and were in a position of being able to deploy the proceeds somewhere else, in some other takeover candidate somewhere down the line.

CASE STUDY: THE ALARMING STORY OF PROTECTION ONE

Here's another horror story that illustrates a grand acquisition/diversification strategy gone awry.

Between 1996 and 1998, the security alarm business experienced the Domino Effect as a series of companies—including ADT, Holmes Protection, Alarmguard, and others—were acquired in rapid-fire order. All of these were on my takeover list (see Introduction), and all were taken over one after another.

Among the takeover targets was Protection One (NYSE: POI), which was acquired by Western Resources in July 1997. Protection One was recommended as a takeover candidate in January 1997 at a price of $9½. In July 1997, Western Resources, a midwestern utility, offered to buy 80 percent of Protection One by making a special one-time $7 per share cash payment to Protection One shareholders and then combining Western Resources' own home security operations with those of Protection One, creating a much larger company that could benefit from—you guessed it!—economies of scale.

At the time, I had just had a pleasant experience with Western Resources, which led me into a successful takeover recommendation of ADT Ltd (see Chapter 9). Western was run by David Wittig, who had been lured from his investment banking duties at Salomon Brothers to lead Western Resources into a brave new world of diversification following the deregulation of the utility industry. One of Wittig's first moves was an audacious 1996 hostile takeover bid for Kansas City Power & Light. What made this bid audacious, other than the fact that hostile takeovers in the genteel utility industry were rare, was that Kansas City Power & Light had already agreed to be acquired by a neighboring utility, Utilicorp United. A nasty fight ensued, with charges and countercharges flying all over the place among the three combatants. But in 1997, Western Resources and Kansas City Power & Light reached a friendly merger agreement. That deal unraveled 11 months later, in December 1997, when the stock price of Western Resources got too strong, rising from the low $30s to the low $40s.

As a result of Western's rising stock price, Western's investment bankers decided that Kansas City Power & Light stockholders were getting too good a deal—so the terms were revised.

In light of what was about to happen, this proved to be the ultimate irony.

Western Resources had been trading around $30 a share when 42-year-old David Wittig arrived as its CEO in 1995, charged with transforming Western Resources from a sleepy utility into a lean, mean acquisition machine.

After Western Resources bought and sold a huge stake in home security company ADT in 1996, turning an $864 million profit when ADT was ultimately acquired by Tyco International, Wittig decided that Western Resources' major push into the home security industry would be accomplished through the acquisition of Protection One. Western had previously purchased the home security business of Westinghouse Electric, and Wittig now sought to combine those operations with Protection One and then use the new company as a vehicle to further expand into that business.

The move made strategic sense to almost everybody. Here was a utility company that ran lines into a home and provided a service for which it was paid on a monthly basis, like clockwork. As Western and Wittig saw it, the home security business was little different: An initial marketing push and the onetime expense of installing an alarm system would then yield to a steady stream of "monthly recurring revenues," and it would all have to be supported by the sort of infrastructure that a utility company like Western Resources already had in place. So, the theory went, Western could cross-market its utility services to its home security customers, and vice versa. In interviews, Wittig was talking about further diversifying Western Resources along the same lines into areas such as telecommunications or cable TV.

And so, when Protection One soared from the original recommended price of $9½ in January 1997 to $21 in July of that year, following the Western Resources takeover bid, shareholders faced a choice: Should they simply take the profit and move on? Or should they stick around for the $7 per share cash payment and then hold the ex-dividend shares of Protection One for the long haul, betting that Western Resources, as POI's new majority shareholder, could successfully implement its growth strategy?

The Western Resources strategy seemed like a good one, but with more than 100 percent profit in only 7 months in a stock that had correctly been predicted as a takeover target, the decision was to take the profit and get out of Dodge.

I told my subscribers: "Since I am focusing mainly on takeover candidates, I am going to bid farewell to Protection One. If you were prescient enough to own Protection One, I would suggest a switch to either Holmes Protection or Alarmguard," two other security alarm takeover candidates.

This turned out to be the correct move. Both Holmes Protection and Alarmguard ultimately received takeover bids and the Domino Effect continued to sweep through the security alarm business.

Western Resources, pleased with the reception that its growth strategy had received on Wall Street, promoted David Wittig to chairman and CEO in May 1998. Western's stock price had jumped from $30 when Wittig arrived in 1995 to a high of $48⅞ in March 1998—not bad for a conservative utility company in the midst of metamorphosis.

In October 1998, Western Resources kept the dominoes falling in the alarm industry when its now 85 percent-owned Protection One unit agreed to acquire Lifeline Systems, a company that provided alarm-paging services to elderly people through a nationwide network of hospitals. Lifeline customers wore paging pendants around their necks, which could be activated if they needed medical assistance. A signal would then be sent to a Lifeline Systems control center, which would then alert the nearest hospital to the emergency situation.

To David Wittig, this was a natural offshoot of the home security alarm expansion program that Western Resources had been pursuing through Protection One. In announcing the deal, he also told *The Wall Street Journal* that Western was on the lookout for still more acquisitions outside the electric utility industry, possibly including bottled water companies, which struck me as a dangerous mix with an electric company.

The Wall Street Journal noted that utility companies had tried once before to diversify and "had failed at it in the 1980s, when they bought companies such as savings & loans, a drugstore chain, and even an insurance company." But *The Journal* reported that unlike the past, Mr. Wittig said that "Western is investing in businesses that are similar in terms of the relationships we're having with the customers."

The Journal also noted that Protection One had nearly tripled its customer base since being acquired by Western, *and that it had spent about $1 billion on acquisitions, buying 20 security companies in the U.S. and also overseas in the year since it was bought by Western.*

Meanwhile, Protection One stockholders were beginning to hear alarm bells of their own. Following the $7 per share cash payment, the stock fell from its "ex-dividend" high near $14 throughout 1998. By year-end, the steady price erosion had taken Protection One down to the $8 area. Early in 1999, Protection One shares plunged rapidly, falling as low as $5, before stabilizing in the spring.

Obviously, Wall Street sensed a problem.

By mid-1999, the festering problems finally came to the surface: Protection One announced that its cash flow had turned negative, that it was suffering from a growing rate of customer attrition, that its accounting practices had come under the scrutiny of the Securities & Exchange Commission, that the company would lose $16.9 million in the third quarter, and that it had failed to meet the terms of its banking lending agreements. Then, Protection One terminated its previously announced acquisition of Lifeline Systems.

Finally, in October 1999, Western Resources acknowledged that it had erred in its belief that Protection One would become a vehicle for growth in the security alarm business. "Western Resources has experienced some short-term financial challenges with regard to its Protection One investment," the company said in a press release, which had to be in the running for "Understatement of the Year." Western added that "while the security alarm business generates strong cash flow, it has not generated net income." Therefore, said Western, it was now "considering alternatives" for its 85 percent-owned security alarm business, which had by this time declined to under $2 a share—a sickening 85 percent decline from its $14 peak in less than 2 years in the midst of one of the greatest bull markets of all time.

While Western Resources was "considering alternatives," what alternatives were available to loyal shareholders of Protection One who had decided to hold their shares following the takeover and go along as minority shareholders for the growth ride envisioned by David Wittig and Western Resources?

The sad truth was that there *were* no alternatives anymore, other than taking a tax loss and chalking it up to experience. Like an opportunity that comes along and is then gone forever, the alternative was available only for a brief time when Protection One rose to its ultimate high following the takeover bid. Those Protection One shareholders who seized the alternative had sold their shares on the open market and walked away.

Meanwhile, in the ultimate irony, by December 1999, Western chairman and CEO David Wittig was hosting investor and analyst dinner meetings in New York City trying to drum up support for his badly sagging stock price. Western had plunged 46 percent in 1999 to around $18, and at that low price Western's merger with Kansas City Power & Light—which had been held in regulatory purgatory for nearly 3 years—was now in jeopardy.

Just 2 years earlier the deal had almost fallen apart because Western's stock price had risen too quickly based on Wall Street's perception of David Wittig as an astute deal maker. The terms had been negotiated downward in deference to Western shareholders, who owned an increasingly popular stock and did not want to give too much of it away to Kansas City Power & Light stockholders. Now, the opposite was taking place: Because of the Protection One disaster, Western's stock price had slumped so far that the deal was in danger of coming apart once again.

On January 3, 2000, Kansas City Power & Light announced that it had terminated its merger pact with Western Resources. After nearly 3 years of negotiating, regulatory red tape, and untold millions in legal fees, the Western Resources–KCP&L merger was undone, in large part, by the Protection One fiasco—a takeover that turned out very badly for the acquiring company and its shareholders.

Indeed, as the 1990s drew to a close it was becoming increasingly apparent that it is a lot easier to take a company over than it is to run it in a manner that creates any long-term value for the "gobbler."

But of all the ironic developments that took place during the disastrous diversification adventure of Western Resources, the final plot twist topped them all: On March 29, 2000, 4 years after Western Resources made its first move to diversify out of the utility industry by purchasing its initial stake in ADT Ltd., and less than 3 years after acquiring Protection One, Western Resources announced that it had come to the conclusion that it would be better off as—drum roll, please—*a pure play!*

Proving once again that there is virtually nothing new under the sun, and that every innovative new concept eventually runs its course and recycles itself, Western Resources admitted that its investors would be better off if the company concentrated on a single business and that its grand strategy to become a 1960s style "conglomerate" had been a failure.

In a press release, Western Resources chairman and CEO David Wittig announced that the company would split itself into two companies: an electric utility company named Westar Energy, and another company to be named later, which would consist of everything the company had acquired over the past few years, in an attempt to diversify itself and get its stock price higher.

"We believe," said Mr. Wittig, "that a *pure play electric utility company will unlock the value* associated with our electric assets by providing shareholders an investment opportunity exclusively in our electric utility operations."

The press release stated that Westar Energy, the new "pure play" utility company, would consist of two electric utilities, Kansas Power & Light and Kansas Gas & Electric, which provide electric service to 628,000 customers in Kansas. The nonelectric utility company, which was yet to be named, would consist of Western's 85 percent ownership in Protection One, its 100 percent interest in Protection One Europe, a 45 percent interest in NYSE-listed natural gas transmission company named Oneok (more about this later), and a 40 percent interest in a direct market company called, ironically, Paradigm Direct LLC.

By the time Western Resources decided to change paradigms by going back to the strategy of being a "pure play" (which is what the company was in the first place) rather than a collection of unrelated businesses, Western's stock price was scraping along near its lows under $15, down from a peak of nearly $40 in early 1998 when the initial giddiness over its new relationship with Protection One was still masking the festering problems that would soon come to the surface and cause Western's stock price to unravel.

This press release from Western Resources, meanwhile, was a gold mine of clues, information, and Telltale Signs for superstock sleuths. For one thing, as we have learned, *when a troubled company starts taking steps to return to its roots by jettisoning noncore operations and turning itself into a pure play, its often a sign that the ultimate plan is to sell the company.* This is especially true when the company operates in an industry that is already trending toward consolidation.

In the case of Western Resources, it was a company that had been doing perfectly well as a pure play Kansas-based utility. Had Western just sat there and done nothing but make its utility operations more efficient and profitable, there is a very good possibility that the takeover wave, which struck the utility industry during the late 1990s, would have engulfed Western Resources, much to the delight of its shareholders.

But Western did not want to become a "gobblee"; in fact, the company aspired to be a "gobbler," and it wound up undoing itself and its shareholders by removing itself from its position of being directly in the path of the regional electric utility takeover wave and diversifying into a business—security alarms—that turned out to be a disaster for everyone except the shareholders of Protection One *who decided to take the money and run.*

Now, having come full circle, Western Resources issued a press release that contained three code phrases, or Telltale Signs, that would immediately pique the interest of a superstock sleuth: *pure play, core business,* and *unlock the value.* These three phrases would have immediately aroused the takeover antenna of any investor browsing the financial news who was familiar with the way of thinking you have learned about here.

Western was about to create a new company that consisted solely of two Kansas-based electric utilities—about as pure a play as you can get. Not only that, having produced and directed the utility industry version of *Titanic,* one would have to assume that Western's management would be in no position to fend off a takeover attempt of this new pure play electric utility should some other utility company make an offer for this company once it was separated from the rest of Western's operations. In fact, the press release issued by Western Resources chairman and CEO David Wittig implicitly stated that *pressure from shareholders to create an electric utility pure play was one of the driving forces behind the decision to split the company in two parts.*

So, the logical assumption would be this: It's very possible that separating the electric utility assets was the first step in having these assets acquired, and even if that were *not* the primary purpose of creating the utility pure play, Western's management, having lost most of its credibility with its shareholders, would certainly seem to be in no position to reject a reasonable takeover bid for the newly separate utility company should one ultimately emerge.

In other words: Westar Energy, once it began trading separately, would have to be viewed as a potential superstock takeover candidate—and this stock should have been added to your universe of potential superstocks to keep a close eye on.

On the other side of the equation was the company that would own Western's nonelectric utility assets—temporarily nameless but certainly not without interest to a superstock sleuth, *because one of its major assets would be a 45 percent interest in Oneok (OKE), a NYSE-listed natural gas transmission company.*

A well-trained superstock sleuth—which would be you, by this time—would immediately ask: What is Oneok? How did Western Resources wind up with this 45 percent stake? Is it possible that this newly independent company without a name might try to buy the rest of Oneok or eventually sell its stake to a third party? Or might Oneok try to buy back that 45 percent stake in some way?

To answer questions like these, the best strategy is to go to the 10-K Report (the annual report filed with the Securities & Exchange Commission) of the company whose stock is owned by the outside beneficial owner. The 10-K Report is available by going to the Web site www.freeedgar.com. It might take you a while, but if you browse through the 10-K, which is considerably more lengthy and detailed than the annual reports published for public consumption, you will eventually find a description of how this outside beneficial owner came to acquire its stock.

In the case of Oneok, by checking out the company's most recent 10-K, you would have learned that this company provided natural gas transmission and distribution services to 1.4 million customers *in Kansas and Oklahoma—right in Western Resources' neck of the woods.* And you would also have learned that, in 1998, Oneok acquired the natural gas distribution assets of Western Resources in exchange for Oneok stock—and that is how Western Resources wound up with its 45 percent stake in Oneok. In other words, when Western's diversification-minded management decided to branch out from the utility business, one of its early moves was to sell its natural gas transmission business to Oneok.

In reading the history of this transaction in the Oneok 10-K, you would also have learned that there was a "standstill agreement" between Oneok and Western Resources that prevented Western from increasing its ownership above 45 percent. And you would also have learned that Oneok's stated corporate strategy was to "acquire additional distribution and transmission facilities and other assets," and in fact Oneok had recently announced the $307.7 million purchase of the natural gas processing plants plus the Kansas and Oklahoma transmission systems of a company called Dynergy (DYN). The 10-K revealed that Oneok had agreed to buy Southwest Gas, a natural gas utility serving customers in Arizona, Nevada, and California, in 1999, but that Oneok had recently cancelled the merger agreement.

By checking out the insider trading data on Western Resources and Oneok, you would have learned that Western Resources had been regularly selling off small chunks of its Oneok stake late in 1999.

A superstock sleuth trained to look for situations like this would see several possibilities, *but no clear picture as yet to the ultimate outcome of this situation.* But let's put it to you this way: *This situation would appear to be pregnant with possibilities—and both the Western Resources companies and Oneok should have been immediately placed on the superstock sleuth's list of stocks to monitor just in case future Telltale Signs were to emerge.*

The fact that Western Resources had been selling off some Oneok stock, combined with the fact that Oneok appeared to be a company determined to acquire other companies—a "gobbler," in other words—would seem to make it unlikely that the new Western Resources spinoff would seek to buy the rest of Oneok. This would be especially true in light of the "standstill agreement."

But that would not prevent Western from selling its stake to a third party, which would then bid for Oneok. Or perhaps Oneok might turn around and acquire the new Western spinoff to get that 45 percent stake back. Or perhaps some third party would acquire the Western spinoff to get a stake in Oneok as a prelude to a hostile takeover bid.

Who knows?

The point is this: There were possibilities here, a situation to be monitored just in case one or more additional Telltale Signs were to emerge that might point you toward a clear and logical opinion as to what happened next.

And the best part is, had you been a Protection One shareholder who took the money and ran, you would have had the capital to take a position in one of these stocks if and when further clues emerged which made it seem logical to do so.

On the other side of the equation, those Protection One shareholders who hung on to their shares after the Western Resources takeover by buying into the growth/diversification strategy would have been reduced to wishing and hoping while watching their investments shrink dramatically in value.

The other aspect of this situation to remember is this: You will find, as you utilize the thought processes and strategies outlined for you here, that familiar names will reappear over time, drawing your attention to out-of-the-way news items you may not have noticed had you not been involved with a certain situation at a prior time. Over time, in other words, accumulated experience will become a valuable ally and will in turn lead you to further interesting—and hopefully profitable—situations.

CASE STUDY: HOW MATTEL GOT PLAYED BY THE LEARNING COMPANY

In December 1998, Mattel announced that it would acquire The Learning Company for $3.6 billion in Mattel stock. The Learning Company was a seller of educational software and entertainment programming, including Sesame Street and Reader Rabbit. The proposed acquisition of The Learning Company was viewed as an attempt by Mattel to transform itself from a traditional toy manufacturer into what the company called "a global children's products company." In announcing the acquisition, Mattel called The Learning Company "an excellent strategic fit" and said it would immediately add to Mattel's earnings.

Some observers were not so sure. Among them was Herb Greenberg, columnist for TheStreet.com, who wrote at the time that The Learning Company had attracted an unusually large and sophisticated legion of detractors. These skeptics, said Greenberg, had for some time been questioning The Learning Company's "aggressive accounting." They also believed that The Learning Company was having difficulty moving products, that its distribution channel was clogged with inventory, and that the company was headed for trouble.

Greenberg openly questioned Mattel's judgment in paying $3.6 billion for The Learning Company when the deal was announced. As it turned out, these were the very issues that would shortly return to haunt Mattel and its stockholders.

On October 4, 1999—just 5 months after the transaction was completed—Mattel unleashed a bombshell, disclosing that The Learning Company would lose between $50 and $100 million in the third quarter of 1999 compared to an expected profit. The problems that were surfacing were some of the very issues openly discussed by Herb Greenberg and The Learning Company skeptics before Mattel even arrived on the scene. Yet Mattel went ahead with the acquisition and was apparently blindsided by the problems it had inherited.

Mattel shares, which had peaked near $30 earlier in 1999, plunged 5 points to $11⅞ following the announcement, wiping out over $2 billion in shareholder value in a single day.

The only winners in the Mattel takeover of The Learning Company were those Learning Company shareholders who took the money and ran following Mattel's takeover bid. Those who opted to accept Mattel stock and hold on for the fruits of the synergistic melding of these two companies wound up with huge losses.

However, as in the case of Western Resources–Protection One, the Mattel–Learning Company fiasco also had an ironic ending in which several Telltale Signs emerged.

When a widely publicized acquisition turns out badly, the media generally has a field day, and there seems to be a certain satisfaction in seeing high-paid corporate movers and shakers knocked down a few pegs when they must face the music and admit they have just lost hundreds of millions or even billions of their stockholders' money on an ill-advised acquisition. This can be especially galling when, as in the case of Mattel, the acquisition turns sour in a breathtakingly short period of time.

But as we have just seen in the case of Western Resources and Protection One, the unraveling of an acquisition strategy can provide more than a means for journalists to rake the "gobbler" over the coals; sometimes the final chapter of an acquisition that has gone bad can turn out to be the opening chapter of a superstock story.

The key, as usual, is to *watch for the Telltale Signs*.

In the case of Mattel, soon after its stock collapsed on the news of The Learning Company's losses, a group of Mattel insiders began buying large chunks of stock on the open market. This is a variation of one of the Telltale Signs, which is that when a company announces a big "restructuring" charge or some sort of corporate reorganization—or some other piece of bad news that takes Wall Street by surprise—you should keep an eye out for insider buying, which can often be a clue that the problem will be short-lived and that Wall Street is taking an inordinately short-term point of view.

Shortly after The Learning Company debacle, a massive wave of insider buying began, with several Mattel insiders buying a total of 464,000 shares between October 25 and November 24, 1999, at prices between $13 and $14½.

Nevertheless, Mattel shares continued to fall below $10, even though these insiders—which included Mattel director John Vogelstein, the powerful vice chairman of the investment firm Warburg-Pincus—had paid much higher prices for the stock they purchased on the open market.

In an interview following The Learning Company news, Vogelstein categorically rejected comparisons to Mattel's troubles in the late 1980s, telling a questioner, "This company is not broken. It has a *core business* that is vital and well-run."

"Core business?" By now that term should be music to your ears.

Here was a sophisticated, well-connected Mattel insider who certainly should have had the ability to force the stock market to place a higher value on Mattel shares, which would better reflect its value *as a business*. He was buying stock on the open market and talking about Mattel's "core business."

When you get a situation like this, where a well-known company with a valuable franchise makes a major misstep, you very often wind up with a takeover candidate because there are usually "bottom fishing" turnaround investors lurking around waiting, based on the premise that they can come in, take the company over, and restore it to its former luster.

Also, by February 15 *the American Federation of State, County and Municipal Employees Pension Fund announced on Valentine's Day that it wanted to have a heart-to-heart talk with Mattel's Board of Directors about several matters, including the possibility of dismantling Mattel's takeover defenses. The pension fund owned around 3.7 percent of Mattel's stock.* Here was another Telltale Sign: An outside beneficial owner was getting restless and urging the Board of Directors to take steps and to make Mattel more takeover-friendly.

Nobody cared, and Mattel stock continued to languish below $10.

In March 2000, John Vogelstein had purchased another 100,000 Mattel shares on the open market, this time at a price of $10⅜.

In April 2000, two more insiders had purchased an additional 56,750 shares at prices ranging from $9.69 to $11.12 per share. Also, in April 2000, *Mattel had decided to bite the bullet by selling The Learning Company. The Wall Street Journal* had reported on the morning of April 3 that Mattel would soon announce that The Learning Company was for sale, and estimated that company, for which Mattel had issued $3.5 billion worth of its own stock just a year earlier, would probably fetch between $500 million and $1 billion—which has to rank as one of the most striking examples of how rapidly an acquisition can go bad in the annals of American business.

Later that day, Mattel confirmed that it had retained Credit Suisse First Boston to sell The Learning Company, but Mattel went out of its way to make it clear that it did not intend to sell any of its "core brands."

In other words, Mattel had decided to revert to being a pure play toy company.

One would think that Mattel shares might have sagged on the news that the company would soon lose as much as $3 billion in one year on its acquisition of The Learning Company—but instead Mattel shares jumped 30 percent on this news. Why? Because the Telltale Signs were accumulating, and some investors apparently were beginning to get the feeling that The Learning Company disaster would ultimately be the catalyst that could turn Mattel into a takeover target.

On September 29, 2000, Mattel announced that it would virtually give away The Learning Company by "selling" it to a private company in return for a share in any future profits. In reporting this transaction, the Associated Press called Mattel's acquisition of The Learning Company "one of the worst deals in recent corporate history." This was almost certainly true—unless you were a shareholder of The Learning Company who took the money and ran.

The Mattel–Learning Company saga is important for three reasons: First, it illustrates why it's almost always better to "take the money and run" when a stock you own receives a takeover bid. Second, it shows how accumulated experience with various companies and individuals can lead you to anticipate future developments, which you might perceive in a different light than almost everyone else because of your awareness of Telltale Signs. And third, it illustrates how the seeds of a future superstock can be planted in the midst of a barrage of bad news and ridicule from the financial press, whose incessant harping on what has gone wrong creates the very stock market bargains that can bring you profits in the long run—if you're willing to think "outside the box" when it seems like nobody else around you can.

The list of takeover blunders that occurred in the mid-to-late 1990s could be a book in itself. In 1999 alone, of the 10 worst-performing stocks in the Standard & Poor's 500, at least seven could be traced directly to acquisitions that turned out badly or, at the very least, did not deliver the benefits Wall Street expected: JCPenney, Waste Management, Allied Waste Industries, HealthSouth, McKesson HBOC, Rite Aid, and Service Corp. International.

All of these companies were gobblers that suffered a bad case of indigestion when their grand plans for synergy, economies of scale, or whatever it was that motivated them to make these acquisitions turned out to be off the mark.

As an investor searching for potential superstock takeover targets, you should not underestimate the lemminglike mania that at times can overpower corporate executives. The more you understand the impulsive manner in which decisions like this can be made, the less surprised you are apt to be at the speed and scope at which a takeover wave can engulf an entire industry, turning a highly competitive industry landscape into a barren wasteland consisting of a handful of behemoths with stomach pains.

Remember this: Do not assume that the takeovers that take place in the midst of a lemminglike mania will make any long-term sense, or that these takeovers occurred based on a rational decision-making process. The waste management industry is an example.

CASE STUDY: WASTE MANAGEMENT AND ALLIED WASTE INDUSTRIES

As a group, the waste management stocks were trashed in 1999, tumbling nearly 60 percent. They were led on the way down by the two industry giants, Waste Management and Allied Waste Industries, both of which spent most of 1998 leading the way toward consolidating the garbage industry. The fact that both of these companies turned up on the list of the 10 worst-performing stocks in the S&P 500 one year later tells you all you need to know about how *that* strategy turned out.

The trend toward garbage company takeovers was initiated in July 1998 when USA Waste bought Waste Management in a $19 billion takeover. The new industry giant kept the Waste Management name, and then one month later announced the acquisition of another garbage company, Eastern Environmental Services, for $1.5 billion.

Got it so far? Two megamergers, back-to-back, started the dominoes falling in the waste management industry. Suddenly, little garbage companies were being acquired left and right, and every investment banker on Wall Street was looking for a garbage pickup. In October 1998, Allied Waste announced the takeover of American Disposal Services for $1.1 billion, which everybody on Wall Street agreed was a sound move because of the obvious "economies of scale," and you know the rest by now. On October 21, 1998, just a couple of months before these stocks would enter the record books as one of the worst-performing groups of 1999, *Investor's Business Daily* reported that "analysts continue to see the waste management companies as a safe haven that can be counted on to generate double-digit earnings growth."

On March 8, 1999, Allied Waste struck again when it agreed to buy Browning-Ferris Industries for $7.3 billion, another megamerger that created ripples of excitement in Wall Street investment banking circles but apparently created little else of value, since Allied Waste shares fell sharply on the news and have never been as high since.

Remember, all of this frantic takeover activity was touched off by the USA Waste–Waste Management–Eastern Environmental Services triple merger, which served as the role model for garbage industry consolidation and established both the rationale as well as the valuations that would be used in future deals.

Trouble is, the premise turned out to be a bit shaky.

On December 30, 1999, Waste Management filed a lawsuit alleging that it had been defrauded into overpaying for Eastern Environmental Services. The lawsuit came about as a result of a Special Audit Committee established by Waste Management's Board of Directors, who were trying to figure out why chaos had ensued at Waste

Management almost immediately after the three companies were combined.

"The lawsuit," said *The Wall Street Journal*, "arose out of a sprawling effort by Waste Management's Board of Directors to determine how the company's $19 billion merger with USA Waste Services went wrong, and how the company's management lost control of its operations and accounting systems in the months after the July 1998 merger." In a follow-up story on February 29, *The Journal* reported that Waste Management executives were still assuring company directors as late as mid-June 1999 that the acquisition was going well and that it appeared the company would meet its earnings forecast for the second quarter.

The first hint of trouble—and it was quite a hint—came on July 6, 1999, when Waste Management shares dropped from $53 to $25 in a single day, following word that the company's third-quarter revenues and earnings would be far less than expected. The company announced massive management changes. The new group soon discovered massive disarray in such areas as receivables, billing, and inventory—almost all a result of the chaos surrounding the company's inability to integrate its acquisition.

To help sort out its problems, Waste Management enlisted the services of Roderick M. Hills, former chairman of the Securities & Exchange Commission, who wound up as chairman of the Audit Committee. "The big story here," Mr. Hills concluded, "is that they made terrible acquisitions and didn't know how to run the merged company."

The most telling comment of all from *The Wall Street Journal* was: "And the pioneers of the practice proved not much better at figuring out when to run for cover than the average investor." This was a reference to the fact that insiders of the acquiring company either continued to buy stock or failed to sell prior to the ultimate unraveling of these highly touted mergers.

Shortly thereafter, Allied Waste—the other serial garbage acquirer—announced it would miss its earnings estimates for the fourth quarter of 1999 and also for the year 2000 due to "costs associated with the Browning–Ferris acquisition."

Stewart Scharf, an analyst at Standard & Poor's, commented that "companies need to ensure what they are acquiring is a good fit."

Another analyst, Jaimi Goodfriend, told CBS Marketwatch, "Over the course of the last couple of years, these companies have made massive amounts of acquisitions in order to try to stimulate the top line revenues growth. In doing so, it's sort of been more of a 'buy now, integrate later' strategy. They would buy a lot of companies and acquire all of this new revenue—but in doing that, they neglected the systems integration."

When you throw in the additional allegations of fraud that Waste Management says caused it to overpay for Eastern Environmental Services, you can see that the deals that paved the way for garbage industry consolidation in 1998–99 turned out to be based on a foundation that was about as solid as a landfill. Which explains why the "safe" waste management stocks dropped over 60 percent in 1999.

Meanwhile, keep in mind that any Eastern Environmental shareholder who accepted $29.87 worth of Waste Management stock in December 1998 and held it until year-end 1999 wound up seeing the value of that investment decline by around 60 percent, which once again illustrates the danger of believing that the acquiring company in a takeover transaction necessarily knows what it is doing.

The purpose of this chapter was to illustrate, in no uncertain terms, that "brilliant" corporate executives often make dumb acquisitions for poorly thought-out reasons, and that they are advised and encouraged to do so by "brilliant" investment bankers who are just out there taking their best guess like the rest of us, at best—and who, at worst, are motivated in part by the desire to generate investment banking fees, which cannot be generated unless transactions like these take place.

Meanwhile, "analysts" who are compensated in large part based on their ability to bring investment banking business to their firms, and whose bonuses depend in large part on investment banking fees earned by their firms in general, disseminate voluminous research reports that may say a "buy," "strong buy," "accumulate," "outperform," or "neutral"—but only say "sell" 0.9 percent of the time.

You should keep these cautionary tales in mind the next time you turn on CNBC and discover that one of your stocks has received a takeover bid, and the CEOs of both companies are sitting there trying to convince you to become a long-term stockholder of the combined entity based on their visions of the future and the "analysis" of some investment banker that the deal makes all the sense in the world and that it will turn out just peachy.

The next time you are in a situation like that, do what chocolate baron Milton Hershey did: Sell your ticket on *Titanic* to someone who is frantically bidding for a chance to go on the Synergy Cruise, and use the techniques I have outlined for you in this book to find another possible takeover target.

In the summer and fall of 2000 the Domino Effect was in full force as banks and insurance companies paid all-time record prices in their rush to acquire securities brokerage firms. PaineWebber; Donaldson, Lufkin; Advest; Daine-Raushcer; J.P. Morgan; and others were all acquired at valuations that would have been considered pie-in-the-sky 2 or 3 years ago. These brokerage firms were bought despite the fact that there seemed to be growing evidence of (1) a weakening tech sector, which would probably reduce the number of IPOs in the foreseeable future; (2) cutthroat commission competition from online brokerage firms; (3) growing worries that brokerage firms that have provided bridge financing to private companies might wind up with burgeoning bad debts; and (4) weakening earnings from "Old-Economy" companies, which could be an early warning of an economic downturn and possibly a bear market.

None of that mattered to the "gobblers," however. Buying a brokerage was the "in" thing to do, and independent stockbrokers started disappearing like puddles on a sunny afternoon.

(One notable exception to the lemming syndrome was France's AXA Group, a multinational insurance company that decided to take advantage of the mad rush to buy stockbrokers by *selling* its stake in Donaldson, Lufkin to Credit Suisse First Boston.)

All of which should reinforce the following concepts:

1. The "Domino Effect," or the "Lemming Effect," or whatever name you want to attach to this phenomenon of a takeover frenzy running rampant through a certain industry, is as powerful as it is because sometimes corporate executives can get emotionally carried away and make silly and impulsive shopping decisions, just the way we do when we have a credit card burning a hole in our pocket and too much time on our hands at the mall. This is one major reason why so many takeovers in a certain industry can occur in such a hurry, and why the prices paid for companies can often exceed the estimates of sober Wall Street analysts and sometimes even the wildest dreams of the controlling shareholders of the target companies themselves.

In other words, if you smell a Domino Effect in the making, don't be afraid to buy any logical takeover candidates you uncover, and do not be surprised if you receive more for your shares than you expected if a takeover bid does emerge.

2. If you *do* buy a stock because you are betting on a Domino Effect takeover wave, and you're fortunate enough to wind up with a takeover target, you should take the money and run rather than accept stock in the acquiring company and stick around to see if the business geniuses who offered to buy your company turn out to be right.

Let the mutual funds and the institutional money managers who absolutely must own the big-cap stocks take the risk that the "gobblers" will be right. Because very often, in fact, more than you might expect, they won't.

3. The same holds true for the high-publicity "mergers of equals" like AOL–Time Warner/Daimler–Chrysler, or any future combination of two huge companies that results in no premium being paid to any shareholder of either company. More often than not, these deals take place because (a) neither company can figure out how to grow its business in a significant way, therefore they decide to combine operations and attempt to create cost efficiencies that will lead to higher earnings, or (b) both companies are fearful of being acquired, so they decide to merge with each other to protect themselves. In either instance, there is no money to be made for shareholders of either company, so you should ignore such deals. If you own stock in either company involved in a "merger of equals," sell it and move on. Despite the fact that you read about these megadeals ad infinitum, and you will hear chatter among television analysts day in and day out involving the nuances of these deals and the exciting plans and "synergies" that will result, the basic rule of thumb is that there is no money to be made for you, as an individual investor. Therefore, ignore them, and ignore the Wall Street spin machine as it attempts to lure you and others into these deals based on some pie-in-the-sky projection of what will happen years into the future.

Just give us the premium for our takeover target, thank you very much, and we will be on our way to browse for the next potential target.

By the end of 1999, the Wall Street shell game involving mergers of equals had worn thin with investors. Instead of bidding up the stock prices of companies that simply exchanged pieces of paper with each other without offering a takeover premium to anybody, based on the premise that two plus two equals five, companies that proposed mergers of equals began to find that their stock prices declined on the news.

On Christmas Day 1999 the Associated Press ran a story entitled "Drug Deals Stumble as Shares Fall," which discussed the fact that the Monsanto–Pharmacia & Upjohn merger of equals as well as the Warner-Lambert–American Home Products merger had received a collective thumbs-down from Wall Street in the form of falling stock prices for all four companies.

"The Warner-Lambert and Monsanto transaction raises fundamental questions regarding the viability of mergers of equals," said Tom Warnock of Credit Suisse First Boston. "Given the market reaction to both of these deals, Boards of Directors will be more circumspect before pursuing such a partner."

The Associated Press concluded that "investors want a merger to offer them a premium for their shares in the target company."

No kidding.

You can't have a true takeover if everybody wants to be the gobbler, and with nothing but gobblers, you have no superstock. Therefore, any merger without a true "gobblee" is not a takeover that should interest you.

CHAPTER EIGHTEEN

Look for Multiple Telltale Signs

I have owned a lot of race horses in my life and I've met some very smart horse bettors. One bettor I know had an uncanny knack for picking horses that would win races at 8-to-1 or 10-to-1—not outrageous long shots by any means, just decent horses with ability that were perfectly capable of winning and had been overlooked by the crowd.

I asked him how he managed to come up with so many winners at such generous odds.

"It took me a long time to learn this," he said, "but I finally learned to trust my instincts.

"I see a lot of races," he said. "I notice things, and after a while I learned that if I see certain things, a certain result usually follows. But it took me a long time to learn to trust in what I have observed, because when I see something and then I look up and a horse is 10-to-1, I used to think, 'Well, I must be missing something, otherwise the horse would be 2-to-1 or 3-to-1.' And then the horse wins, and I realize that I am just more experienced than the other bettors. I have seen more than they have seen, and I pay attention to what has worked in the past. I can see meaning in a piece of information that they think is irrelevant, if they notice it at all. And after a while I just gained confidence in my own judgment, and now it doesn't bother me at all to put my money on a 10-to-1 shot if I see something I know is meaningful and which suggests that the horse has the best shot to win. I just don't care about the odds anymore. Why should I? The

odds only reflect what everybody else thinks, and I am more interested in what I think. I've learned to trust my own judgment."

Once you become accustomed to reading the financial news in
terms of the list of Telltale Signs, you will begin to understand what
my friend the horse bettor was talking about. You'll begin to notice
small items which, to most readers of the financial news, are insignificant—but they will be of great significance to you. You will be seeing them in a totally different light than virtually everyone else
because you'll be operating in a different paradigm.

Eventually you will encounter situations where more than one
Telltale Sign is present. These can sometimes be the most profitable
situations of all because there will be no one outstanding or terribly
unusual development that would attract the attention of the financial community, thereby leading them to suspect that a superstock
takeover is brewing. However, when taken together, a combination
of several apparently unrelated developments—all of which are on
the list of Telltale Signs—can clearly point you in the direction of a
winning stock.

The trick is: When you *do* see these multiple Telltale Signs popping up, you will have to trust your instincts, even though you'll
have virtually no support from the "experts" everybody else seems
to look to for analysis. You may have to endure a long period of frustration as the clues pile up and nobody else is paying attention. But
if you can do this—if you can recognize the sign and have the courage
to stick to your guns as long as the evidence is on your side—you can
often run rings around the Wall Street professionals.

Here are several examples of how I zeroed in on takeover candidates that were overlooked by Wall Street simply by noticing multiple Telltale Signs.

CASE STUDY: SUGEN, INC.

On December 21,1995, Sugen Inc. (SUGN) was recommended as a
takeover candidate at $11½. Sugen was a development stage biotech
company working mainly on innovative anticancer therapies. There
was really nothing to separate Sugen from a hundred other biotech
companies with big ambitions, except for this: Britain's Zeneca Ltd.,
a large pharmaceutical company, had purchased 281,875 Sugen shares
on September 29, 1995, at $12 per share. Some further research

revealed that Zeneca had already held a stake in Sugen, and that this new purchase had increased Zeneca's interest in the company to around 20 percent.

Part of the reason I took special note of the Zeneca purchase was that Zeneca had made a takeover bid for one of my recommended stocks, Salick Health Care, earlier in 1995 (see Chapter 15). Zeneca was in an acquisition mode, and the fact it was increasing its stake in Sugen was a Telltale Sign.

Looking into Sugen a bit further revealed that Amgen, another large biotech company, also owned a 3.5 percent stake in Sugen. This was not terribly unusual because many development-stage biotech companies attract investments from larger pharmaceutical companies hoping to own a stake in a small company that makes a big discovery. And although Amgen's stake fell below the 5 percent threshold that makes an outside company an "official" beneficial owner, the fact of the matter was that Sugen had attracted not one but two major outside investors, each of which was perfectly capable of buying Sugen at some point in the future.

What finally led to my recommendation of Sugen, however, was the news on December 6, 1995, that Asta Medica, a German pharmaceutical company, had purchased 495,000 Sugen shares. This purchase was made as part of an agreement that gave Asta Medica the right to jointly develop, manufacture, and market Sugen's anticancer drugs in Europe, and it gave Asta Medica a roughly 5 percent stake in Sugen.

This development gave Sugen a total of *three* outside beneficial owners, each of which was a legitimate candidate to someday take over Sugen.

And that wasn't all: The final Telltale Sign in a series of Telltale Signs was the fact that Asta Medica had purchased those 495,000 Sugen shares at an above-market price of $20.88 per share—which was two times the prevailing market price of Sugen's stock at the time of the purchase.

Sugen shares had briefly spiked up to the $14 area from around $10½ when the news broke of Asta Medica's above-market purchase, but the stock quickly dropped back to the $11 area, providing an entry point and proving, once again, that when you are dealing with underfollowed stocks, the market can be remarkably accommodating in providing tuned-in investors with one excellent buying opportunity after another, even in the face of a news development that makes it highly likely that something very bullish is brewing.

Nearly 1 year later, Sugen had gained exactly one-eighth of a point from the recommended price. So far, I did not look like a genius. But I had enough experience with the Telltale Signs to know that the odds were on my side, and I continued to recommend Sugen.

In December 1996, 1 year after the initial recommendation, Zeneca purchased another 509,000 Sugen shares at $12, raising its stake to 24.9 percent of the company. I also noted that Allergan (AGN), another large drug company, had purchased 191,000 shares of Sugen at the same above-market price of $20.88 that Germany's Asta Medica had paid a year earlier.

These new Telltale Signs now gave Sugen a total of *four* outside "beneficial owners," two of which had paid nearly twice the value of Sugen's current stock price for their stock. And every one of these four companies was a large pharmaceutical company perfectly capable of making a takeover bid for Sugen should they have desired. These multiple Telltale Signs strongly suggested that Sugen's research was promising and that these outside shareholders suspected that a marketable drug would be created as a result of this research. These multiple signs also strongly suggested that Sugen had the potential to become a superstock takeover target.

By January 1997, another Telltale Sign appeared: Sugen's stock price was starting to sketch out a potential "superstock breakout" pattern, a pattern that often signals a significant accumulation of the stock taking place in anticipation of some sort of major bullish development on the horizon.

Toward the end of 1996 a Sugen director bought nearly 22,000 shares at $12⅛ on the open market—*flashing yet another Telltale Sign, which was the strongly bullish combination of insider buying and multiple outside beneficial owner buying.* Sugen was piling up Telltale Signs all over the place—but the stock was still stuck in neutral.

Still, the signs kept coming on: On November 13, 1997, Zeneca purchased another 456,000 Sugen shares, paying $16 a share. On January 16, 1998, another Sugen director bought 20,000 shares of stock on the open market at $12⅝ to $12¾.

On May 8, 1998, we reported that Sugen was in later-stage trials for several antiangiogenesis agents designed to kill cancer tumors. The reason for this story was that on May 3, 1998, *The New York Times* had run a front page story about antiangiogenesis, a process that literally starved tumors by cutting off their blood supply. *The Times* had focused on a company called Entremed (ENMD), whose stock soared from $12 to $85 following the story.

We had noted that Sugen was also in the forefront of antiangiogenesis research, yet Wall Street had not yet focused on this fact, even though Entremed stock had gone through the roof following *The New York Times* story.

It wasn't really necessary, though, to focus on Sugen's leadership in developing antiangiogenesis drugs because Zeneca, Asta Medica, Amgen, and Allergan—the four outside beneficial owners—had taken stakes in Sugen. And when they all moved into Sugen by purchasing stock, that was the clue to follow their lead.

This is the logic and the advantage of following outside "beneficial owners" when they take positions in a company—*you may not know what they know, but you can know what they do—and sometimes that is all you really need to know.*

On June 2, 1998, Sugen's CEO appeared for an interview on CNBC. He talked about Sugen's innovative anticancer therapies, adding that he expected Sugen to be profitable within 2 to 3 years.

It is especially important to watch CEO interviews when they involve companies you are following for one reason or another. There are two reasons for this. First, if you have the right interviewer who asks the right questions in the right way, you would be surprised at what you can learn not only from a CEO's answer, but also from the CEO's body language. You can learn to "read" these interviews, looking for subtle clues that might help in your search for superstock takeover candidates.

For example, there have been a number of occasions on which the CEO of a company that has been an active acquirer of other companies has given just enough information about his company's future acquisition plans that you could actually narrow the list of potential targets down to two or three companies. There have also been occasions on which a CEO has given a not-so-convincing answer about his company remaining independent, or has chosen to answer a question about whether his company is a takeover candidate by using his words so carefully that you just know he cannot deny the possibility outright, because there is something going on. (Later in this chapter, in fact, you will learn about an interview with the CEO of Frontier Corp. which led to a recommendation that Frontier would become a takeover target.)

In the case of the interview with Sugen's CEO, what struck me most of all was the fact that he was highly confident, yet not going out of his way to convince anybody that Sugen was going to make anybody rich overnight. It was more the quiet confidence of someone who knew that he had "the goods," as they say at the racetrack when somebody has a really good horse. He was, in other words, acting like the cat that swallowed the canary—and my confidence in Sugen went up a notch after watching his performance on CNBC.

At the time of the interview with Sugen's CEO, the company was trading around $16, compared to the original recommended price of $11½, 30 months earlier. This was an okay but not great performance up to that point. But by September 1998, Sugen's shares plunged all the way from $17¾ to $10. Despite the fact that there was far more evidence in September 1998 than in December 1995 that Sugen was a potential superstock takeover candidate, the stock was trading at a lower price than I had first recommended it.

Pretty discouraging, wouldn't you say?

Well, yes.

So what do you think I did?

I stuck my neck out even further because I had the evidence to back up my opinion and I was willing to reaffirm my recommendation based on what I believed I knew, regardless of what the stock market seemed to think.

By December 1998 two Sugen directors had purchased a total of 21,000 shares on the open market a few weeks earlier at $10 to $10¾. Not that we needed it, but Sugen had just flashed another in a seemingly endless series of Telltale Signs.

In April 1999, Sugen was featured on a CBS *60 Minutes* segment which discussed the promising potential of the company's anticancer drugs. During a period of four trading days prior to the *60 Minutes* segment, Sugen shares soared from $14 to $23¾! Following the program, the stock promptly fell back to the $15 area.

As it turned out, that was the final buying opportunity in Sugen for those who had been following the avalanche of clues along the way.

On June 16, 1999, Sugen jumped 7 points in one day, a gain of 31 percent in a single trading session, following an announcement that Pharmacia & Upjohn had agreed to buy Sugen at $31 per share.

That takeover price represented a 72 percent premium over Sugen's trading price at the time of my final front-page recommendation just two weeks earlier. It also represented a more than 200 percent premium over Sugen's trading price as recently as September 1998, just 9 months earlier, when Sugen had briefly dropped below the original recommended price.

It came as no surprise that Sugen finally received a takeover bid. The only surprise was the identity of the buyer: Pharmacia & Upjohn had emerged out of nowhere to become the acquirer of Sugen.

The Telltale Signs had been everywhere, from multiple beneficial owners raising their stakes to these same beneficial owners paying above-market prices for stock. When Sugen insiders began buying stock in conjunction with outside beneficial owner buying, this was another Telltale Sign—and remember, Sugen had sketched out a "superstock breakout" pattern along the way, which is usually a sign of major accumulation in anticipation of some major bullish event.

All of these Telltale Signs foreshadowed the takeover bid for Sugen. None of them, viewed in isolation, would have been enough to get any mainstream Wall Street analyst interested in Sugen. But taken together and viewed from the perspective of experience, they provided a clear and comforting "road map" to recommend Sugen despite the frustration of seeing all of the obvious signs and having the stock market completely ignore them.

There were literally hundreds of biotech companies floating around, and there still are. But not many of them got acquired. Sugen did—and the Telltale Signs were there to foreshadow the takeover bid for those who knew what to look for.

And as you can see, it was a long road between the first Telltale Sign to the final takeover bid. A superstock investor would not only need to know what to look for, he or she would also have needed confidence as well as patience and the resilience to weather one false start after another. It took about 3½ years from the original recommendation of Sugen for that takeover bid from Pharmacia & Upjohn to create a 169 percent profit. And remember, if you were *extremely* confident (and how could you not have been with all of the Telltale Signs?)—you could have bought Sugen in the $10 to $11 area in September 1998 and wound up with a nearly 200 percent profit in just 9 months.

No index fund could have matched that return.

Granted, superstock investing requires a little more mainte-
nance and a lot of patience. In the end you have to look at it this
way: If you believe something to be true based on experience, and
if you have the courage to make a decision based on that knowledge, the longer it takes for the stock market to recognize what you
already see, the more of an opportunity you will have to accumulate
shares at bargain prices—especially if the price of the stock continues to languish even as the multiple evidence continues to accumulate, making you even more certain of your original premise.

And that is really the only way to look at it. Do not be frustrated when others fail to see what is obvious to you. Instead, look at it
as an opportunity—and be thankful that you have developed an
insight that others simply do not have.

CASE STUDY: FRONTIER CORP.

In December 1996 a developing takeover trend was taking place in
the telecommunications industry. Ironically, the very news item that
led to the recommendation of Frontier Corp. as a takeover candidate was viewed by Wall Street as a huge negative when it was
announced: Frontier stock plunged 6 points in one day following
word that its earnings would come in below expectations, due in
part to a "restructuring" charge.

Frontier, it seemed, was biting the bullet in certain areas, taking
write-offs and redirecting the company toward more profitable and
promising "core"operations. By this time, that sort of news would
probably prick up your ears and you would look at this announcement
as a signal to look into the company as a potential takeover target,
especially since Frontier was operating in a consolidating industry.

Wall Street did not see it that way, however, and Frontier shares
plunged from $27 to $21 in a single day, when we added the stock
to the Master List of Recommended Stocks on December 20, 1996.

Frontier was the nation's fifth largest long distance company. As
recently as mid-1996 the stock had been trading at $33½. And yet,
even though a takeover trend had already developed in the telephone industry (Bell Atlantic had just announced a deal to merge
with Nynex), and even though the sort of "restructuring" moves

that Frontier had announced were one of the Telltale Signs of a company preparing to sell itself, Wall Street took completely the opposite view of Frontier and knocked the stock down to the $21 area, providing a great entry point.

And there was more to the recommendation: In a mid-December CNBC interview with Frontier's chairman, CNBC reporter David Faber conducted a terrific "new paradigm" interview. Instead of asking all sorts of generic questions about the industry, Faber zeroed in on the developing takeover trend in the telecom industry and asked if Frontier had received any takeover inquiries as a result of its recently falling stock price. *Frontier's chairman replied, "We are not in any active merger discussions at this time."* David Faber did not move on, as most interviewers would have; he sensed that the answer was carefully phrased, and he pressed Frontier's chairman with a follow-up question: Are you saying you have not been approached about a takeover? Frontier's chairman replied: "I am saying we are not in active discussions at this time."

What David Faber had done in this interview was elicit valuable information for any superstock sleuth who was paying close attention: He asked the correct question, received an answer that begged a follow-up question, *and he had asked the logical follow-up question.* The clear impression from this interchange between David Faber and Frontier's chairman was that Frontier had been approached about a takeover but that there were no talks going on right now. This impression, combined with Frontier's restructuring moves and the fact that Frontier's industry was seeing a number of takeovers, led me to recommend Frontier as a takeover candidate.

By June 1997, Frontier's stock had dropped again, this time to the $16 to $18 area. Earnings continued to come in at disappointing levels—but again, the bulk of the earnings disappointments were due to the fact that Frontier was repositioning itself, jettisoning non-performing operations, taking the appropriate write-downs, and investing large amounts in a new infrastructure that would allow the company to expand its Internet capabilities as well as enhance its long distance infrastructure. Everything Frontier was doing would make it more attractive as a takeover candidate.

In June 1997 the takeover trend in the telecom industry was continuing, with a proposed merger of AT&T and SBC Communications.

They say that beauty is in the eye of the beholder. On Wall Street you can say the same thing about "bad"news. *Each time Frontier announced another restructuring-related write-off, Wall Street dumped Frontier stock—yet each of these announcements was a thing of beauty because they were Telltale Signs that this company was setting itself up to be acquired.*

By October 1997 it was apparent that the takeover wave in the telecom industry was accelerating. Among the deals, Worldcom had just bid for MCI Corp., Excel Communications had agreed to acquire Telco Communications, a combination of long distance carriers; and LCI agreed to buy USLD Communications, another merger of long distance companies. Clearly, Frontier was a restructuring company in a consolidating industry.

On October 31,1997, another Telltale Sign emerged: the "multiple bidders" signal. Three bidders emerged to buy long distance telecom company MCI Communications: British Telecom, WorldCom, and GTE. The multiple bidders concept is *a strong signal that the takeover wave in that industry will continue in full force.* Usually, the "multiple bidder" Telltale Sign involves two companies trying to take over a company. In this case there were *three* multiple bidders—a rare development that indicated the takeover wave among telecom companies in general, and long distance companies in particular, was still in its early stages.

In November 1997 Frontier's newly installed CEO, Joseph Clayton, was interviewed. Again, it was remarkable what could be learned simply from paying attention to what was said and the manner in which Clayton said it. In a remarkably straightforward response to the right question, he said that Frontier "could be acquired" but that *he believed the company would be able to deliver more value to its shareholders by first turning the company around.* He predicted that the restructuring Frontier was currently implementing would improve Frontier's results by the end of the first quarter of 1998. In other words, the CEO of Frontier confirmed the suspicion that *all of the restructuring moves and write-offs that were causing the lemmings to dump Frontier stock were, in reality, Telltale Signs that Frontier was about to become a takeover target!* This was an excellent illustration of the difference between "new paradigm" and "old paradigm" thinking: The same piece of information can lead to diametrically opposed conclusions about the future depending on what you know, what you have experienced, and how the information is interpreted.

Nearly a year later, in October 1998, Frontier stock was trading in the high $20s. We reported in *Superstock Investor*:

> Frontier's new CEO Clayton has been selling off noncore and under-performing operations, which is often a *telltale clue* that a company is putting itself in better shape for a potential sale in the not-too-distant future. Given the rapid consolidation in the telecommunications industry and the evolution of this business into a small group of multinational behemoths, a takeover bid for Frontier seems quite possible.

In light of what was about to happen, those comments were about as close to the mark as you can get in this business.

In February 1999 a spokesperson for Frontier Corp. delivered another Telltale Sign by uttering the words "restructuring options" and "increase shareholder value," which are two key phrases to look for when you are looking for companies that believe their stock is undervalued and that intend to do something to rectify the situation. At the time, Frontier was trading at $35½.

The interview with Frontier's CFO Rolla Huff, in which Mr. Huff made these statements, did not appear in the national media. In fact, the interview appeared in a Rochester, New York, business publication—another example of how browsing through out-of-the-way publications can sometimes lead you to a perfectly exquisite gem of information that can lead to big stock market profits. In the interview, Huff said that Frontier was frustrated by the relatively low valuation being accorded its stock, and he said that "the company is evaluating a number of options, including spinoffs, initial public offerings, and mergers."

In particular, Huff pointed to Frontier's data and Internet business, which was hidden beneath the company's image as a long distance telephone company, as being worth far more than the stock market was giving Frontier credit for.

In March 1999 we reported that Frontier was attempting to break out of a superstock breakout pattern: "The entire price range between roughly $34 and $37 is the upper end of a trading range trading back to 1996. Each time Frontier threatened to break out above this range the stock was blindsided by an earnings setback. But the recent move up to $39¼, combined with the willingness of Frontier management to make the bold forecast mentioned earlier, strongly implies that this break-in process is the real thing."

It had been 27 months since the original recommendation of Frontier Corp. The original recommendation had been based on a Telltale Sign of a company in a consolidating industry announcing restructuring moves designed to rid itself of underperforming operations and make it more of a "pure play." This was followed by another Telltale Sign: multiple bidders for MCI Corp., which strongly implied that more takeovers of long distance companies would take place. This was followed by Frontier officials using buzzwords like "increase shareholder value" and "restructuring options," which are often code phrases used by managements who believe their stock is badly undervalued and who are searching for a catalyst to force the stock market to push the stock higher. And finally, Frontier had broken out of a "superstock" trading range by crossing the $34 to $37 area.

By March 1999, Frontier received a $62 takeover bid from Global Crossing. Frontier was originally recommended in December 1996 at $21, when it was viewed as a hopelessly troubled company with erratic earnings and very little going for it. The momentum players hated it, and the Wall Street lemmings sold it.

The purpose in telling you about the Sugen and Frontier takeovers is to illustrate how seemingly insignificant news items can accumulate, one after another, to form a giant flashing arrow pointing directly to a superstock takeover. In the case of Frontier, what was especially ironic was that some of the Telltale Signs that led to Frontier in the first place with increasing confidence were precisely the news developments that caused the Wall Street lemmings to dump Frontier stock!

All of which proves one thing:

Wall Street is a lot like horse racing, and also a lot like life, in that experience makes a huge difference. Like my friend who was able to pick those 8-to-1 shots at the track, if you give two people the identical information or circumstances, you will sometimes find that one of them is able to see something that the other simply cannot see.

That is a huge advantage, and by becoming a "new paradigm" thinker, you can create this advantage for yourself when it comes to picking superstock takeover candidates.

CASE STUDY: WATER UTILITIES

Once you get used to the idea of reading the financial news in terms of the Telltale Signs, certain news items that don't register at all with most investors will literally jump out at you as a guidepost and precursor to future takeover developments in a particular industry, or for a certain company within that industry. Often you will find that it's not just one news item but an accumulation of small items, or clues, that when taken together begin to form a clear picture of what lies ahead. Like the straw that broke the camel's back, it was not the straw that finally touched off the event—rather, it was the accumulation of straws, one after another, that did the camel in. Similarly, there will be times when you notice one item, then another, and then another, and based on an accumulation of evidence you'll finally decide that a certain industry or a certain stock deserves your close attention.

On Wednesday, October 14, 1998, an item appeared on page B-26 of *The Wall Street Journal*. The very fact that it appeared on page B-26 tells you how high up on the list of major financial news developments this story stood on that particular day. But by this time you will understand *everything* in the financial news comes to you in a pre-filtered manner. After all, somebody, somewhere, has to decide which news developments are at the top of the list in terms of significance and general interest, and which will be buried somewhere inside the newspaper—or possibly not even reported at all.

The headline on this particular story was, "American Water Agrees to Acquire Utility for Stock," and the gist of the report was that American Water Works (AWK), a water utility, had agreed to buy privately held National Enterprises Inc., another water utility, in a transaction valued at $485.2 million.

There are three probable reasons why this story did not receive very much attention. First, National Enterprises was a privately held company, and therefore the takeover bid did not involve a big jump in anybody's stock price. Second, the value of the transaction was not exactly an eye-opener in an era of multibillion-dollar mergers. And third, these were water utility companies, for heaven's sake—and how exciting is that?

But anyone who took the time to read this story would have found several Telltale Signs that suggested a potentially profitable takeover wave was about to unfold in the previously sleepy water utility industry. The story, written by Allanna Sullivan, pointed out that this takeover was part of a recently developing trend toward consolidation in the water utility industry, and that a number of private water companies had already been bought by publicly held water companies.

The story mentioned that smaller water companies were being hurt by increasingly stringent environmental laws, which had increased operating costs, and that these smaller utilities were deciding to sell out to larger, better-financed water utility companies. The story also pointed out that American Water Works had purchased a Hawaiian water utility just several months earlier, and it quoted an American Water Works spokesperson as saying that other potential acquisitions were being considered.

It might have been easy to miss this story if not for an excellent report that appeared in the *Investor's Business Daily* "Companies in the News" section just a month before. The IBD "Companies in the News" section is an excellent "browsing" place and it can often provide invaluable information for superstock browsers, not only because it provides in-depth discussion of the thinking that goes into various corporate maneuvers (such as takeovers), but also because its "Industry Group Focus" table, which usually accompanies its reports, gives you a top-to-bottom look at the various publicly traded companies that comprise the industry being discussed.

This particular "Companies in the News" item dealt with Philadelphia Suburban Corp. (PSC), a large water utility that had just grown larger by announcing that it would acquire Maine-based Consumers Water Co. (CONW). That merger, said the IBD report, would move Philadelphia Suburban from its present ranking as the third largest water company (behind American Water Works and United Water Resources) into the number two position. The IBD report described the reasoning behind this takeover, alluding to the burden of rising regulatory costs being borne by smaller water utilities, and also made reference to the economies of scale that could be achieved by merging water utilities.

The IBD story quoted Philadelphia Suburban's CEO as follows: "Since this is such a highly fragmented industry, the acquisition gives us a head start in the consolidation phase." He added that he expected the combined Philadelphia Suburban–Consumers Water to "take advantage of what we think will be great opportunities for buying up smaller companies in the future."

This IBD story was reminiscent of the dominolike takeover wave that had recently engulfed the drugstore industry (see Chapters 14 and 17), and so the water utility industry became a possible candidate for the Domino Effect.

And after reading the report on Philadelphia Suburban and noting that the list of publicly traded water utility stock in the accompanying table was rather small, it seemed that the water industry might be about to undergo the same sort of consolidation wave that had recently struck the drugstore industry.

The combination of these—one in IBD and the other in *The Wall Street Journal*—two items appearing less than a month apart, is what finally led me to take a long, hard look at the water utility industry.

The list of publicly traded water utility stocks was similar to the drugstore industry just prior to the "dominolike" takeover wave that shrunk the number of public drugstore companies down to a handful. There were a total of 15 public water utility companies, and after some research focusing on the region of the country where they operated and a comparison to the larger takeover-minded industry leaders, it became obvious that this industry could evolve into a handful of large regional companies—just as the drugstore industry had.

Moreover, when the stock price values of the public water utilities were compared to the takeover values being placed on water utilities that had recently been acquired, it became startlingly obvious that the smaller publicly traded water utility stocks, which were the most obvious takeover candidates, were trading at values far below their potential takeover values.

And these water stocks had an added attraction: Because they were utilities, they carried high dividend yields, generally between 4 and 5 percent, which were a juicy bonus in an environment of ultralow interest rates.

Finally, several of the water utilities on the list were already partially owned by an outside "beneficial owner," which was one of the Telltale Signs to always look for—the fact that two of these outside beneficial owners were acquisition-minded European companies was also a major plus.

In December 1998, I presented a front-page report in *Superstock Investor* entitled "Water Utility Industry Could Be on the Verge of a Takeover Wave." The report compared the state of the water utility industry to the drugstore industry back in 1996, just prior to the barrage of takeovers that reduced that formerly fragmented industry to a handful of regional giants.

In December 1998 nine water utilities (and one water services stock) were recommended (Table 18–1), and we suggested a cross section of these stocks, thinking of the portfolio as a sort of "mutual fund" of water utility takeover candidates. We noted that two of the water utilities in the portfolio were already partially owned by outside beneficial owners: 29.1 percent of United Water Resources was owned by a French company, Lyonnaise des Eaux; and 8.7 percent of California Water was owned by SJW Corp., a neighboring California water utility.

The beauty of this situation was that these water stocks were *utilities*. And if ever there were an example of how a takeover trend could turn previously unexciting stocks into "superstocks," this would be it. Historically, utility stocks tend to be viewed as low-growth income vehicles whose dividend yields are the most important part of their investment profile. As the stock market soared in the mid-to-late 1990s, dividend yields began to wane in importance as investors increasingly sought growth and capital gains. Some utility companies, in fact, actually reduced or eliminated their dividends and sought to become growth companies by diversifying away from their core business. (For more on *that* strategy, take a look at what happened to Western Resources in Chapter 17.)

So, the concept of buying a stock for its dividend yield had become a hopelessly out-of-favor investment strategy, which is one of the major reasons why the water utilities, which were not diversifying like the electric and gas utilities, were completely unloved and virtually unfollowed among the traditional Wall Street investment firms.

The concept of buying these stocks as potential *takeover candidates* had not yet emerged as a strategy at the time of the original recommendation and in the months that followed, which meant that the water utilities simply moved inversely with interest rates, much as traditional utility stocks had always done. When interest rates rose, the water stocks fell, so their dividend yields would rise along

Table 18–1

Water Utility Stocks as of 12/98
(original recommended prices)

United Water Resources (UWR)	$20¹⁄₁₆
California Water (CWT)	$26⅞
E'town Corp. (ETW)	$45⅛
Aquarion (WTR) (adjusted for 3-for-2 split)	$24¾
American States Water	$28½
SJW Corp. (SJW)	$60
Connecticut Water (CTWS)	$27½
Middlesex Water (MSEX)	$24½
Southwest Water (SWWC) (adjusted for two 3-for-2 splits)	$6⅝

with interest rates in general. When interest rates fell, the water utility stocks bounced up a bit, so their dividend yields would fall.

But, as a superstock sleuth who was focusing on the takeover aspects of these stocks, it seemed the water stocks would soon be marching to the beat of a very different drummer. Based on experience in picking takeover candidates and noticing characteristics of industries and stocks that were about to become takeover targets, these stocks appeared in an entirely different light. Each time the water utility stocks fell back in response to rising interest rates, it became yet another opportunity to buy more, because their dividend yields would soon become completely irrelevant. And, *these stocks would soon be valued on the basis of their takeover values.*

It was also an easy matter to calculate what each of these water stocks would be worth in a takeover situation because the water utility takeovers that had occurred up to that point had been trending higher from a valuation of 2.5 times book value to the area of 2.9 times the book value. So it was a fairly simple matter to determine that most of the water utility stocks had the potential to rise 50 percent or more in the event of a takeover—an incredible risk/reward situation since we were talking about *water utilities,* for heaven's sake.

How often in the stock market are you offered the chance to make 50 percent on your money with minimal downside risk? That was the appeal of the water utility stocks—and yet, for several months these stocks could have easily been purchased at or below the original recommended prices.

In February 1999, in an off-the-record conversation I had with an executive at one of the water utilities on the takeover list, the executive asked to remain anonymous but gave me permission to use his comments. He told me that my analysis was "right on target," and listed a number of logical reasons why smaller publicly traded water utilities would opt to be acquired by larger companies. The list of reasons sounded quite familiar to a seasoned takeover sleuth, and, in fact, read like a list of reasons to expect another lemminglike, Domino Effect takeover wave to strike this industry.

1. As the competitors become larger, they will achieve a competitive advantage as their cost of capital is lower. Because the water utility industry is capital-intensive, this is a major issue to smaller companies.

2. The water utility industry is particularly suited to economies of scale resulting from combining companies, which include elimination of general office operations, billing operations, lab expenses, and the day-to-day expenses of running a business such as engineering costs, purchasing, accounting, insurance, and so forth.

3. The increasing costs of complying with environmental requirements, *especially in the eastern United States*, could drive smaller water companies to merge with larger companies.

This conversation with a well-positioned water utility executive, even though it was off-the-record, was an excellent example of something I learned over the years, which is that *you would be amazed at what an officer, director, or spokesperson for a publicly traded company might tell you if you just took the time to ask*. Not inside information about revenues or earnings, but rather, background information regarding business strategy, industry conditions, opinions about competitors and what they may be up to, and even the relative valuations of stock prices compared to potential takeover value.

Remember, *it is a natural inclination for a person to want to talk about what he or she knows best*. Whenever you ask a person to discuss a topic that is near and dear to that person's heart, or one that person spends most of his or her time dealing with on a daily basis, you will find that you are requesting information that the giver is naturally inclined to impart to you.

The same holds true in the world of business, but there are variations on this theme. Some officers and directors of publicly traded companies are ultracautious and will answer questions from a stockholder (or a newsletter writer) only in a thinly veiled prescripted way. This is generally the case with larger companies or very popular stocks that are attracting a great deal of analyst and investor attention. You will find that the more popular a stock has become, the less information you are likely to elicit from that company's investor relations spokesperson. Many times you will get the feeling that this person receives hundreds of inquiries per day and probably wishes that talking to shareholders and analysts were no longer part of his or her job description.

But you will also find that, as you begin dealing with companies whose stocks are unloved and out of favor—as will be the case much of the time if you put these principles and thought processes to work for you—you are very likely to elicit interesting and valuable information simply by picking up the phone and calling the company. Often you'll find that these companies have attracted so little investor interest that they do not even have a full-time investor relations person, and you will wind up speaking to the company treasurer, a vice president, or some other officer who doubles as the investor contact.

In cases like this, you will often discover that these people are perfectly willing and even anxious to discuss and explain their business and industry to an outsider, especially a stockholder who seems genuinely interested. It often seemed that some of these people were just sitting there *dying* for someone to call and express an interest in their company. And, when they finally heard an interested and receptive voice on the other end of the phone, they were more than willing to tell that person almost anything they might want to know.

This may seem like an exaggeration, but it is not. You should try it sometime.

This was the distinct impression I received in a conversation with the water utility executive in January 1999. Here was a guy who was an officer of a water utility that had operated in an industry that is about as predictable as you can get in the world of business. People need water, all the time, every day. You provide it. When your costs go up a little, you apply for a rate increase. You pay out a certain percentage of earnings as dividends, people who are seeking income buy your stock, and that's that—what more is there to say?

Suddenly, the landscape changed. Several water utilities had been purchased by larger companies and consolidation was in the air. The stocks perked up a bit as a handful of investors who appeared to be paying attention began to suspect that these formerly sleepy stocks might become takeover targets. The industry itself was abuzz with questions: Who might be the next target? What might these companies be worth as takeover targets? Some of these companies also owned large tracts of real estate—could these parcels inject a valuable "wild card" into potential valuations?

Suddenly, the water utility business was getting very interesting—but virtually nobody on Wall Street was paying attention. This water utility executive had a lot to say and was more than willing to discuss the industry and the "new paradigm" that was emerging for all of its players. In fact, he was so pleased that someone outside the industry had noticed what was going on that *he actually called me back later to add some thoughts that he had failed to mention.* What are the odds that an executive at General Electric would call you back just to talk a little more?

The executive deflected the question about whether his water utility might wind up as a takeover target, as well he should have. (Sometimes that question is not deflected, however, so it never hurts to ask.) But his comments about the reasons behind the recent water utility takeovers and his view that these rationales made sense and would continue to make sense provided more confidence in the scenario I had already painted.

Perhaps the juiciest nugget of information obtained from this conversation involved the potential valuations of future water utility takeovers. In such a conversation with an executive of a company, it is important to ask the most pertinent questions first, even though they are usually unlikely to be answered directly. But don't give up if you don't get the direct answers you are hoping for. And always greet whatever response you receive in an understanding, good-natured way. If you don't get what you were after, try to keep the conversation going in terms of more general industry questions that relate in some way to what you are trying to determine.

Sometimes an executive will give you a "Yes" for an answer when asked if his company has received a takeover bid. More often, the question must be couched in different terms, such as: "If you received a takeover bid would you reject it out of hand, or would you consider what is in the best interest of shareholders?" Or, if a company already has an outside "beneficial owner," the question might go like this: "Have you ever discussed the possibility of being acquired by XYZ?" Or: "Is it possible they might want to buy the rest of the shares they don't own?" Or: "Would it make any sense for them to eventually want to buy you outright?" Or: "Are there any understandings or agreements that would prevent XYZ from acquiring the rest of your company?"

The point is that there are a number of different ways to ask the same question without directly asking if a company is likely to become a takeover target, and if you phrase the question carefully, you leave the executive enough "wiggle room" to respond to you in a manner that you may gain the information you are looking for in a roundabout way—or possibly even other information that you had not even considered asking about.

In the case of the water utility executive, in addition to learning all of the excellent reasons why water companies would continue to be acquired, two additional things were revealed by just keeping the conversation going: First, water utilities located in the eastern United States might be under a bit more pressure to sell out to a larger company; and second, it would be fair to assume that most of the water utilities on the list would be worth between 2.5 and 2.9 times book value if they were to be acquired—with the potential valuation moving up toward the upper end of that range as time went on and fewer acquisition candidates were available.

This interview led me to focus on the valuation question, comparing the stock prices of the recommended water utility stocks to their potential takeover values. What I was looking for was the biggest "gap" between a company's stock price and its possible buyout value—in other words, the most undervalued water utilities in the group. Three water utilities appeared to be particularly undervalued: E'town Corp., SJW Corp, and American States Water. SJW Corp. also owned an 8.7 percent stake in California Water, which could give SJW an added attraction as a takeover candidate.

Within 10 months two of these three water companies had received takeover bids.

By May 1999, using a technique that has often pointed directly toward a takeover target, I made note of stocks that were performing noticeably better than other stocks in their industry group.

The two stocks in question were both water utilities: Aquarion (WTR), a Connecticut-based water company, and E'town (ETW), a New Jersey water company. Generally, stocks within a well-defined industry group will tend to move in the same general direction; not every day, certainly, but over time. When you have a situation where a certain stock in an industry is moving up consistently, while its peers are doing nothing or even declining, it can often be a sign that something very bullish is brewing.

Both Aquarion and E'town were examples of this principle. Also, Aquarion had large real estate holdings, which could add to its takeover appeal—something I learned from the water company executive a few months earlier. And, both of these water utilities operated in the eastern United States, where I'd discovered that water companies might be under more pressure to sell themselves, due to more stringent environmental regulations and higher compliance costs.

You can see that a combination of various factors—lessons learned, comments heard—led to focusing directly on both Aquarion and E'town.

On June 1, 1999, Aquarion announced that it had agreed to be acquired by Yorkshire Water PLC, Britain's largest utility, for $37.05 per share. Aquarion, a Connecticut water company, was one of the water utilities that owned large tracts of real estate.

That $37.05 takeover price represented a premium of nearly 70 percent above Aquarion's trading price as recently as March 1999, and it represented a 50 percent gain above the initial recommended price in December 1998. Once again the stock market had obligingly allowed tuned-in superstock investors to buy a stock at a bargain price even after, in the case of Aquarion, it became obvious that water utilities were about to become takeover targets, as demonstrated by the fact that Aquarion slipped significantly below the original recommended price even in the face of gathering evidence that a takeover trend in this group was already under way and would very likely continue. *I cannot overemphasize this point: You will be astonished at how often the stock market disregards Telltale Signs that are perfectly obvious to you, and how long genuine superstock takeover candidates will remain on the bargain counter right up until the takeover occurs.*

This was a boring, high-yielding water utility—and yet superstock analytical techniques led directly to the takeover of Aquarion. The concept of risk vs. reward—in which an investor considers not only the potential profit but also the potential risk—was a lost art for a time in the late 1990s, and making 50 percent in a stock was not especially impressive in some circles. But to those investors who had been around long enough to understand that risk is usually commensurate with reward, the idea that one could make 50 percent in 6 months on a water utility stock should have been a wake-up call that there were tremendous opportunities to be found in other water utility takeover candidates.

That message, however, did not sink in. The other water stocks in the portfolio bumped up briefly on the Aquarion takeover, but soon settled back to levels that *still* left huge gaps between their stock price levels and their potential takeover values. Was this frustrating? No. This just meant that the opportunity for profit was hanging around longer—all the better for investors. Even the fact that Aquarion had been acquired at 2.7 times book value—which confirmed the takeover value range I had been using—was not enough to bring the water utility stocks significantly closer to their takeover values. As a result of that 2.7 times book value figure, in June 1999 the potential takeover values of the water utility stocks in the portfolio were estimated. And once again, E'town, SJW Corp., and American States Water were the three water utilities that seemed to be selling at the biggest discount to their potential buyout prices.

On August 24, United Water Resources announced that it had agreed to be acquired by Suez Lyonnaise des Eaux, a French company, for $35.48 per share. That takeover price represented a 77 percent premium over the original recommended price for United States Water just 9 months earlier. The takeover bid for United Water Resources certainly came as no surprise—especially since Suez Lyonnaise was already an outside "beneficial owner" of United Water with a 32 percent stake in that company. As any seasoned superstock takeover sleuth might have expected, the accelerating trend toward water company takeovers had resulted in a "me too" type takeover bid in which an outside owner who already owned a large stake in United Water decided to join in the takeover parade by bidding for the rest of the company. It was not a coincidence that a European water company that owned a stake in United Water would decide to buy the rest of the company just weeks after Aquarion had been taken over by Yorkshire Water, a British company. The "lemming" effect, or the Domino Effect, or whatever label you might want to put on this tendency of corporate decision makers to play follow the leader, was alive and well, and it was playing out perfectly in the water utilities industry, to the delight of those handful of investors who had recognized the signs early and had the foresight and confidence to buy these stocks when nobody else wanted them.

For virtually all of 1999 an investor could easily have purchased United Water Resources in the $19 to $22 range, receiving a hefty yield to boot, and wound up with a superstock takeover target valued at over $35. All that you, as an investor, would have needed was a familiarity with a thought process, a way of looking at the financial news, that would have made it crystal clear that water utility takeovers would be taking place. From there it would have been an easy matter to zero in on a company already partially owned by an outside "beneficial owner." United Water, in fact, traded in that $19 to $22 range right up until the last week of July 1999, just prior to the takeover bid, despite mounting evidence that water utilities were becoming takeover targets. This was another clear example of how the stock market overlooks values in sleepy, out-of-favor industries to such an extent that individual investors can beat the Wall Street experts at their own game simply by being willing to go off the beaten path in search of stock market "inefficiencies."

On October 29, SJW Corp. announced that it had accepted a $128 takeover bid from American Water Works—*the very same company whose CEO had managed to get through an entire interview on CNBC without being asked a single question about water industry consolidation* (see Chapter 4). That $128 takeover price represented a 113 percent premium over the original recommended price for SJW of $60 just 11 months before.

Less than 1 month later, on November 22, 1999, E'town Corp. announced that it would be acquired by Britain's Thames Water PLC for $68 per share, a premium of 50.6 percent above the original recommended price 12 months before. E'town jumped over $10 per share in a single day on this news.

It had been less than a year since we recommended the water utility portfolio, and already four of the nine stocks on the list had received takeover bids, at premiums ranging from 50.6 percent to 113 percent above the original recommended prices. Moreover, in each case these takeover targets could have been purchased at prices significantly *below* the original recommended price, even as the evidence mounted that water company takeovers were coming, resulting in greater percentage gains.

An article in *The Wall Street Journal* the day after the bid for E'town was announced clearly spelled out the reasons for the takeover wave in the water stocks. It all seemed so obvious—but it would have been just as obvious one year earlier if you'd been using many of the techniques discussed in this book about spotting this developing trend. The difficult part, you see, is not always seeing the handwriting on the wall. Sometimes the difficult part is believing what you see and having the courage to act on what you believe, even though the stock market is paying no attention to this evidence whatsoever. You have to "know what you know," in other words, and you have to have the confidence to act accordingly even if it seems that you are out of step with everyone else around you.

A Superstock Shopping List

As you have seen, an important part of my approach has been to make special note of companies that are partially owned by outside "beneficial owner" investors. I am particularly interested when one of these partially owned companies exhibits one or more additional Telltale Signs—especially when the outside beneficial owner had both the ability and the desire to maximize the value of its investment.

To help you start your own "research universe," we have compiled a sampling of companies that are partially owned by either another company or a private investor or what I would call a "financial" investor, such as a brokerage firm or buyout firm which would presumably know how to take advantage of any opportunity to maximize the value of its stock. By listing these firms as outside beneficial owners, our assumption is that should the opportunity present itself, these "financial" outside owners would be ready, willing, and able to cash out of their investments at a nice premium.

We have also elected to include several stocks in which a significant ownership stake is held by a family trust, in some instances involving descendants of the founding family. As in the case of outside "financially oriented" owners, companies that are partially owned by a family trust are also candidates for "value maximization" when the timing is right.

This list was compiled from the most recent data available at the time this book was published—but as we have learned, things change. I'd suggest, therefore, that before you make any investment decisions based on the following information, you should make certain that there have been no material changes in the data we've provided here.

There are two ways to determine the very latest ownership stakes of these "beneficial owners": You can either call the company directly or you can go to www.freeedgar.com on the Internet. Once you access freeedgar.com, simply enter the trading symbol of the company and click on "view filings." You will then see a list of the company's Securities & Exchange Commission filings. The best filing to check would be the most recent Proxy Statement, listed on the site as "Form DEF-14A–Definitive Proxy Statement." Within that filing you will find a section listing all of the company's major shareholders, including "beneficial owners" with more than a 5 percent stake. You should also make note of any recent Form 13 filings, including not only 13-D's but also Form 13-G's, which are filed by investment advisers. These filings may indicate that an outside owner had either increased or decreased its position, or that a new outside owner has surfaced.

As you scan this list you will see that these partially owned companies span a multitude of industry groups. You will find stocks on this list that will fit almost any conceivable investment criteria, and I would urge you to study this list and become familiar with it for two reasons.

First, all things being equal, if you are looking to invest a portion of your investment funds in a certain industry, why not include a stock or two within that industry that is already partially owned by an outside beneficial owner? You will pay nothing extra for the privilege, and you just may wake up some morning to find that the outside beneficial owner has come up with a way to maximize the value of its investment, which would also maximize the value of *your* investment.

The second reason you should become familiar with the companies on this list is that as you scan the financial news in search of the Telltale Signs, you will eventually find some of these companies popping up on your radar screen. Remember, any of the Telltale Signs combined with an outside beneficial owner is a potential signal that you may have a superstock takeover candidate on your hands.

I want to make it clear that this is not a recommended list of stocks, and you should not view this list in that way. Rather, it is a starting point for further research if you have the inclination to use the tools that have been described to you and apply them to these companies that are already partially owned.

Our goal in writing this book was to describe a personal perspective on the financial news that I have developed over the past 26 years. In a way, I have tried to provide you with a new set of lenses that will enable you to filter out significant elements of the financial news that most investors, including most "professionals," tend to overlook. As I said at the outset, I make no claim that this is any sort of "foolproof system," and I readily acknowledge that it takes a lot of effort. But I am confident that if you learn to recognize the Telltale Signs and if you take the time to study and remember the actual case studies of successful takeover recommendations I have related to you here, you will soon find yourself zeroing in on seemingly innocuous news items that will have little or no meaning to most investors but will have a great deal of meaning to you. You will view these news items in a totally different light—and if you take the time to delve further into these situations as they present themselves, you will soon be wending your way toward finding your own superstock takeover targets.

Shopping List of Potential Superstocks
Information as of 10/17/00

Company	Symbol	Partial Owners
21st Century Insurance Group	TW	American International Group (62.1%)
Abercrombie & Fitch	ANF	J.P. Morgan Co. (7.7%)
ABM Industries	ABM	Rosenberg Family Trust (21%)
Acmat	ACMT	Queensway Financial *Canada* (19.8%)
Actrade Financial	ACRT	NTS Corporation (29.2%)
ACTV, Inc.	IATV	Liberty Media (23.8%)
Advanced Magnetics	AVM	BVF Partners (13.6%)/ Eiken Chemical, Ltd. *Japan* (5.6%)
Advanced Tissue Sciences	ATIS	Smith & Nephew, Inc. *England* (7.95%)
Aegon Insurance Group	AEG	Vereniging NV *Netherlands* (34.4%)
AEP Industries	AEPI	Borden, Inc. (32.4%)
Allied Waste Industries	AW	Apollo Advisers L.P. (17.2%)/ Blackstone Mgt. LLC (11.9%)
Ambac Financial	ABK	J.P. Morgan (10.4%)
AMC Entertainment	AEN	Fairmac Realty Group (11.3%)/ Syufy Century Corp.(7.2%)/ Durwood Family Heirs (5.8%)
American Classic Voyages	AMCV	Sam Zell Group (36%)
American Express	AXP	Berkshire Hathaway *Warren Buffett* (11.4%)
American Locker Group	ALGI	Estate of Harold Ruttenberg (22.5%)
Ann Taylor	ANN	Morgan Stanley (5.4%)
ARI Network Services	ARIS	Briggs & Stratton (13.6%)/ Witech (21.3%)/ Vulcan Ventures (8.7%)
Aristotle Corporation	ARTL	Geneve Corporation (50.8%)
Astoria Financial	ASFC	J.P. Morgan (9.9%)
Atchison Casting Corporation	FDY	Edmundson International, Inc. (11.8%)
Autozone	AZO	ESL, Ltd. (16.2%)
Bancwest Corporation	BWE	Banque National de *Paris* (45%)
Barnes & Noble	BKS	Forstman-Leff Associates (15.7%)
Barrick Gold	ABX	Trizec Hahn *Canada* (8%)
Battle Mountain Gold	BMG	Noranda Inc. *Canada* (28.4%)
Beringer Wine	BERW	Texas Pacific Group (51.7%)
Berlitz International	BTZ	Soichiro Fukutake/ Benesse Corporation *Japan* (61.6%)
Biosphere Medical	BSMD	Sepracor, Inc. (58%)

Continues

Shopping List of Potential Superstocks
Information as of 10/17/00 (continued)

Company	Symbol	Partial Owners
Blockbuster, Inc.	BBI	Viacom, Inc. (82.3%)
California Water	CWT	SJW Corporation *Being acquired by American Water Works* (8.5%)
Campbell Soup	CPB	Dorrance Family Heirs (38.8%)
Catalina Marketing	POS	General Electric (7.6%)
CDI Corporation	CDI	Garrison Family Trust (29.2%)
Centex Construction Products	CXP	Centex Corporation (61.5%)
Cerus Corporation	CERS	Baxter Healthcare (16.2%)
Chart House Enterprises	CHT	Samstock, LLC (27.1%)
Chiron	CHIR	Novartis (44%)
Churchill Downs, Inc.	CHDN	Duchossois Industries (24.2%)
CIT Group	CIT	Dai-Ichi Bank *Japan* (26.8%)
Clorox	CLX	Henkel K GaA *Germany* (26.5%)
CNAFinancial	CNA	Loews Corporation (86.8%)
Coca-Cola	KO	Berkshire Hathaway *Warren Buffett* (8.1%)
Coca-Cola Bottling	COKE	Coca-Cola Company (31%)
Coca-Cola Enterprises	CCE	Coca-Cola Company (40.3%)
Cognizant Technology	CTSH	IMS Health (61%)
Congoleum Corporation	CGM	American Biltrite (68.3%)
Conmed Corporation	CNMD	Bristol Myers Squibb (6.13%)
Continental Airlines	CAL	NWA Corporation (84.6%)
Cooper Industries	CBE	J.P. Morgan (7.1%)
Coventry Health Care	CVTY	Principal Life Insurance Co. (25.5%)/ Warburg, Pincus Ventures (30.6%)
CPC of America	CPCF	CTM Group, Inc. (39.5%)
Curtiss-Wright	CW	Unitrin (43%)
Darden Restaurants	DRI	Prudential Insurance (13.6%)/ American Express (9.3%)
Dave & Busters	DAB	LJH Corporation (11.3%)/ Mandarin, Inc. *United Kingdom* (10.6%)
Dawson Geophysical	DWSN	Pebbleton Corporation (18.1%)
Detroit Diesel	DDC	Daimler Chrysler (21%)
Devon Energy	DVN	Santa Fe Synder Corporation (16.6%)
Diamond Offshore	DO	Loews Corporation (51.7%)
Donnelly Corporation	DON	Johnson Controls, Inc. (15.1%)

Continues

Shopping List of Potential Superstocks
Information as of 10/17/00 (continued)

Company	Symbol	Partial Owners
Dreyers Grand Ice Cream	DRYR	Nestle (21.8%)/General Electric (18.8%)
DST Systems	DST	Kansas City Southern Industries (32.3%)
Dynergy	DYN	Chevron (28.9%)
E*Trade Group	EGRP	Softbank Holdings (26.1%)
Ecolab	ECL	Henkel K GaA *Germany* (13.6%)
Electric Lightwave	ELIX	Citizens Communications (10.2%)
Entrust Technologies	ENTU	Nortel Networks (31.8%)
Euronet Services	EEFT	DST Systems (11.7%)
Excite @ Home	ATHM	AT&T (23.8%)/Comcast (4.6%)/ Cox Communications (7.3%)/ Cablevision Systems (5.2%)
Family Dollar Stores	FDO	Bank of America (8.2%)
Federal Realty	FRT	Morgan Stanley Dean Witter (14.9%)
Fiberstars, Inc.	FBST	Advanced Lighting Technologies (33%)
Fifth Third Bancorp	FITB	Cincinnati Financial Corporation (15.6%)
Fleet Boston Financial	FBF	Kohlberg Kravis Roberts (5.5%)
Footstar, Inc.	FTS	ESL Partners (22.1%)
Franklin Electronics Publishers	FEP	Bermuda Trust Company (21.6%)
Freeport McMoran Copper	FCX	Rio Tinto Indonesia, Ltd. (37%)
Friendly Ice Cream	FRN	Prestley Blake (11.4%)
Galey & Lord	GNL	Citicorp Venture Capital (47.2%)
Galileo International	GLC	UAL Corporation (17%)/Swiss Air (6.7%)
Garden Fresh Restaurant Corporation	LTUS	D3 Family Fund L.P. *David Nierenberg* (14.3%)
General Binding	GBND	Lane Industries (62.8%)
Gillette	G	Berkshire Hathaway (9.1%)/ Kohlberg Kravis Roberts (4.9%)
Golden State Bancorp	GSB	Mafco Holdings *Ronald Perelman* (32%)
Great Atlantic & Pacific	GAP	Tengelmann Group *Germany* (54%)
Great Lakes Chemical	GLK	Berkshire Hathaway *Warren Buffett* (13.9%)
GTS Duratek	DRTK	The Carlyle Group (23.1%)
Guitar Center	GTRC	Chase Capital Partners (23.2%)
Hagler Bailey, Inc.	HBIX	Cap Gemini S.A. (14.4%)
Halifax Energy	HX	Research Industries (34.9%)
Hanover Compressor	HC	GKH Investments (39%)

Continues

Shopping List of Potential Superstocks
Information as of 10/17/00 (continued)

Company	Symbol	Partial Owners
Harleysville Group	HGIC	Harleysville Mutual Insurance (56.6%)
Hearst Argyle TV	HTV	Hearst Broadcasting (63%)
Heska Corporation	HSKA	Novartis (11%)/Ralston Purina (6.7%)
Hispanic Broadcasting	HSP	Clear Channel Communications (26%)
Houston Exploration	THX	Keyspan (70.3%)
Human Genome Sciences	HGSI	Bass Group (15.3%)/ Merrill Lynch (6.6%)
ICN Pharmaceuticals	ICN	Special Situation Partners (8.5%)
IDEC Pharmaceuticals	IDPH	Genentech (6.7%)/Citicorp (7.7%)
IDEX	IEX	Kohlberg Kravis Roberts (28.7%)
IIC Industries	IICR	Kenyon Phillips, Ltd. *England* (77.8%)
Immunex	IMNX	American Home Products (55.3%)
Impco Technologies	IMCO	BERU Aktiengesellschaft *Germany* (12.1%)
Insurance Management Solutions	INMG	Bankers Insurance Group (62.7%)
International Home Foods	IHF	Hicks, Muse (42.6%)
International Multifoods	IMC	Archer Daniels Midland (8.6%)
Interstate Bakeries	IBC	Ralston Purina (29.5%)
Intrusion.com	INTZ	Science Applications International Corporation (15.6%)
Isis Pharmaceuticals	ISIP	Novarits *Switzerland* (7.2%)
Kemet Corporation	KEM	Citicorp (7.6%)
Keystone Consolidated	KES	Contran Corporation (40.8%)
Kohl's Corporation	KSS	AXA *France* (14.9%)/ Prudential Insurance (5.4%)
Laboratory Corporation of America	LH	Roche Holdings (46.2%)
Ladish Company	LDSH	Grace Brothers (28.4%)
Lafarge Corporation	LAF	Lafarge S.A. *France* (52.2%)
Legg Mason	LM	AXA Financial (16.7%)
Liberty Financial	L	Liberty Mutual (71.4%)
Lifeway Foods	LWAY	Danone Foods (Dannon) *France* (20%)
Ligand Pharmaceuticals	LGND	ELAN International Services (19.3%)
Lilly (ELI) & Co.	LLY	Lilly Foundation (15.4%)
Lincoln National	LNC	Dai-Ichi Mutual Life Insurance (7%)

Continues

Shopping List of Potential Superstocks
Information as of 10/17/00 (continued)

Company	Symbol	Partial Owners
Linens 'N Things	LIN	Marsh & McLennan (12.2%)/ American Express (5.3%)
Litton Industries	LIT	Unitrin (27.8%)
Lone Star Technologies	LSS	Alpine Capital (38.2%)/ Keystone, Inc. (9.7%)
Loral Space & Communications	LOR	Lockheed (15.5%)
Magnum Hunter Resources	MHR	Oneok, Inc. (38%)
Mascotech	MSX	Masco Corporation (17.5%)
McMoran Exploration	MMR	Alpine Capital (27.7%)
Mediquist	MEDQ	Koninklijke Philips Electronics NV *Netherlands* (68.5%)
Meemic Holdings	MEMH	Professionals Group, Inc. (82%)
Midway Games	MWY	Sumner Redstone *National Amusements* (25%)
Millennium Pharmaceuticals	MLNM	Bayer AG *Switzerland* (11%)
Mylan Labs	MYL	American Express (10.5%)
Neiman Marcus	NMGA	Harcourt General (18.1%)
Neurogen	NRGN	Pfizer (18.4%)
Nextel Communications	NXTL	Motorola (13.1%)
Noland Company	NOLD	Edmundson International (16.4%)
OMI Corporation	OMM	Mega Tankers *Norway* (11%)
Oneida Corporation	OCQ	National Rural Electric Co-Op (8.6%)
Oneok, Inc.	OKE	Western Resources (45%)
Overseas Shipholding	OSG	Archer Daniels Midland (16.8%)
Owens-Illinois	OI	Kohlberg Kravis Roberts (24.5%)
Panamsat Corporation	SPOT	General Motors *Hughes* (80.8%)
Payless ShoeSource, Inc.	PSS	ESL Partners (14.3%)
People's Bank	PBCT	People's Mutual Holdings (59.7%)
Petrocorp	PEX	Kaiser-Francis Oil Company (49.8%)
Petsmart	PETM	Carrefour SA *France* (11.7%)
Philadelphia Suburban	PSC	Vivendi *France* (18%)
Phillips Van Heusen	PVH	Vaneton International *Hong Kong* (18%)/Mellon Financial (5.1%)
Picturetel Corporation	PCTL	Intel (9.9%)
Primedia	PRM	Kohlberg Kravis Roberts (72%)
Prodigy Communications	PRGY	SBC Communications (41.9%)

Continues

Shopping List of Potential Superstocks
Information as of 10/17/00 (continued)

Company	Symbol	Partial Owners
Protective Life Corporation	PL	Amsouth Bancorp (9.6%)
RCN Corporation	RCNC	Level 3 Telecom Holdings (32.8%)/ Vulcan Ventures (27.9%)
Redhook Ale Brewery	HOOK	Anheuser-Busch (25%)
Regis Corporation	RGIS	Curtis Squire (15.7%)
Ribozyme Pharmaceuticals	RZYM	Elan Int'l *Ireland* (15.9%)/ Chiron Corp (8.6%)
Rosetta Inpharmatics	RSTA	Vulcan Ventures (12.7%)
Royal Caribbean Cruises	RCL	A. Wilhelmensen A.S. (25%)/ Pritzker Family (28%)
Russell Corporation	RML	Merrill Lynch (8.1%)
Safeway	SWY	Kohlberg Kravis Roberts (10%)
Samsonite	SAMC	Artemis America *France* (30.2%)
Scitex Corporation	SCIX	Merrill Lynch (6.07%)
Scripps (E.W.)	SSP	E.W. Scripps Trust (49.3%)
Seacor Smit	CKH	Geocapital Corporation (8.6%)
Smart & Final	SMF	Groupe Casino *France* (60.2%)
Sodexho-Marriott Services	SDH	Sodexho Alliance S.A. *France* (48%)/ TransAmerica Investments (12%)
Sport Supply Group	GYM	Emerson Radio (23.2%)
Sterling Sugars	SSUG	M.A. Patout & Sons, Inc. (62%)
Stolt Offshore	SCSWF	Stolt Nielson S.A. *Luxemburg* (44.9%)
Sunrise Assisted Living Centers	SNRZ	Morgan Stanley (10.8%)
Supergen, Inc.	SUPG	Abbott Labs (49%)
Swiss Army Brands	SABI	Victorinox *Switzerland* (40.2%)/ Brae Group (23.8%)
Talbots, Inc.	TLB	Jusco, Inc. (61.3%)
Targeted Genetics	TGEN	Immunex (7.2%)/Elan Int'l *Ireland* (5.9%)
Tiffany & Co.	TIF	Jennison Associates LLC (10.4%)
Timberland	TBL	Swartz Family Trust (36.9%)
Titanium Metals	TIE	Tremont Corporation (39.1%)
Transatlantic Holdings	TRH	American International Group (60%)
Tremont Corporation	TRE	Valhi, Inc. (78.9%)
Triton Energy	OIL	Hicks, Muse (38.9%)
True North Communications	TNO	Publicis S.A. *France* (9.4%)
U.S. Cellular	USM	Telephone & Data Systems (43.1%)
Ultramar Diamond Shamrock	UDS	Total Finance/TOTAL *France* (8.04%)

Continues

Shopping List of Potential Superstocks
Information as of 10/17/00 (continued)

Company	Symbol	Partial Owners
UnionBanCal	UB	Bank of Tokyo–Mitsubishi (64.6%)
United Park City Mining	UPK	Loeb Investors (66.1%)/ Farley Group (12.6%)
UNOVA	UNA	Unitrin (22.7%)
USG Corporation	USG	Knauf International (9.99%)
V.F. Corporation	VFC	Barbey Trust (19.9%)
Valhi, Inc.	VHI	Contran Corporation (78.9%)
Venator Group	Z	Greenway Partners LP (14.4%)/ AXA *France* (10.4%)
Vicorp Restaurants	VRES	SE Asset Management (19%)/ Quaker Capital (12%)
Washington Post Company	WPO	Berkshire Hathaway *Warren Buffett* (18.3%)
Westfield America	WEA	Westfield America Trust (64.7%)
Westwood One	WON	Viacom, Inc. (17.3%)
White Mountains Insurance	WTM	Berkshire Hathaway *Warren Buffett* (19.9%)
Whitman Corporation	WH	PepsiCo, Inc. (39.6%)
WMS Industries	WMS	Sumner Redstone *National Amusements* (25%)
Worldtex, Inc.	WTX	Lockheed Martin Investment Management (21.5%)/ EGS Partners (34.2%)
Yonkers Financial	YFCB	Gould Investors LP (16.2%)

Note: This data has been obtained from sources believed to be reliable, but its accuracy cannot be guaranteed. This data is subject to change at any time and may have changed already subsequent to this compilation. Readers are advised to independently verify this data and conduct their own research.

RESOURCES

Barron's, published by Dow Jones & Company, Inc., New York.

BusinessWeek, published by The McGraw-Hill Companies, New York.

Byrne, John, *Chainsaw* (New York: HarperCollins, 1999).

Cerf, Christopher, and Victor Navasky, *The Experts Speak* (New York: Pantheon Books, 1984).

FreeEDGAR.com, a product of EDGAR Online, Inc., is the market leader in EDGAR data retrieval.

Goldman, William, *Adventures in the Screen Trade* (New York: Warner Books, 1989).

Griffin, Nancy, and Kim Masters, *Hit & Run* (New York: Simon & Schuster, 1996).

Investor's Business Daily, published by William O'Neil & Co., Los Angeles, California.

JagNotes.com, JAGfn.com, a product of JAG Notes, is a financial network.

Kahn, Herman, *The Next 200 Years* (New York: William Morrow & Co., 1976).

Kiplinger's, published by The Kiplinger Washington Editors, Inc., Washington, D.C.

The Mansfield Chart Service, published by P.W. Mansfield & Co.

Nathan, John, *Sony: The Private Life* (Boston: Houghton Mifflin, 2000).

The New York Times, published by The New York Times Co.

Rudd, Terry R., *1929 Again* (Lewiston Idaho: Bell Curve Research Foundation, 1986).

Smith, Adam, *The Money Game* (New York: Random House, 1967).

Smith, Adam, *Supermoney* (New York: Random House, 1972).

Superstock Investor, published by Superstocks, Inc., Rochester, New York.

Vickers Weekly Insiders Report, published by Argus Research, Baltimore, Maryland.

The Wall Street Journal, published by Dow Jones & Co., New York.

Woodward, Bob, *The Agenda* (New York: Pocket Books, 1995).

Yahoo! Finance, a product of Yahoo! Inc.

INDEX

ABOUT THE AUTHORS

Charles M. LaLoggia is the editor and publisher of *Superstock Investor*, a monthly stock market newsletter he has published since 1974. He has also written numerous newspaper columns and magazine articles on investing. Charles LaLoggia's stock market views and stock recommendations have been reported in virtually every major financial publication in the world, including *BusinessWeek*, *The Wall Street Journal*, *Barron's*, *The New York Times*, *Kiplinger's Personal Finance*, *Money*, *Fortune*, *Newsweek*, and many others. He has appeared on numerous television and radio programs, including *Wall Street Week With Louis Rukeyser*, *The Nightly Business Report* on PBS, and CNBC. During his 26-year career as a stock market analyst, Charles LaLoggia has developed a reputation for being able to identify future takeover targets in their early stages, before they become widely recognized. In 1999, financial columnist Dan Dorfman called Charles LaLoggia "unquestionably one of the country's hottest—if not the hottest—takeover picker." In a December 2000 article entitled "Riding the Buyout Wave," *Fortune* magazine said that Charles LaLoggia's *Superstock Investor* newsletter "has a solid record for predicting buyouts."

    Cherrie A. Mahon is copublisher and director of research of the *Superstock Investor* newsletter. Prior to that she was a stockbroker at a major Wall Street firm.

    Further information regarding the monthly *Superstock Investor* newsletter is available by e-mailing ssinvestor@aol.com or calling 1-800-450-0551 or writing to *Superstock Investor*, P.O. Box 30547, Rochester, New York 14603.